Catiline: Rebel of the Roman Republic

Catiline: Rebel of the Roman Republic

Lucius Sergius Cailina & His Conspiracy

James T. Carney

First published in Great Britain in 2023 by
Pen & Sword History
An imprint of Pen & Sword Books Limited
Yorkshire – Philadelphia

Copyright © James T. Carney 2023

ISBN 978 1 39906 789 8

The right of James T. Carney to be identified as
Author of this Work has been asserted by him in accordance
with the Copyright, Designs and Patents Act 1988.

A CIP catalogue record for this book is
available from the British Library

All rights reserved. No part of this book may be reproduced or
transmitted in any form or by any means, electronic or mechanical
including photocopying, recording or by any information storage and
retrieval system, without permission from the Publisher in writing.

Typeset by Mac Style
Printed in the UK by CPI Group (UK) Ltd, Croydon, CR0 4YY.

Pen & Sword Books Limited incorporates the imprints of After
the Battle, Atlas, Archaeology, Aviation, Discovery, Family History,
Fiction, History, Maritime, Military, Military Classics, Politics,
Select, Transport, True Crime, Air World, Frontline Publishing, Leo
Cooper, Remember When, Seaforth Publishing, The Praetorian Press,
Wharncliffe Local History, Wharncliffe Transport, Wharncliffe True
Crime and White Owl.

For a complete list of Pen & Sword titles please contact

PEN & SWORD BOOKS LIMITED
47 Church Street, Barnsley, South Yorkshire, S70 2AS, England
E-mail: enquiries@pen-and-sword.co.uk
Website: www.pen-and-sword.co.uk
or
PEN AND SWORD BOOKS
1950 Lawrence Rd, Havertown, PA 19083, USA
E-mail: Uspen-and-sword@casematepublishers.com
Website: www.penandswordbooks.com

Contents

Chronology viii
Acknowledgements xi
Introduction: Catiline's Ghost xiii

Chapter I Catiline's Family and Youth: 106–89 1

Chapter II Catiline and the *Sullani*: 89–73 7

Chapter III Catiline: Politician: 73–63 16

Chapter IV Catiline: Candidate for Consul: 66–65 30

Chapter V Catiline and Cicero: 65–63 39

Chapter VI Catiline: Rebel: Autumn 63 59

Chapter VII Lentulus' Blunder: November–December 63 81

Chapter VIII The End of the Conspiracy: December 63 92

Chapter IX Marius Eagle: December 63 – January 62 107

Chapter X Historical Sources for Catiline and the Catilinarian Conspiracy 115

Chapter XI Catiline's Ghost in the Arts, Letters and History 134

Notes 140
Bibliography 196
Index 205

Chronology

753	Founding of Rome (Tr.)
509	Establishment of Republic (Tr.)
494–287	Five Secessions of Plebeians
264–241	First Punic War
218–201	Second Punic War
149–146	Third Punic War – Destruction of Carthage
146	Fall of Corinth and Roman Conquest of Greece
133	Murder of Tiberius Gracchus
122	Murder of Gaius Gracchus
112–106	Jugurthine War
113–101	War with the Teutones and Cimbri
106	Catiline's birth
91–87	Social War (War with Italian Allies)
89	Siege of Asculum – Catiline on Strabo's *consilium*
88	Sulla consul
89–85	First Mithridatic War
87	Sulla leaves for the East (with Catiline?)
83–82	Sullan Civil War
83–81	Second Mithridatic War
82–79	Sulla in Power
81–71	War with Sertorius in Spain
78	Sulla's death
	Catiline elected *quaestor* for 77
77	Lepidus' revolt (Catiline with Catulus?)
77–71	Pompey and Metellus in Spain (with Catiline to 74?)
73	Crassus and Catiline charged in the Vestal Virgin affair and both are acquitted
70	Pompey and Crassus consuls
69	Catiline elected *praetor* for 68
68	Catiline *praetor*

67–66	Catiline *pro praetor* in Africa (Tunisia)
July 66	Autronius and Sulla elected consuls
Autumn 66	Election of Autronius and Sulla overturned; Catiline returns from Africa, attempts to stand in second election but his candidacy is denied.
Late Autumn 66	Torquatus and Cotta elected consuls
December 66	So-called 'First Catilinarian Conspiracy'
29 December 66	Disruption at the trial of Manilius
Spring 65	Piso sent to Spain
Summer 65	Cicero contemplates *coitio* (coalition) with Catiline
Autumn 65	Catiline acquitted of extortion
Spring 64	Piso killed in Spain
1 June 64	Sallust's date for formation of the second Catilinarian Conspiracy
July 64	Cicero and Antonius elected consuls for
Spring 63	Catiline acquitted of involvement in Sullan proscriptions
July 63	Consular elections postponed by Cicero
September 63	Murena and Silanus elected consuls Conspiracy begins
19 October 63	Crassus and the others give Cicero letters warning about the conspiracy
20 October 63	Cicero reads letters to senate; Arrius reads letter from Etrurian friend warning of plans for a rising; senate passes a decree of *tumultus*; Fulvia betrays the plans of the conspirators
21 October 63	Cicero tells senate Manlius will take the field on October 27; senate passes the *senatus consultum ultimum*
27 October 63	Manlius takes the field
28 October 63	Alleged date for murder of the optimates; Cicero sends Sestius to Capua to repress the conspiracy there
1 November 63	Conspirators' plan to seize Praeneste foiled; senate instructs military leaders to go to various parts of Italy and suppress the conspirators
6–7 November 63	First meeting at Laeca's home
8 November 63	*First Catilinarian*

8–9 November 63	Second meeting at Laeca's house; Catiline leaves Rome
9 November 63	Catulus reads Catiline's letter to senate; *Second Catilinarian*
10 November 63	Catiline arrives at Arretium
Early November	Manlius sends message to Marcus Res
Mid-November 63	Catiline arrives at Manlius' camp; Catiline and Manlius are declared *hostes*; Murena's trial for bribery; conspirators contact the Allobroges; military leaders suppressing conspiracy in various parts of Italy.
Late-November 63	Catiline moves camp from Faesulae to evade approach of Antonius and prepares to march on Rome
End of November	Gabinus brings Allobroges into plot
	Allobroges betray plot to Sanga and others
1 December 63	Final meeting of Allobroges with conspirators
2 December 63	Allobroges leave Rome and seized at Mulvian Bridge
3 December 63	Cicero arrests the conspirators; *Third Catilinarian*
4 December 63	Optimate attempts to bring down Crassus and Caesar
5 December 63	Senate debate; *Fourth Catilinarian*; Execution of Conspirators
Mid-December 63	News of the uncovering of the conspiracy reaches Catiline's camp; Catiline attempts to evade Antonius and escape to Transalpine Gaul; Celer moves to block the road to Gaul
31 December 63	Tribunes prevent Cicero from making farewell address to Roman people
1 January 62	Nepos attacks Cicero in senate
3 January 62	Nepos attacks Cicero in senate; move to recall Pompey to suppress the conspiracy
Mid-January 62	Battle of Pistoria; Catiline slain
Later January 62	Catiline's head brought to Rome
Spring 62	Cicero prosecutes the remaining Catilinarians
62	Last Catilinarians in central and southern Italy dispersed by government forces

Acknowledgements

I first want to acknowledge the impact of my parents on my appreciation for learning in general and for my wider interest in classical civilization. I want particularly to acknowledge the efforts of my mother who, in the summer of 1959, had me do a paper a day which she subjected to rigorous criticism, thus improving my writing abilities – however limited initially – to a level of competence which I have tried – often unsuccessfully – to meet ever since. I want to acknowledge the efforts of my father, who spent every weekend of my senior year in high school serving as an extra debate coach and judge so that I could participate in debate or extemporaneous speaking. His actions led to my ultimately wise decision to go to law school and practice law, to the benefit of the academic profession and the loss of the legal profession. Having spent some thirty-three years of my career in the U.S. Steel Law Department negotiating with the United Steelworkers of America, it is safe to say that some of my union friends would have preferred that I had chosen the groves of academe. I have a number of grey hairs on my head from my battles with them, but they have more.

I want to point out that this work would never have been published except for the assistance and encouragement of my sister, Elizabeth Donnelly Carney, who is the real scholar in the family and the world's greatest expert on women in ancient Macedonian society. I benefitted from the teaching of two great classical scholars at Yale University – Francis Oates and Larry Richardson – the latter of whom convinced me that I did not have the language abilities/interest to continue on in Classics. I also want to thank my Yale classmate – Harry Edwards – who turned away from the dark side of the Force to become an eminent scholar, and made some – but not enough – critical comments on drafts of this work. I had sent out two chapters of this book to various classical journals, which rejected them, but sent me critical comments from unnamed reviewers whose thoughts benefitted my revision not just of those chapters but of the book as a whole. I also want to thank my first cousin, Nancy Matthews Handlin for her suggestions that for the benefit of non-experts I should include a map and chronology.

Next, I want to thank my editor, Philip Sidnell, who suffered through my pangs as a first-time author reluctant to let his baby venture forth into the world but who forced the delivery. I also want to thank my secretary form the U. S. Steel Law Department, Connie Kelley, who typed the last manuscript of this work until I took it up again following my retirement from U.S. Steel. Now, I am supposed at this point to say that, despite all the help I have received, I am solely responsible for any errors in the work. Well, I may not be a good lawyer, but I know enough not to make any damaging admission and will not do so now. One well-known historical fiction author who focuses on the last century of the Roman Republic – Philip Matyszak – has graciously reviewed the work and pointed out several errors which I have corrected. However, I am sure that he has missed a number of them. Under the ancient legal doctrine of last chance – which means that the last person who had an opportunity to avoid an accident is responsible for the same– he is responsible for any errors which remain in this work.

Finally, I want to thank my beloved wife Donna, whose interest in Roman history is nil, as well as my two great sons – James F. Carney and Daniel P. Carney –for their forbearance in my endeavours and my four grandchildren – Teddy, Squiggles (aka Frankie) Mario and Dani – one of whom, if I am lucky, will actually read this book.

Introduction

Catiline's Ghost

I have been fascinated by Catiline since 1958 when, entering Mt. Lebanon High School as a transfer student, I turned left in the hallway to the office and noticed a large, six by four foot picture showing an orator addressing the Roman senate, with one senator sitting alone on a bench far apart from the others. I did not know it at the time, but it was a copy of the famous nineteenth century fresco from the Palazzo Madama in Rome showing Cicero delivering his *First Catilinarian* (i.e. Oration Against Catiline). (A copy of the section of the fresco showing Catiline is on the cover of this book.) I felt a wave of empathy for the man who was as isolated as I felt upon entering a new school.

I first learned the story of Catiline when I was a third year Latin student. At that time, I read Cicero's *First Catilinarian* denouncing Catiline as a dangerous revolutionary and translated Sallust's famous description of Catiline as a man who was

> born of a noble clan, was of great strength of mind and body, but possessed of an evil and depraved character. From his youth, he loved civil discord, murder, pillage and political dissension; and among these he spent his early manhood. His body could endure hunger, cold, and lack of sleep to a degree which was unbelievable; his mind was reckless, cunning, changeable, capable of any form of pretence or concealment. Covetous of the possessions of others, he was wasteful of his own. Violent in his passions, he possessed a great deal of eloquence but little wisdom. His disordered mind always desired the monstrous, the gigantic and the incredible. After the dictatorship of L. Sulla, he was seized by a great desire to take over the Republic, little reckoning the means by which he would achieve this goal as long as he attained power himself.[1]

While fascinated by the portrait of Satan incarnate painted by Cicero and Sallust, I grew sceptical of its accuracy and started off defending him. I focused on Catiline's early life and background. Over the years I continued in my scepticism about the classical picture of Catiline, but developed a more realistic concept of my 'hero'.

This book reflects my examination of recent scholarship dealing with Catiline and the Roman Revolution which saw the fall of the Republic. This process started in 133 with Tiberius Gracchus' efforts at agrarian reform and ended in 31 with Octavius' victory at Actium and the establishment of the Principate/Empire. What caused this development is one of the most controversial topics in Roman historiography. This issue has led to a divergence in view among the three preeminent twentieth century scholars of this period: P.A. Brunt, Christian Meier and Erich Gruen.[2]

However, there is a general consensus that the Romans during this period were confronted with a large number of problems created by the city-state's expansion beyond Italy. Among the key issues created by Rome's expansion were (1) proper governance and taxation of the provinces so that the provincials were not subjected to extortion by Roman governors or bankruptcy by the *publicani* (Roman tax collectors), (2) corruption in both the law courts and in the political process due in large part to the riches available to those who were elected to office which was a prerequisite to becoming a provincial governor, (3) lack of a system to compensate the Roman armies which were no longer composed of citizen but rather of professional soldiers, (4) the demands of the non-Roman Italians, the friends and allies of the Senate and Roman People (*amici et socii Senatus Populusque Romanus*) for admission to full Roman citizenship, (5) the decline of small farmers in some parts of Italy due to their inability to compete with the slaves in *latifundia* (slave plantations owned by the members of the senatorial and *equites* classes – i.e. the rich elite),[3] and (6) the rise of the urban proletariat in Rome itself. These issues were not of easy solution; neither were they incapable of it. A few Roman statesmen of differing political philosophies made efforts to deal with one or more of these problems, but they met with little success.[4]

Why were these statesmen unsuccessful? The basic obstacle to any reform is that it requires sacrifices on the part of one or more groups of citizenry. Thus, extension of the franchise meant dilution of voting power and consequently a loss of practical power by all Romans. Extension of the franchise downgraded the status of the poorer Roman citizens just as freedom for African American slaves downgraded the status of poor white people in the South. Agrarian reform involved a loss of income to both the senatorial class and the *equites* who had occupied the public lands in exchange for the payment of a small fee and who would lose the income they made from the lands if these lands were divided up into small farms and given to members of the urban proletariat. Any method of providing for compensation of legionnaires upon completion of service would also come at the expense of the two upper classes and deprive generals of a tool which they used to leverage leadership of unpaid soldiers into political power. Reform failed because the majority of the elite (and also the public at large) were unwilling to pay the price to solve these problems. Brunt[5] recognizes that the ruling class' 'inability to solve problems that arose from Rome's expansion…was a critical factor in the fall of the Republic.'

Brunt contends that by the time Caesar crossed the Rubicon and sought to overthrow the Republic, all elements in Roman society were so alienated from the current political system because of its failures that they were willing to tear it down or at least abandon it.[6] Meier agreed with Brunt about the fragmentation of the various elements in Roman society, but disagreed with the conclusion that the various components of the Roman populace were out to destroy the Republic. Meier argued that the negligent failure of the elite to solve the problems and to change the outmoded existing political system led to the fall of the Republic.[7] Gruen agreed with Meier that no group desired to destroy the Republic; however, he argues that Sulla had essentially restored a stable Republic which would have endured had not Caesar decided to overthrow it in 49.[8] Thus, he sees Caesar as responsible for the overthrow of an otherwise stable political system. In this Gruen disagrees with both Brunt and Meier. Gruen's theory that the Republic was stable between Sulla and Caesar seems to be undercut by the fact that during this period of 'stability', the Republic was disturbed by at least two attempts to overthrow the government by force: the first by M. Aemilius Lepidus (in 78) and the second by Catiline (in 63), as well as by the period of near anarchy in the 50s. Contrary to Gruen's argument, it seems likely that, Caesar or no Caesar, the Republic would not have survived.

The problem of why the Romans were unable to pull together for the common good is inseparable from the question of why the Republic was replaced by the Principate/Empire. A major factor in the failure of Romans to stand together was the absence of a common enemy following the end of the Second Punic War. Perhaps Cato the Censor's efforts in the second century to create continued fear of Carthage by ending each speech with a declaration *Ceterum (autem) censeo Carthago delenda est* (Among other things I think that Carthage must be destroyed)[9] reflected his recognition that the existence of a common enemy was necessary to unify the Roman citizenry. Certainly, Sallust viewed the downfall of the Republic as beginning with the destruction of Carthage, which eliminated any possible threat to Roman supremacy in the Western Mediterranean.[10]

A second major factor in the failure of Romans – and particularly the Roman elite – to preserve the Republic was the willingness of the elite to break accepted political conventions in their struggle for power. As Robert Dahl has pointed out,[11] democracy in the United States has always depended on the members of the political elite – even more than the general public – accepting the norms of democracy. Similarly, the survival of the Roman Republic depended on the willingness of the political elite to keep political struggles within certain bounds. This first step in the actual Roman Revolution occurred when Ti. Gracchus proposed an agrarian law in the popular assembly which the senate had not previously approved.[12] The second step came when Octavius the tribune vetoed the agrarian law which had been approved by the popular assembly. The third step occurred when Ti. Gracchus persuaded the popular assembly to remove Octavius from office for his veto of legislation which the popular assembly had approved.[13] The fourth step occurred when the elite (the oligarchs) organized Gracchus' murder under the guise of the *senatus consultum ultimum consules ne quid res publica detrimenti caperet* (a senate resolution that the consuls should take care that the Republic should suffer no harm) and in effect declared martial law thus providing political cover for members of the oligarchy to use force to maintain order in the Republic and to eliminate their opponents.[14] Ti. Gracchus' murder initiated a vicious process: a resort to violence by all, corruption of both the electoral and judicial processes, and ultimately reliance on armies who owed their allegiance more to their generals than to the elected government. This cycle ended only when the Republic was replaced by the Principate/Empire.

Catiline embodied the virtues and vices of members of his class and generation. The picture of Catiline which will emerge in this book is neither that of a villain depicted by Cicero or Sallust nor that of a principled *popularis* (someone who advanced popular causes opposed by the elite) portrayed by some historians. Nor will it show him as a puppet of more prominent figures such as Crassus or Caesar or as a bogeyman of Cicero's imagination.

In short, this picture of Catiline is of one of the *Sullani* (a follower of Sulla). Catiline was a conservative who was as ambitious as Sulla, but not as lucky. Catiline's oldest political supporter was the *princeps senatus* (leader of the senate) Q. Lutatius Catulus who was perhaps the most prominent of the conservative *Sullani* (*optimates*). Catiline's military experience seems always to have been under commanders who were *Sullani*. There is no evidence that Catiline espoused any *popularis* (reform) programs during his first campaign for the consulship. Indeed, it was unlikely that Cicero would have considered combining with Catiline in the 64 consular elections had the latter been a *popularis* since Cicero was a conservative at heart.

It was only after Catiline's defeat in the consular election for 63 that, disheartened by his failure to win when competing with the *novus homo* Cicero,[15] he began to support *popularis* programs. Even then, however, he focused primarily on debt reform and relief for the Sullan veterans (his former comrades in arms) who had been given farms in Etruria by Sulla, but who had fallen on hard times for various reasons. Catiline may have advocated some kind of agrarian reform in his second run for the consulship. It was a second defeat which Catiline attributed to Cicero's chicanery and to widespread bribery by the successful *optimate* candidates that led him to the path of rebellion.[16]

Catiline did not take up arms to lead a social revolution. Rather, he tried to seize by force that which he believed has been unfairly denied to him. Had he succeeded in his second campaign for consul or in his efforts to seize control of the Republic, he would have advanced the debasement of the currency and some kind of agrarian reform but nothing more. Catiline was driven by pride and ambition, not social philosophy. He could not accept defeat. Catiline was remarkable in terms of his charisma, ambition, and force of will, but not in terms of social thinking or ideology. As Cicero predicted, Catiline chose to die as a rebel rather than live as an exile.[17] Catiline R.I.P.

Chapter I

Catiline's Family and Youth: 106–89

L. *Catilina, nobili genere natus* (L. Catilina, born of a noble family) begins the narrative portion of Sallust's *Bellum Catilinae*.[1] This sentence reveals the most significant element of Catiline's character: his consciousness of his noble background and his conviction that, as a descendant of a great clan, he was entitled to election to the offices held by his forefathers – specifically the consulship, which was the highest office in the Republic and was held only by those who had first been elected *quaestor* – an administrative position – and *praetor* which was a legal position. In his campaign against Cicero, Catiline contemptuously referred to his opponent as an '*inquilinus*' (a city boarder who lived outside Rome.)[2] He attacked Cicero on the grounds that the latter was a *novus homo* (new man whose ancestors had never held the consulship) who was not worthy to become consul in the stead of a noble such as Catiline.[3] Sallust claims that Catiline replied to Cicero's *First Catilinarian* by saying that it was inconceivable that a man of a distinguished clan such as Catiline would conspire against the Republic or that an '*inquilinus*' such as Cicero would defend it.[4] Catiline, like every noble Roman, wanted to distinguish himself above all others; his life was dominated by the pursuit of glory.[5]

Catiline went through life convinced that he was destined to become consul. His conviction was unrealistic. Those who reached the consulship generally came from powerful and distinguished clans. Many nobles sought the consulship but very few attained it, since only two consuls were elected in each year.[6] Catiline came from a *gens* (clan) whose members had not reached the consulship for many generations. The odds against his reaching the position were high. He was to face almost as much difficulty in reaching the consulship as did a *novus homo*,[7] particularly because his family was not extremely wealthy.[8] The wonder is not that he failed to achieve his goal, but that he came so close to achieving it. Nevertheless, Catiline's family, contrary to the contentions of his enemies,[9] was not poor. Catiline did acquire a mansion on the exclusive Palatine Hill – probably through inheritance.[10] Catiline always satisfied the property qualifications required of a senator.[11] Accordingly, Cicero's claims that Catiline was consistently on the verge of bankruptcy seem exaggerated.[12]

The Sergii were patricians.[13] The legendary founder of the Sergia *gens* was Sergestus, the companion of Aeneas.[14] The Sergii played a prominent role in the first century and a half of the Republic. Marcus Sergius Esquilinus[15] was among the second set of *decemviri* (ten men appointed to reform the laws) in 450.[16] The first member of the *gens* to obtain the consulship was L. Sergius Fidenas, who in 437 won a bloody victory against the Fidenae and the Veientes.[17] He was twice consul (437 and 429) as well as being made a military tribune with consular power in 433, 428 and 424.[18] Three of his descendants (the Sergii Fidenates) were frequently military tribunes with consular power: Manius Sergius Fidenas in 404 and 402;[19] L. Sergius Fidenas in 397[20] and G. Sergius Fidenas Coxo in 387, 385 and 380.[21]

As the Republic waxed, the Sergii waned; the last famous Sergius was M. Sergius Silus, a legendary hero of the Second Punic War.

> In his second campaign Sergius lost his right hand. In two campaigns he was wounded twenty-three times. Although disabled, Sergius served in many subsequent campaigns. He was twice captured by Hannibal – no ordinary foe – from whom twice he escaped, although kept in chains and shackles every day for twenty months. He fought four times with only his left hand, while two horses he was riding were stabbed beneath him.
>
> He had a right hand made of iron for him and, going into battle with this bound to his arm, raised the siege of Cremona, saved Placentia and captured twelve enemy camps in Gaul – all of which exploits were confirmed by the speech he made as *praetor* when his colleagues tried to debar him because of his disfigurements from the sacrifices.[22]

He served as urban *praetor* (essentially a judicial officer and a subordinate of the consuls) in 197, but failed to reach the consulship – presumably due to his deformity (which the Romans regarded as a mark of moral turpitude).[23] C. Sergius Plautus – possibly a cousin of this great soldier – was urban *praetor* in 200 and *pro praetor* in 199 with the responsibility of assigning land to veterans.[24] (*Pro praetor* and *pro consul* were positions assigned to *ex-praetors* and ex-consuls. These positions normally involved governorship of a province, but could entail special assignments necessitating the appointment of a high-level official.) L. Sergius – possibly Caius' brother – was an ambassador/legate to Carthage in 203.²⁵ Another Sergius involved in the Second Punic War was M. Sergius, a military tribune in 205 who was murdered by the *pro praetor* Q. Pleminius.²⁶

The son of M. Sergius Silus served as a *legatus* under L. Aemilius Paulus during the Third Macedonian War against King Perseus and fought at the Battle of Pydna in 168.²⁷ However, he does not seem to have attained the praetorship, let alone the consulship.²⁸ Catiline's grandfather, the third M. Sergius Silus, served as *quaestor* in 116–115 when, on orders of the senate, he struck a coin in honour of the first M. Sergius Silus.²⁹ The third M. Sergius Silo never held a praetorship. One of his two sons, the fourth M. Sergius Silo, was a *quaestor* in 94 and minted a number of denarii.³⁰ His other son, Catiline's father – L. Sergius Silus –³¹ seems never to have held office.³² The sun of the Sergii had set long before Catiline's birth.³³

Like many a family whose fortunes seemed on the decline, the Sergii may have attempted to improve their situation through matrimonial alliances. Catiline's mother may have come from the ancient Annia *gens* since his maternal uncle seems to have been L. Annius Bellienus. His sister may have married Q. Caecilius, an *eques* (a rich person who had not been elected to public office)³⁴ who may have brought wealth but no distinction to the Sergii. It is unlikely that this individual was a member of the powerful Metellus branch of the Caecilii. Neither of these marriages seemed to have done much to advance the fortunes of the family. The Sergii, more enamoured of their heritage as they became less deserving of it, may have seen in Catiline a boy who could restore the clan to its former glory. Even more than most noble families, they may have emphasized the glory achieved by Catiline's forebears. In accordance with Roman custom, they probably kept life-like waxen masks of their ancestors in their home and took them out on public holidays.³⁵ They may have told Catiline many stories about previous generations of his family. His parents' reverential treatment of their ancestors may have been responsible for Catiline's ingrained conviction that he was entitled to the highest rank in the Republic by virtue of his birth.³⁶ As a young boy, Catiline would have been keenly aware of his family's decline and may have determined to restore the patrician Sergii to their former place in the Republic.

Patrician status had two significances: (1) patricians could run for office earlier than plebeians and (2) only one patrician could be elected consul in any given year. The minimum age requirements under the Sullan constitution were: for *quaestor*, 30; for *praetor*, 39; for consul, 42. However, patricians such as Catiline were certainly permitted to run for the last two offices two years earlier than plebeians – e.g. at 37 and 40 respectively.[37] Given the fact that there had to be a nine year hiatus between quaestorship and praetorship, it seems logical to conclude that patricians were permitted to run for *quaestor* at the age of 28.[38] Normally, nobles would run for offices in the first year in which they were eligible.[39] Since Catiline first ran for *praetor* in 69 (for 68) and first stood for consul in 66 (for 65),[40] he would have been born in 106.[41]

It is likely that Catiline received the typical training accorded to a scion of the nobility. Thus he would have spent his early years with his mother and father who, often with the assistance of a slave, would give him his initial education.[42] As Catiline approached the age of 7, he probably attended a school at which he would have learnt reading, writing and arithmetic.[43] He would have been accompanied to school by a household slave – a pedagogue – who was often Greek in origin.[44] Depending on his educational background, the pedagogue could play an important role in educating the young noble.

Catiline would have had some exposure to a school of rhetoric, since no Roman could aspire to public office unless he was a competent public speaker.[45] In addition, he could have used textbooks on rhetoric to learn oratorical skills.[46] One advantage of textbooks was that they reduced 'the practices of persuasion to a learnable code'.[47] An effective Roman politician did not have to be a great orator like Cicero, but he did have to be able to deliver 'a coherent and well-argued speech'.[48] Possessing a quick but not thorough mind, Catiline probably did well in his studies – or at least those involving rhetoric. Preferring physical activity to mental, however, he may have spent much of his youth outdoors, acquiring at that time the ability attributed to him by both Cicero and Sallust to endure *inediae, algoris, vigiliae* (hunger, cold and lack of sleep) to an almost incredible degree.[49]

Upon reaching the age of 16 or 17, Catiline would have assumed the *toga virilis* (an adult's garment).[50] In the normal course of events, he would have entered military service shortly thereafter,[51] since most members of the Roman nobility who wanted to pursue political careers performed ten years of military service.[52] In 91 the Social War had broken out, when Rome's Italian *socii* (allies), denied any opportunity to become Roman citizens, revolted and attempted to establish a non-Roman Italian state. The outbreak of this war may have accelerated Catiline's assumption of the *toga virilis* and his entry into military service. Catiline was placed on the *consilium*[53] (staff) of Gn. Pompeius Strabo, who was in command of the Roman army on the northern Italian front and besieging the city of Asculum.[54] This appointment was almost certainly the result of some connection between the Sergii and Strabo, since members of a general's *consilium* were often the commander's friends or relatives of his friends.[55]

Strabo scored a significant victory by first defeating the Italian army sent to break the siege of Asculum and then capturing the town.[56] On 17 November 89, following the capture of Asculum, Strabo, with the approval of his *consilium*, granted Roman citizenship to a group of fifteen Spanish cavalrymen for their services in the campaign.[57] The inscription recording this event lists all the members of Strabo's *consilium* including Catiline and Gn. Pompeius, Strabo's son, who became entitled *Pompeius Magnus* or Pompey the Great for all of his victories as a general. Both men are listed as *eques* because, while wealthy, they had not been elected to any office and thus had not attained senatorial rank. The inscription identifies Catiline as the son of Lucius and a member of the *tribus* (electoral district) Tromentian.[58] It is unclear what relationship, if any, existed between Pompey and Catiline at the time of the Asculum campaign or later.[59] There is no evidence that they ever became friends.

Ironically, a third famous Roman – M. Tullius Cicero – served under Strabo in 90 when he witnessed a meeting between Strabo, Strabo's brother, and T. Vettius Scato[60] who was one of the three Italian generals who had defeated Strabo at the Battle of Mt. Falernus in 90.[61] However, by the spring of 89 Cicero had transferred to the command of P. Cornelius Sulla and served with him in his unsuccessful effort to capture Nola.[62] He certainly was not part of Strabo's *consilium* at the fall of Asculum. The prolific and loquacious Cicero never referred to Sulla's military service with Strabo or with Sulla until the end of his career. The only three references that Cicero ever made to his time in the army were incidental.[63] It was not likely that his military service was distinguished, since Cicero was a *vir nihil minus quam ad bellum natus* (a man born for anything other than war).[64]

Did Cicero serve with Pompey and Catiline? B. Levick paints a picture of the three youths serving together.[65] However, there is no solid evidence that Cicero served on Strabo's staff at the same time as the other two young men. The known dates of service of the three men do not coincide. Contrary to Tatum[66] the inscription does not list Cicero as serving with Pompey and Catiline at the siege of Asculum. What makes it unlikely that

Cicero served with Pompey and Catiline is that Cicero never claimed any early acquaintance with either of them. If there had been a connection with either or both, it seems probable that Cicero would have referred to it at some point in his voluminous letters, speeches, and books. In the 64 consular campaign Cicero sought the support of the Pompeiians, pointing out that he had praised Pompey, he had defended Pompey's supporters in court[67] and he had endorsed laws giving Pompey special military commands.[68] If Cicero had been a companion in arms with Pompey during the Social War, he would have shouted that fact to the rooftops. Similarly, if he had served with Catiline, he would have denounced the latter for betraying an earlier *amicitia* (friendship). Cicero's silence with respect to both men indicates the absence of any joint service or early acquaintanceship with either.

The inscription, while showing that Catiline served with Pompey during the Asculum campaign, does not indicate how long the two men served together in that campaign or thereafter. After celebrating a triumph at the end of December 89, Strabo was succeeded by the new consuls, P. Cornelius Sulla and Pompeius Rufus. On Sulla's order, Strabo turned over command of his army to Pompeius Rufus who was murdered by his new troops a few days after he took command. It was widely believed that this murder was instigated by the unscrupulous Strabo.[69] At some point Strabo took over the army again and led it in a campaign against Cinna in 87. Pompey served with his father in this campaign.[70] Shortly after the start of this campaign, Strabo was removed from the scene by a bolt of lightning; his funeral was disrupted by a mob, which dragged his body from the bier and heaped insults on it.[71] When Catiline left Strabo's staff, or what he did immediately upon leaving it is unknown.

Chapter II

Catiline and the *Sullani*: 89–73

A. Catiline, Catulus and Sulla: 89–82

'L. Cornelius Sulla, born of a noble clan…'[1] Thus Plutarch begins his life of Sulla with a conscious imitation of Sallust's portrayal of Catiline,[2] hinting at the similarities between the two men. Sulla and Catiline came from obscure noble families. While the Sullan family was part of a patrician clan and prominent throughout the entire Republican period,[3] its Sullan branch had never been distinguished. No one bearing the name of Sulla had ever achieved any office higher than the praetorship.[4] Like Catiline, Sulla throughout his life manifested a great aristocratic pride which was not commensurate with his familial circumstances.[5] Also like Catiline, Sulla was poor (by the standards of the Roman nobility).[6] Both men were determined to assume the place in the political arena to which they believed themselves to be entitled by birth; ambition was their driving motivation.[7] Both were gifted with great personal charm which they used to their political advantage.[8]

Sulla's striking features – his golden red hair contrasting with his white face – with the entire head being dominated by piercing blue eyes and an overall hawk-like demeanour –revealed a man who was intelligent, courageous, unyielding and totally ruthless.[9] Sulla first achieved prominence in the war with Jugurtha (a ruler of an area in North Africa) when, as a subordinate of C. Marius, he persuaded one of Jugurtha's allies to hand Jugurtha over to the Romans.[10] Originally on good terms with Marius, the first vain, self-seeking *novus homo* from Arpinum (Cicero being the second), Sulla quarrelled with Marius over credit for ending the war with Jugurtha. The great families of the nobility, without necessarily accepting Sulla as one of their own, began to support him as a way of opposing Marius, whom they hated.[11]

Sulla played an important part in the ultimate Roman victory in the war with the Teutones and Cimbri (two German tribes who invaded Roman territory in the hopes of seizing land on which they could settle).

This war had broken out in 113 and continued until 101. Following the war, Sulla was elected *praetor* in 98. After his praetorship, in 97 Sulla was assigned the province of Cilicia (in southcentral Turkey bordering on the Mediterranean) and led his small army to defeat a force of the archenemy of the Romans – Mithridates (king of Pontus in northern Turkey bordering on the Black Sea). Sulla then returned to Rome only to find his political ambitions thwarted for several years by the enmity of Marius. However, following the outbreak of the Social War, Sulla achieved a significant victory over the Samnites and was elected consul by a grateful populace. Following his consulate, he was assigned Asia as a province as *pro consul* to direct the renewed war against Mithridates.

Marius, seeking further glory, then combined with the tribune P. Sulpicius to have the popular assembly transfer the command of the war against Mithridates from Sulla to himself. Sulla, who had not yet departed for Asia, became enraged by this act and called upon his soldiers to uphold his *dignitas* (honour) and march on Rome – thus starting another act in the death spiral of the Roman Republic. Sulla seized Rome, outlawed Marius, and executed Sulpicius. Sulla then saw to it that legislation was passed that gave him back command of the forces against Mithridates. He forced the enactment of other legislation to reform the state and solidify power in the hands of the nobility. In a revulsion against Sulla's actions and his treatment of Marius and Sulpicius, the populace then elected L. Cinna, a Marian, as consul. Thus, as Sulla departed for the East, the Roman government fell into the hands of his opponents.

Meanwhile, what of Catiline? It is highly likely that Catiline joined Sulla's staff and served in the war against Mithridates. Catiline was always regarded as a brave and capable soldier;[12] he certainly must have served many years in the army besides his two-year stint in the Social War. Now both Badian[13] and Keaveney[14] contend that Catiline stayed in Italy during the Mithridatic War. However, Keaveney explains that after Sulla's *legati* (lieutenants) deserted him during his march on Rome

> a glittering opportunity presented itself to the ambitious. Here, for those who would fill the empty places, was a chance to acquire wealth in the East and fame that would unlock the doors to high office. It is not surprising that a number of men elected to seize the opportunity.[15]

Given Catiline's character it is inconceivable that he would have lingered in his home while L. Cornelius Sulla was on the march to the East. It is also likely that, during the Mithridatic war, Catiline became a friend of Sulla:[16] This would have been a natural relationship given the similarity between the two in terms of background and nature. It would be hard to account for Catiline's exaggerated role in the Sullan proscriptions unless one assumes that he had served under Sulla in the Mithridatic War and earned the latter's confidence.

Catiline may have married before leaving Rome for the East; Sallust indicates that Catiline's son had reached adulthood before Catiline's efforts to attain the consulship in 66.[17] Nothing is known of Catiline's first wife. Syme suggests that she may have been a sister of M. Marius Gratidianus, the nephew of C. Marius, and one of the significant leaders of the Marian faction in the decade of the 80s.[18] This seems unlikely, since Catiline had no connections in the Marian camp. As an undistinguished aristocrat, he was not a likely husband for the niece of the most prominent man in Rome.[19] At some point in time his first wife disappeared with as little fanfare as she had arrived – something which suggests that she did not come from a prominent family.[20] Given the short-lived nature of Roman marriages, it is quite possible that Catiline divorced her. On the other hand, given the mortality rates in ancient Rome, she may have died of natural causes.

After Sulla's departure, Marius returned from exile and, joining Cinna, seized Rome and launched a reign of terror, killing those whom he hated until his own death left his son to succeed him in his murderous role.[21] Among the victims was Q. Lutatius Catulus (cos. 102) who had served with Marius during the war with the Cimbri and the Teutones, but who had later turned against him.[22] When faced with a political prosecution by M. Marius Gratidianus that would have resulted in his execution, the elder Catulus committed suicide.[23] The charge against the elder Catulus was probably *perduellio* (treason) and a conviction would have resulted in his being scourged to death at the stake.

This incident is not comprehensible without an understanding of the difference between the Roman judicial system and the Anglo-Saxon system. While both systems made a distinction between civil law and criminal law, the Roman system regarded most of what we would consider criminal offences involving persons or property as civil matters. The only Roman criminal cases involved offences against the Republic. There were no officials in the Republic whose duty it was to prosecute these offences. Prosecution was a private undertaking.[24] There were two basic motivations for prosecution. First, young men – often in their teens or early twenties

– who were seeking to make a reputation for themselves would bring prosecutions against various public officials in order to advance their own careers.[25] Second, more experienced politicians would sometimes bring prosecutions for personal or political reasons.[26] An example of a political prosecution was Cicero's famous prosecution of Verres, the corrupt governor of Sicily. Cicero at that time was 33 and relatively well known. He was not trying to make a name for himself; rather, he was advancing his political career by undertaking an attack on a leading *optimate* and an extremely corrupt governor. He did so at the behest of Pompey, with whom Cicero always attempted to ally himself.[27] (There was only one other occasion in the course of an extremely successful and lengthy legal career that Cicero was a prosecutor.)[28]

This death of the elder Catulus led his son, Q. Lutatius Catulus, (cos. 78) to follow in the footsteps of many of the nobility and seek refuge with Sulla in the East.[29] It was probably during the younger Catulus' exile and his service with Sulla that he met Catiline and the two formed a permanent *amicitia*, which was as much personal as political.[30]

Following the recovery of all Roman territories previously taken by Mithridates during the early years of the war, Sulla negotiated a peace that left him free to settle the administration of the Roman provinces in Asia Minor and then to turn his attention to the political situation at Rome. Unable to reach accommodation with the Marians, Sulla led his army back to Italy. After a bloody civil war (83–82) ('the Sullan civil war'), he defeated the Marians and seized Rome.[31]

Catiline and the Proscriptions
What role did Catiline play in the violence which followed Sulla's victory? The most frequent charge is that he killed Marcus M. Gratidianus.[32] The latter's death had been foreordained given his role in the prosecution and suicide of the elder Catulus, as well as Sulla's determined policy of rewarding his friends and punishing his enemies.[33] It seems probable that on Sulla's orders Catiline executed Gratidianus,[34] although he would have been happy enough to perform on his own accord a feat so desired by his friend Catulus. It is likely that Catiline executed Gratidianus on the senior Catulus' tomb to emphasize the fact that Gratidianus was being killed as punishment for his role in the latter's death.[35] The story of Catiline's execution of Gratidianus became embroidered with the telling, each version containing more gore and imagined details than the last.[36]

This development, however, should not obscure the basic substance to the charge.³⁷

A case can be made that Catiline was not involved in the death of Gratidianus. Some scholars³⁸ argue for Catiline's innocence based on the fact that the claim that Catiline murdered Gratidianus did not surface until Cicero raised it *In Toga Candida* and that it is never mentioned by Sallust. In addition, the fragments of *In Toga Candida* quoted in Asconius' commentaries do not mention Catiline by name; the identification is supplied by Asconius. Finally, Gratidianus was a relative of Cicero;³⁹ given the general Roman allegiance to family ties, Cicero should not have been willing to form a *coitio* (political alliance) with Catiline in 65 if Catiline had murdered his cousin.⁴⁰ In addition, other executioners have been named for Gratidianus. The *Adnotationes super Lucanum* names Catulus as the executioner of Gratidianus.⁴¹ Valerius Maximus, on the other hand, claims that notoriously cruel Sulla personally killed Gratidianus.⁴² Livy follows Valerius Maximus in naming Sulla as the executioner.⁴³

This case for exculpating Catiline is not convincing. The fact that no one alleged that Catiline had killed Gratidianus before the delivery of *In Toga Candida* or that Sallust did not record Gratidianus' execution means little given the fact that no campaign speeches by Catiline's opponents other than Cicero have survived and since Sallust did not relate any specific information about Catiline's early career. The failure of the surviving fragments of In *Toga Candida* to name Catiline specifically as the murderer of Gratidianus is not significant given the fact that Q. Cicero⁴⁴ identifies Catiline as the executioner of Gratidianus,⁴⁵ thereby providing a contemporary basis for Asconius' identification in his commentary on *In Toga Candida*. The principle that no Roman would ally themselves with an individual who had killed a relative was more honoured in the breach than in the observance. Given the distant nature of Cicero's relationship with Gratidianus (first cousin once removed),⁴⁶ his disapproval of Gratidianus' actions,⁴⁷ the hostility between the Gratidiani and the Cicero family in in the late 90s and early 80s,⁴⁸ and Cicero's occasional lack of scruples, it is likely that Cicero in 65 was more than willing to overlook Catiline's role in Gratidianus' execution.⁴⁹ As for the *Adnotationes super Lucanum* naming Catulus as the executioner, it is quite possible that a scribe had miscopied Catulus for Catilina. Finally, and most importantly, it is impossible to explain the close connection between Catiline and the younger Catulus which existed until Catiline's death unless Catiline had avenged the death of the senior Catulus by executing Gratidianus.

It is likely that Catiline executed Gratidianus immediately after Sulla took Rome and before the infamous proscriptions,[50] vividly described by Plutarch, began.[51] Keaveney, who is extremely supportive of Sulla admits that the proscriptions '...remain forever as a blot on his character and a career so admirable in many other ways.'[52] Proscriptions (from the Latin word write down) started when Sulla began to post in public places a list of those of his enemies who were to be captured and executed. However, the process of placing names on the list was subject to corruption and many found their names inscribed on the lists by personal enemies or by individuals jealous of their wealth.[53] Someone who killed an individual who was on a list would be entitled to a share of that person's estate. The remainder of that estate was forfeited to the Republic, which then sold it at very low prices to Sullan supporters.

Among the various scurrilous charges made against Catiline was that he murdered his brother-in-law and covered up by the crime by having his brother-in-law's name placed on the proscription list retroactively.[54] Cicero's brother, Quintus alleged that Catiline's

> ...first appearance in the state had been in killing Roman *equites*. For you will remember that Sulla placed Catiline in charge of the Gauls who cut off the heads of the Titinni, Nannii and Tanussi. ...[55]

However, one cannot determine who the Titinni, the Nanni and the Tansussi were – a fact which raises questions about the credibility of this charge.[56] Another fact which suggests that Catiline was not deeply involved in the proscriptions is that he was not removed from the rolls of the senate in 70, when the censors removed forty-one individuals for various misdoings, generally in connection with the proscriptions.[57] Moreover, Cicero would probably not have contemplated a *coitio* with Catiline if Catiline had been notorious for his role in the proscriptions.[58] Indeed, it was only after this prospect of combining with Catiline was dashed that Cicero *In Toga Candida* charged that Catiline had played a major role in the proscriptions and had been involved in the gruesome execution of Gratidianus and other individuals.[59] One thing is clear; there is no evidence that Catiline emerged from the proscriptions rich,[60] as did some of the other *Sullani* such as M. Licinius Crassus.[61]

At the expiration of his consulship in 80, Sulla retired to private life only to die in his sleep in the spring of 78, leaving his supporters (the *Sullani*) to maintain the constitution which he had imposed on the Republic.[62] There were probably several groups of *Sullani*; (1) the soldiers (such as Catiline) who had been part of Sulla's cadre in the Mithridatic War, (2) men (such as Catulus) who joined Sulla during this period to escape the Marian-Cinnan regime, (3) others (such as Crassus) who went into exile during the Marian-Cinnan regime but who did not join Sulla's camp immediately, (4) moderates like Hortensius who remained in Rome during the Marian-Cinnan regime but were unsuccessful in conciliating the *Sullani* with the Marians and joined Sulla when he arrived in Italy and (5) a group of Cinnans (such as Pompey) who deserted to Sulla when he landed in Italy and appeared certain to win.[63]

Most members of the great houses of the nobility who dominated the political scene during the 70s and 60s were *Sullani*. However, the *Sullani* were united simply by their opposition to the Marian-Cinna regime and their allegiance to Sulla as the regime's opponent; once the Marians and Cinnans were destroyed and Sulla resigned as dictator, the *Sullani* group began to disintegrate, since the members had no other ties to bind them together.[64] Not unsurprisingly, the constitution that Sulla had re-established was undermined over the years by the actions of individual *Sullani* who placed their own interests above those of the Republic.[65]

B. Catiline Post Proscriptions 81–73

Chief among the *Sullani* was Catiline's friend the younger Catulus, who had been elected consul in 79 for 78 along with M. Aemilius Lepidus. The latter was supported by Pompey over Sulla's misgivings.[66] Sulla's concerns proved to be well founded; Lepidus ultimately led a rebellion designed to overthrow the Sullan constitution. This revolt was put down in 77 by the younger Catulus as *pro consul* with the assistance of Pompey.[67] Catiline, who had attained the age of 28 in 78, was presumably elected to the one of the twenty *quaestor* seats open in that year.[68] Nothing is known about Catiline's activities as *quaestor* for the year 77; this is hardly unusual since such office had limited power. It is likely that he joined the army of Catulus and assisted in putting down Lepidus's rebellion in 77. As a personal friend of Catulus, he probably would have been a member of Catulus' *consilium*. What Catiline did upon the end of his quaestorship is not known.

It is probable, given Catiline's military skills, that following his quaestorship he followed the normal path of going abroad to serve as a legate with a governor of a province or with a prominent general in command.[69] There is a fragment of Sallust's *Historiae* which states that *magnis operibus perfectis obsidium cepit per L. Catilinam legatum.* (having prepared great siege works, he began the siege through L. Catilina, his *legatus*).[70] Unfortunately, the fragment does not indicate who Catiline's superior was, what town was being besieged, or when this event took place.

Maurenbacher has suggested that this fragment refers to the successful siege of Praeneste in 82 during the Sullan civil war.[71] Keaveney and Strachan suggest that this is a reference to sieges of Nola and Aesernia in 80 in the same war.[72] Since Sallust's *Historiae* dealt with the history of Rome starting in 78,[73] it seems highly improbable that the fragment refers to any event which occurred during the Sullan civil war. In addition, Catiline at the age of 23 (in 82) or 25 (in 80) was rather young at that time to have been given a command as a *legatus*.[74] Finally, to be a *legatus*, Catiline should have been at least a *quaestor*.[75] Since he could not have served as *quaestor* until 77, logic indicates that the reference is to an event occurring after the end of the Sullan civil war.

Cichorius suggests that in 77 Catiline joined the staff of Sullan P. Servilius Vatia (cos. 79), who was sent out in 77 to deal with the pirates who were based in Cilicia and to subdue the fierce tribes in the mountain hinterland surrounding the region.[76] Therefore, Cichorius theorizes that this quotation refers to an action under Vatia's command. The problem with this theory is that it is unlikely that either the Cilician pirates or the hill tribes would have had towns which need to be besieged and captured.

Badian suggests that Catiline spent a large part of the 70s serving under Pompey in Spain against the Marians led by Sertorius and that this statement refers to an event occurring during this period.[77] There are several facts in favour of this theory. Catiline certainly knew Pompey by reason of their service together in the Social War and could have used this acquaintanceship to obtain a position on Pompey's staff. Moreover, since Pompey spent five years in Spain (76–71) fighting Sertorius and the Marians, this theory accounts for Catiline's activities during much of this period.

The major difficulty with this theory is that Catiline never seems to have been allied to Pompey. Rather, his associations in later years were with Cn. Piso, an enemy of Pompey,[78] with Crassus, Pompey's rival,[79] and with

Catulus who, as leader of the *optimates*, was opposed to Pompey in fear that he would establish one man rule in Rome.[80] Nevertheless, it is possible that despite his later anti-Pompeian alliances, Catiline may have served as an effective lieutenant for Pompey in Spain. It is more likely, however, that he served in Spain under a fellow *Sullani* and *optimate*, Q. Caecilius Metellus Pius, who had a command which was separate from Pompey's, although the two sometimes cooperated in the campaigns against Sertorius.[81] Metellus was certainly involved in the siege of a number of Spanish towns,[82] which would be consistent with the statement in Sallust's *Historiae* that Catiline conducted a siege as a *legatus*.

A potential drawback to this theory, however, is that Metellus prompted the prosecution of Catiline for extortion in later years when Catiline was *pro praetor* for Africa.[83] Metellus Pius was the patron of Africa both because of his own connections and those of his father[84] and thus was obligated to defend his *clientes* against what they perceived as oppression. Normally, commanders supported their subordinates in their later careers as did Lucullus in the case of Murena.[85] However, Catiline and Metellus may have had a falling out while in Spain together. Metellus Pius was a difficult character; it is not hard to imagine a hot-headed Catiline quarrelling with him.[86] Such an argument could have involved conflicting claims for credit for a particular victory.[87] Certainly, Metellus' hostility to Catiline suggests an *inimicitia* (personal enmity) between the two, which could have arisen during the war against Sertorius. Of course, if Catiline had in fact murdered his own brother-in-law, Q. Caecilius, who was a member of Metellus' clan, this action may have caused the *inimicitia* between the two men. Since Metellus Pius was a prominent *optimate* leader, this *inimicitia* was not a good development for Catiline's future.[88] In all events, Catiline completed his regular military service by the mid 70s and then returned to Rome to resume his political career.

Chapter III

Catiline: Politician: 73–63

A. The Roman Political Framework: 73–63[1]

The Rome to which Catiline returned after his military service was a limited democracy.[2] It was a democracy in that all public officials were elected.[3] It was a limited democracy in several respects. Like America in 1789, there were many large groups – women, slaves, non-Italians – who were ineligible to vote. Roman democracy was limited in another respect as well. Most Roman citizens could not exercise their franchise. There were approximately 910,000 Roman citizens, according to the 70/69 census, almost all of whom lived in Italy.[4] They were all eligible to vote for consul and the other officials elected by the *comitia centuria* (the electoral assembly).[5] In practice, however, only one in five hundred had a realistic opportunity to vote, because voting had to be done in person on the Campus Martius (the election field) in Rome. Only citizens living in the city, or well to do citizens living outside of it, and who could afford to make the lengthy journey to Rome and stay there for the elections, were likely to vote. Accordingly, the number of citizens who actually voted in a consular election was quite small. That was just as well, since the Campus Martius could only hold about 25,000 citizens.[6]

Roman citizens were divided into tribes (*tribi*, sing. *tribus*) – four urban tribes (consisting of those citizens from the city) and thirty-one rural tribes (consisting in theory of citizens located outside the city, even though some of them certainly moved to Rome, but kept their original rural tribe enrolment). At one point the tribes had been geographically based; however, the addition of non-Roman Italians to the various tribes (particularly as a result of the Social War) had eliminated much of their original geographic identity. Voting in the *comitia tributa* (popular or legislative assembly) was done on a tribe by tribe basis with the tribe casting its vote for the measure approved by the majority with each member of the tribe having one vote.[7]

Voting in the *comitia centuria* (the assembly which elected *praetors* and consuls) was much more complicated. The *comitia centuria* was stacked in favour of the wealthy, whose votes were given far more weight than those of poorer citizens – particularly the urban poor.[8] Romans were enrolled in 193 voting units which were called *centuriae*. Twelve *centuriae* were composed solely of *equites*. In addition two *centuriae* each were assigned to the ancient clan tribes of the Tities, Ramnes and Luceres. The other 175 *centuriae* were composed of non-equestrians. Each tribe had two *centuriae* for the citizens in the first class or a total of seventy *centuriae*; only the wealthiest non-equestrians were assigned to the first class. First class members below the age of 45 were assigned to the tribe's junior *centuria* and citizens aged 45 and older were assigned to the tribe's senior *centuria*.[9]

Citizens in the second, third and fourth rank were assigned to one of the twenty *centuriae* for each rank. Citizens in the fifth rank were assigned to one of the five *centuriae* reserved for them with the poorest citizens (approximately half of the population) being assigned to just one *centuria*.[10] It was for this reason that Q. Cicero advised his brother that he 'should pay special attention to the *centuriae* that represent the *equites* and moderately wealthy citizens.'[11] Poor citizens had little political power.

The *centuriae* functioned in the same way that American states do in presidential elections. Each *centuria* would cast its electoral vote for the candidate who had the most votes in the *centuria*.[12] The votes in the *centuriae* which contained the wealthy were counted first. Any candidate who carried ninety-eight *centuriae* was declared to have won, regardless of the number of citizens enrolled in, or even voting in, such *centuriae*, or how the voters in the other *centuriae* had voted. As a result, the votes of the fourth and fifth *centuriae* were counted only if they were needed for a candidate to secure a majority – something which occurred infrequently.[13]

To win an election, a candidate had to win popular support – particularly among the wealthy.[14] In an era when there were no political parties, each candidate 'was a one-man band.'[15] A candidate had to spend a great deal of time campaigning; a consular candidate in particular would campaign for almost the entire year before the election.[16] Politics were not only local, as Tip O'Neill said: they were also extremely personal. There were two types of campaigning – public and private.[17] Public campaigning was done to obtain the support of reasonably well-to-do citizens who were not reached by private campaigning.[18] Public campaigning – like American campaigning – was focused on name recognition, creation of a favourable public image and attacks on one's political opponents. There were several keys to successful public campaigning.

1. An individual who came from a *gens* whose ancestors were well known would have instant name recognition. This factor would have been of little benefit to Catiline since the Sergii had not been prominent for several generations. Of course, Cicero's *gens* – Tullius – was unknown.
2. An individual could become well known and attract favourable public attention by military service which conveyed *dignitas* on the soldier. Little is known about Catiline's military career, but he had been a *legatus*, which means that he had commanded at least a legion. Cicero's remarks in the *First* and *Second Catilinarians* about Catiline's ability to endure *famis frigoris inopiae rerum ominium quibus te brevi tempore confectum esse sentie* (hunger, cold and lack of all necessities of life)[19] as well as Cicero's later statement *vigilant etiam studia rei militaris* that Catiline (was an expert in military matters) demonstrated that Catiline had a well-deserved military reputation[20] and indicated that he was well known for his military exploits[21] and benefited from this reputation. Another very acceptable way to attain *dignitas* was through accomplishments at the bar;[22] this, of course, was Cicero's path.
3. A candidate who had been elected to the curule aedileship and as part of this office had sponsored at his own cost munificent gladiatorial contests would benefit from gratitude for his expenditures.[23] There is no evidence that Catiline – unlike Cicero – sought the curule aedileship – presumably because he did not have sufficient financial resources to sponsor such events. Cicero had obtained such office, but apparently did not spend huge amounts on public entertainment; certainly, his aedileship provided little electoral benefit.[24]
4. Someone running for office would seek endorsements from prominent men hoping that their support and approval would impress the public.[25] In addition, one would post signs reflecting endorsements from local citizens in areas where their friends and neighbours would see the endorsements and be influenced by them.
5. A candidate could attract support by active campaigning. A typical day in the life of a candidate would start with his donning a white toga, greeting friends and clients at his home (*salutatio*), leading a procession of supporters to the forum (*deductio*) and then circulating through the forum (*prensatio*) greeting every person that he knew, or whose name could be whispered to the candidate by his *nomenclator* (name prompter). Anyone running for office would seek support from every citizen, including those who were not respectable.[26] To stand on

Freepost Plus RTKE-RGRJ-KTTX
Pen & Sword Books Ltd
47 Church Street
BARNSLEY
S70 2AS

✂ DISCOVER MORE ABOUT PEN & SWORD BOOKS

Pen & Sword Books have over 4000 books currently available, our imprints include; Aviation, Naval, Military, Archaeology, Transport, Frontline, Seaforth and the Battleground series, and we cover all periods of history on land, sea and air.

Can we stay in touch? From time to time we'd like to send you our latest catalogues, promotions and special offers by post. If you would prefer not to receive these, please tick this box. ❏

We also think you'd enjoy some of the latest products and offers by post from our trusted partners: companies operating in the clothing, collectables, food & wine, gardening, gadgets & entertainment, health & beauty, household goods, and home interiors categories. If you would like to receive these by post, please tick this box. ❏

We respect your privacy. We use personal information you provide us with to send you information about our products, maintain records and for marketing purposes. For more information explaining how we use your information please see our privacy policy at www.pen-and-sword.co.uk/privacy. You can opt out of our mailing list at any time via our website or by calling 01226 734222.

Mr/Mrs/Ms ....

Address ....

Postcode................................ Email address...

Website: www.pen-and-sword.co.uk Email: enquiries@pen-and-sword.co.uk
Telephone: 01226 734555 Fax: 01226 734438
Stay in touch: facebook.com/penandswordbooks or follow us on Twitter @penswordbooks

one's dignity and not beg the support of fellow citizens was to lose an election – as Cato learned to his dismay.[27] Given Q. Cicero's emphasis in his brotherly 'letter of advice' – the *Commentariolum Petitioni* – on the importance of active campaigning, it would seem that Cicero implemented his brother's 'advice' and campaigned actively.[28] It is clear that Catiline was a vigorous campaigner.[29] Both Catiline and Cicero had charismatic personalities and were personally likeable.[30]

6. One could spread vicious rumours about one's opponents and make vituperative attacks on them. Roman customs permitted opposing candidates to engage in extremely defamatory (and false) attacks on the character and history of their opponents.[31] It is questionable how effective these routine charges were, since most voters would recognize them for what they were – campaign propaganda. Posters insulting other candidates and denigrating their *dignitas* were a frequent weapon.[32] One could also threaten competitors with prosecution for alleged bribery.[33] Vituperative attacks and threats of prosecution were among Cicero's favourite tactics.

Probably more important than public campaigning was private campaigning.[34] Given the relatively small number of potential voters, a major part of campaigning involved efforts to attain the support of voters with whom one had some degree of personal contact.

1. One source of such voters would be one's family members (including freedmen)[35] and their connections.[36] Here neither Catiline nor Cicero had much help from their small and undistinguished families which were without a significant number of freedmen.[37] However, even if one was a noble and had a large number of family connections, one could not automatically count on their support; it was necessary to solicit it.[38]
2. Another source of support would be voters from one's own *tribus*.[39] One could legally distribute monies to members of one's own *tribus* – probably the monies went to *sodalitates* (ward heelers) who would ensure the votes of the *tribus* members.[40] It was extremely important to carry one's own *tribus*.
3. A candidate who was seeking support in other *tribi* could get around this prohibition by giving monies to *sodalitates* in other *tribi* who would turn out the votes they controlled for the candidates who had paid them or made deals with them.[41]

4. Another source of support would be one's friends. Q. Cicero lists among Catiline's intimate friends Currius and Annius from the senatorial ranks, Pompilius and Vettius from the equestrian order and Sapala and Carvilius from the auction houses or business places.[42] Cicero's friends included Atticus and Domitius Ahenobarbus.[43]
5. A candidate could obtain support by making promises that he knew he would not fulfil. Q. Cicero wrote that in order to get support one should make whatever promises were requested, since voters would remember a refusal to make a promise, but would forgive the later breach of the same promise.[44]
6. A major source of support would be fellow politicians with whom one made deals.[45] Thus, Catiline certainly made deals with Crassus and Caesar for their support. Cicero, enlisted the assistance of his close friend, Titus Atticus to obtain the support – or at least neutralize the opposition – of the *optimate* leaders who were opposed to his candidacy since he was a *novus homo*.[46]
7. One could extend one's basis of support by entering into a *coitio* with another candidate, as Cicero contemplated doing in the case of Catiline.[47] However, this kind of combination in a consular campaign always left each candidate with the concern that the other would secretly discourage his supporters from voting for the ally and thus ensure that the ally would finish behind his 'partner'.
8. The most significant source of support would be *gratia* (gratitude) from those voters who were under some personal obligation to the candidate as a result of past assistance or other favours.[48] Chief among Catiline's obligees was Catulus. Among Cicero's obligees were those whom he had defended in court.[49] Because of his legal services to clients and his vigorous defence of *equites* and the interest of municipalities, Cicero had a much stronger supply of *gratia* to draw upon. Sometimes these individuals who owed *gratia* to a candidate were known as *clientes* (obligees) and the relationship known as *clientela*. This relationship could be inherited; Gelzer's[50] view that a *clientela* relationship in the hereditary sense was key to electoral success has been rejected.[51] However, there is no doubt that members of the nobility benefited from their families' *clientela* and they, along with members of one's *clientela*, often accounted for a significant number of those greeting the candidate at breakfast, accompanying the candidate to the forum and following the candidate's footsteps as he proceeded through the forum greeting all and sundry.[52]

9. Roman candidates generally had to have a huge supply of cash to influence voters – legally or illegally. To avoid direct violations of the law, a candidate would often give monies to *sequestres* who would then meet *divisores* who would meet with the voters and promise cash for their votes with the cash being delivered to them after the election.[53] Delivery was contingent upon the voters carrying the *centuria* for the candidate and often upon the candidate prevailing in the election as well.[54] It is clear that politics in the last generation of the Republic saw a monetization of the process unknown to prior generations.[55]

A major goal of both public and private campaigning was to convince the public that one was going to win and thus create a bandwagon effect.[56]

The above account does not mention political parties or political platform. Rome did not have political parties as we would know them. Normally, a candidate for office would not advocate the adoption of specific policies let alone have a political platform. However, there were exceptions, including Catiline's consular campaign in 63, when he ran on a platform of debt reform. Although there were different factions in Rome and different interests, a wise candidate tried to avoid taking sides and thus alienating one group or another. Accordingly, Q. Cicero advised his brother that

> On the other hand you should not make specific pledges to the Senate or the people. Stick to vague generalities. Tell the Senate you will maintain its traditional power and privileges. Let the business community and wealthy citizens know that you are for stability and peace. Assure the common people that you have always been on their side, both in your speeches and in the defence of their interests in court.[57]

There was no advantage to the candidate in appealing to the urban poor who had no electoral power.

Nineteenth and early twentieth century historians tended to view Roman politics through the lens of their time and saw the Roman political system as being dominated by two opposing parties: the *optimates*, or the party of the senate and the nobility, and the *populares*, or the party of the people with the *equites*, (the business community) siding with one or the other depending on the issue. This view reflected nineteenth and twentieth century political concepts, which are not applicable to the Republic and did not explain the operation of the Roman body politic.[58]

Now, the Romans were the ones who invented the terms *optimi*, *boni* and *populares*. They had no difficulty in identifying individuals as members of these groups. Thus, Cicero declared in somewhat prejudicial fashion:

> There have always been in this state two kinds of men who are interested in public affairs and who want to direct them: one of these wished to be considered popular; the other wished to be considered the best. The *populares* did and said what they wished to be pleasing to the multitude there; the others however conducted themselves so that they approved plans acceptable to the best men were considered *optimates*.[59]

What these groups represented were not organizations or platforms but 'a set of attitudes, ideas and political techniques'[60] which connected the members. The members of the great houses of the nobility were almost always *optimates* (although the *optimates* included many *equites*) since those in power are normally conservative. However, the *popularis* leaders also came from the ranks of the nobility.

The *optimates* tended to have three major components of their program: opposition to giving extraordinary powers to one individual, support of the *senatus consultum ultimum* as a means of maintaining control of the Republic[61] and hostility to agrarian legislation.[62] They were typical conservatives with a fear of change and a belief that their continuation in power would be in the best interest of the state. Some, such as Cato, had a genuine interest in the non-Roman peoples in the Roman empire, but most had little concern for those outside of Italy, or even for the poorer classes in Italy itself.[63]

The *populares*, on the other hand were less resistant to change; their platform included agrarian reform, food subsidies for the poor and extension of citizenship to all Italians. They believed that their program was necessary to save the Republic from the tyranny of the upper classes. Some had real interest in helping the poor, while others saw a *popularis* appeal as a means of achieving power and wealth.[64] The *populares* were men who believed that the public good – or their own political advantage – would be served by making minor changes which would lessen the tension between various groups in Roman society.⁶⁵ They were open to moderate change, but in no sense were they left wing radicals, let alone revolutionaries.⁶⁶

The *optimates* focused on the senate as the governing body of the Republic with the consuls leading the way to proposed legislation which was then submitted to the *comitia tributa* for approval, whereas the *populares* focused on the tribunes proposing legislation directly in the *comitia tributa* even though such proposals may not have had the approval of the senate.⁶⁷ Emphasizing difference in view of the roles of the senate and the popular assembly may be a more helpful way of distinguishing between the two groups.⁶⁸

In the middle of the twentieth century another school of thought – prosopography – arose. This school viewed Roman politics as being controlled by coalitions of noble families with large *clientes* who supported their political interests and who were bound to them by a feudal like loyalty.⁶⁹ This approach analysed Roman politics in terms of the family connections and geographical origins of the main protagonists rather than political beliefs on the theory that the former factors controlled the political operation of the Republic.⁷⁰

A major shortcoming of this approach was its failure to recognize a fundamental difference between British society in the eighteenth century (the analysis of which by L. Namier gave rise to the prosopographical school) and Roman society during the Republic. Unlike eighteenth century British society and most other societies, the Romans' incest taboos prohibited marriages within the sixth degree of agnatic as well as cognate kin. Thus, women and dowries had to be exchanged not within one kin group, but between different kin groups. The resulting society was one in which relationships between kin groups were more frequent and often more important than relationships within a kin group. Matrimonial alliances were the result of political alliances; not vice versa.⁷¹ Indeed, the nature of the Roman nobility precluded a political system based on family connections and geographical proximity, since almost every member of the nobility would have some relation in one camp or another and anyone who was anyone had a residence in Rome.⁷² P.A. Brunt's examination of the ancient sources has refuted this view that family connections were dominant.⁷³ However, family connections were not unimportant, which is one reason why divorces in the noble families were common, since a frequent way of ending an old political alliance and formalizing a new one was through divorce and remarriage.

A more recent analysis of Roman politics focuses on the formation of *factiones* (political alliances) around one significant figure, such as Pompey. However, these relationships, or alliances, did not dominate the political scene. For example, in the consular election of 65, the supposed *optimate* candidates were L. Manlius Torquatus and L. Aurelius Cotta and the supposed *popularis* candidates were P. Cornelius Sulla and P. Autronius Paetus.[74] R. Syme[75] notes that Sulla was the brother-in-law of Pompey at this time, while R. Seager[76] notes that Torquatus had served with Pompey in the east and was married to a woman from Picenum which was the Pompeian stronghold. Since the two opposing patrician candidates both had Pompeian connections, the existence of a particular connection did not necessarily explain political allegiances or choices. As E.J. Phillips[77] notes, examples such as these 'should be adequate warning against rigid application of the labels Pompeian and anti-Pompeian. While these terms possessed a certain validity, it must be realized that Pompey was only one of a number of factors in the politics of the period.' This does not mean that political alliances were unimportant.[78] There were 'short lived political alliances based on individuals who took punctual decisions about specific issues.'[79] But political alliances did not control the actions of individuals.

The dominant element in Roman politics in the decade of 73 to 63 was not philosophy, family or faction, but personal interest.[80] The reality was described by Sallust:

> For after the office of tribune had been restored in the consulship of Gn. Pompeius and M. Crassus, many young men whose age and disposition made them aggressive, obtained this position and then began to excite the commons by their attacks on the senate and further inflamed the people by bribery and promises so that they could become more influential and powerful. Against these men and their allies, the greater part of the aristocracy strove with all their might, ostensibly on behalf of the senate but actually for the sake of their own power. For, to tell the truth in a few words, all who disturbed the Republic used specious pretences, some declaring that they defended the right of the people; others claiming that they upheld the authority of the senate but all, under the guise of the public good, furthered only their own individual aims.[81]

As P.A. Brunt[82] noted: 'The manoeuvres of such individuals cannot be explained in terms of factional combination, however short lived, or obligations to friends and kin, or in this instance by any principles at all; the personal advantage of the moment was everything.' This is hardly surprising given the fact that Roman politics was dominated by a search for individual glory.[83]

This was the political milieu which Catiline faced.

B. Catiline and Crassus: 73–64.

Whenever Catiline left the military and returned to Rome it is clear that he was there in 73. At this point, he would have been 33 years old. According to Sallust, his ambitions had been greatly influenced by Sulla's example: *Hunc post dominationem L. Sullae lubido maxuma invaserat rei publicae capiundae; neque id quibus modis adsequeretur, dum sibi regnum pararet, quicquam pensi habebat.* (After the dictatorship of L. Sulla, Catiline formed the idea of seizing power in the Republic without regards to the means by which he would succeed.)[84] Sallust also created the classical description of Catiline which is quoted in the Preface to this book, adding on to it his claim that Catiline's

> haughty spirit was goaded further daily by a sense of poverty and a sense of guilt, both of which were augmented by his manner of life. His desires were spurred on also by a corruption of public morals which resulted from two evils of an opposite character – extravagance and avarice.[85]

Cicero claimed that Catiline was a friend of every poisoner, gladiator, assassin, bandit, parricide, forger, cheat, glutton, spend thrift, adulterer, corrupt of youths, rogue and scoundrel in Italy. To this list, Cicero also added charges of pederasty and homosexuality.[86]

Thus, the fable.

What is one to make of these rhetorical descriptions? If one strips away the exaggerations and the biases, it seems clear that Catiline was a very able soldier, a brave man and a good leader. He was industrious in all his undertakings. Like any successful politician, he had a pleasing personality which enabled him to relate to people of all types and conditions. Like many Roman nobles, he was dominated by ambition for the fame and fortune which could be attained by reaching the consulship. He certainly was not regarded as a monster by his contemporaries. In 65 Cicero contemplated running for consul on the same ticket as Catiline[87] and Catulus, the most honourable Roman of his generation, was Catiline's lifelong friend and ally.

For much of the next ten years after Catiline's return to Rome, his career was intertwined with that of M. Licinius Crassus. Crassus was one of the great men of his time, although overshadowed in history by Caesar, Cicero and Pompey.[88] He was an able soldier who was responsible for Sulla's victory at the Colline Gate and who defeated Spartacus and his army of escaped slaves (although Pompey undeservedly received the credit for ending the Servile War when his forces wiped out the remaining insurgents).[89] He was the wealthiest Roman of his generation; however, he obtained much of his wealth at the expense of Marians murdered in the Sullan proscriptions.[90] His avariciousness in this regard was so extreme that he even offended Sulla.[91] Ironically, Crassus lived an extremely simple life for a Roman of his resources and station.[92] His goal was to accumulate wealth not for wealth's sake, but for the sake of the power and prestige which accompanied it.[93] He used his financial resources to advance the careers of men like Caesar and Catiline who could be politically useful to him.[94] He was liked by everyone and trusted by none.[95] He had few enemies – and no friends.

Crassus was a rival of Pompey but not his enemy – as evidenced by the fact that he, Pompey and Caesar combined to form and then reform the First Triumvirate.[96] Pompey' view of Crassus was probably a mirror of Crassus' view of him. Their relationship reflected rivalry but not an *inimicitia*. Each wanted not so much to be a dictator of Rome, but to be recognized as its first citizen.[97] The problem that each of them faced is that the competitive nature of the Roman aristocracy was such that no Roman noble would willingly recognize the primacy of another. The myth that Crassus and Pompey were bitter enemies was created by Cicero in the 50s partly in a bout of wishful thinking and partly in a Machiavellian effort to break up the First Triumvirate by separating Pompey from Crassus and Caesar.[98] On the other hand, Cicero saw Crassus in time as a bitter enemy who was responsible (along with Clodius) for his exile. Crassus, consistent with his character, bore no real animosity towards Cicero despite the latter's hostility.[99]

From Catiline's standpoint, an alliance with Crassus provided him with financial and political backing. This alliance would have been acceptable to Catulus, Catiline's main ally, since Crassus (unlike Caesar) had been a follower of Sulla and kept his foot in all political camps in the years following Sulla's death.[100] Although little is definitely known about

Catiline's alliance with Crassus, the two men were believed to have been closely allied from the late 70s onwards.[101]

Shortly after Catiline's return to Rome in 73, Crassus, Catiline and two others were prosecuted for having had affairs with two Vestal Virgins – Licinia and Fabia (the sister of Cicero's wife, Terentia).[102] The prosecution of Licinia (and presumably of all of the defendants) was brought by a totally unknown Plotius[103] – who was obviously put up to it by one of Crassus' political rivals. The defendants were tried before the pontifical (religious) court.[104] Licinia and Crassus (and possibly the others) were ably defended by M. Publius Piso.[105] The evidence against the two consisted of reports that Crassus and Licinia had been together so often as to arouse suspicion. Crassus' and Licinia's defence seem to have been that Crassus had pursued Licinia incessantly in an effort to persuade her to sell him her beautiful mansion at an extremely low price.[106] That this defence was successful is a tribute to Crassus' reputation for covetousness.[107] Crassus was victorious in yet another respect: after his acquittal, he succeeded in buying the mansion.[108]

The evidence against Fabia and Catiline seemed to be much the same as the evidence against Crassus and Licinia: Catiline had been seen in the company of Fabia on frequent occasions.[109] Indeed, the prosecution of Catiline was probably motivated by the fact that Catiline was an ally of Crassus. Orosius asserts that Catulus enabled Catiline to escape conviction.[110] He does not explain how Catulus achieved this result. Cadoux points out that Catulus was a *pontifex* (priest) and had probably presided over the trial, thus ensuring a favourable judgment for Catiline.[111] It is not likely that Catullus served as Catiline's advocate.[112]

It is unclear whether Catiline's acquittal was before his trial or after it. If Fabia had been tried first and had been acquitted, Catulus may have ruled that Catiline should be discharged as a matter of law.[113] From a purely logical standpoint it would seem that the acquittal of Fabia would have necessitated the dismissal of the charge against Catiline. Consistent with this theory, Lewis pointed out that Cicero, when denouncing Catiline's criminal record, referred only to Catiline's two acquittals – one for bribery in 64 and the other for participation in the Sullan proscriptions in 63 – and not to three acquittals (which would necessarily have involved Catiline's being acquitted for the crime of fornication with Fabia).[114] Accordingly, it seems likely that Catiline was discharged without undergoing trial. Sallust, of course, ignored the outcome of the court proceeding and simply wrote that Catiline had been guilty of adultery with the Vestal Virgin.[115]

This incident illustrates yet another difference between Anglo-Saxon society and law and Roman society and law. Republican Rome had an established religion, although no one was required to adhere to it. However, appropriate deference was paid to it by politicians (particularly Cicero), who often tried to manipulate it for their own purposes.[116] The Roman nobility staunchly believed in the importance of religion as a way of social control over the common people.[117] Accordingly, any open attack on religious institutions was seen as an attack on the Republic itself. Crimes such as adultery with a Vestal Virgin or interference with the festival of the *Bona Dea* were the subject of major prosecutions before religious courts. The common people took religion more seriously that the elite and would be greatly disturbed by a violation of religious norms. There is some evidence that the people had been disturbed by the charges involving the Vestals and that there was a great deal of popular unhappiness over their acquittal.[118]

What Catiline did between 73 and his campaign for the praetorship in 69 is not known. However, given his connection with Crassus and his military reputation, it is likely that he, along with many members of the nobility, joined the army Crassus recruited in 72 to crush the servile rebellion led by Spartacus.[119] He probably served in Crassus' *consilium* since he was both an experienced officer and also an ally of Crassus. Crassus certainly could have used his help, because Spartacus was no mean general and had defeated a number of Roman forces sent against him.

The Vestal Virgin affair did not have any impact on Catiline's candidacy for the praetorship. He ran for this office in 69 when he was first eligible and was elected. For Catiline, election as *praetor* was but a step towards his ultimate goal, the consulship.[120] Attainment of the praetorship in the first year of eligibility was a mark of a successful politician; a mark which Caesar and Cicero had also met. Catiline at this point, like Caesar and Cicero, was on a consulship track having pursued the military/political career path followed by many other young members of the nobility. The consulship was a different matter. While there were eight praetorships open each year, there were only two consulships. That meant that at least six of the *praetors* would not reach the consulship.

Nothing is known about Catiline's praetorship in 68. *Praetors* in general spent their year serving as judges in the urban, peregrine, or criminal courts.[121] Given the nature of their assignment, they had little chance to distinguish themselves. Normally, a *praetor* would be sent out to govern a province as a *pro praetor* following his praetorship.[122] This assignment presented two opportunities: enriching oneself either legitimately (since the *pro praetor*'s share of taxes was quite high) or illegitimately by plundering the provincials or *publicani* (tax farmers) and, in an unruly province, obtaining military glory and additional riches by suppressing rebels and/or conquering neighbouring tribes.[123]

Catiline was assigned the province of Africa (modern Tunisia) for his propraetorship.[124] Africa presented limited opportunities for military glory, but was a reasonably rich province whose taxes could enrich a campaign war chest.[125] Catiline used some of his inherited resources in the campaign for the praetorship and needed, like all but the wealthiest consular hopefuls, to improve his finances for his consular campaign by utilizing the legitimate fees he would earn as a *pro praetor*.

Chapter IV

Catiline: Candidate for Consul: 66–65

While in Africa, Catiline offended some of the *publicani* by taking a greater share of taxes than they believed he was entitled to take, or by forcing them to take less than they wanted to take from the provincials.[1] They sent letters of complaint to the senate, which led several individual senators who were sympathetic to their interests to threaten Catiline with prosecution for extortion.[2] Catiline was probably not too perturbed by these threats Being threatened with prosecution for *res repetunda* (extortion) was a prospect that anyone who governed a province could encounter.[3] Not all threats were carried into action. Moreover, Catiline planned to run for the consulship upon completion of his term as *pro praetor*. If he won the election, he would be immune from prosecution for extortion; following the consulship, he would probably be sent out as a *pro consul* to govern another province with immunity during that term as well.[4] By the time that he returned to Rome, the *publicani* would probably have given up their vendetta. In any event, the odds in an embezzlement case always favoured the defendant, whose defence would involve a recital of his long record of public service (and often of their ancestors' public service as well), a denial of the charges, an attack on the credibility of the witnesses and an argument that conviction would discourage others from taking provincial governorships.[5]

Sometime in the mid-60s, Catiline's son by his first marriage died.[6] Shortly afterwards Catiline married Aurelia Orestilla about whom Sallust primly remarked 'no good man ever praised except for her beauty'.[7] The marriage to Aurelia Orestilla brought Catiline several advantages. His new wife was a member of the powerful Aurelia *gens* and her branch of that clan, the Orestilli, was distinguished; her grandfather had been consul in 103 and her father Gnaeus Aurelius Orestes, adopted into the *gens Aufidia* as Gnaeus Aufidius Orestes, had been consul in 71.[8] Apparently, Aurelia had inherited wealth from her own family and her widowed daughter had inherited wealth from her husband. She and her daughter used their funds to assist Catiline.[9] This marriage improved Catiline's chances of electoral success by giving him the support of another aristocratic family as well as access to the fortunes of both his wife and his stepdaughter.

Cicero, *In Toga Candida,* alleges that Catiline had married his natural daughter by an illegitimate liaison.[10] Asconius states that he could not identify the women in question,[11] although it seems clear that Cicero was referring to Catiline's recent marriage to Aurelia Orestilla. This canard does not hold water given the fact that the Aurelii would hardly have tolerated an incestuous marriage by one of their family. Certainly, after Catiline's death, Aurelia maintained a respectable position in Roman society.[12]

In 66, while Pompey had been absent for three years in the wars with the Mediterranean pirates and Mithridates, the *optimates* had increased their power in the Republic.[13] The consuls elected in the four years following Pompey's and Crassus' consulship in 70 all seem to have been *optimates*. They included the venerable Q. Hortensius, the leader of the Roman bar before Cicero came to dominate it, as well as two members of the Caecilli.[14] For the consular election in 66 the *optimates* had apparently decided to back L. Aurelius Cotta and L. Manlius Torquatus against P. Autronius Paetus and the wealthy P. Cornelius Sulla, who seemed to have been allies of Crassus and possibly Pompey as well.[15] The bribery by the non-*optimate* candidates may have secured their election; indeed, P. Sulla won the vote of every century,[16] which suggested that he had overspent relative to the practical necessities of the election. However, in August-September 66 Torquatus and Cotta prosecuted the successful candidates for bribery and, proving better lawyers than politicians, secured their conviction. As a result, the senate scheduled a second election.[17]

Sometime in 66, Catiline returned to Rome from Africa.[18] Whether he returned in time for the first election (in July) or not is unknown. It is possible that he returned in time to announce his candidacy, but chose not to do so because he feared that he would not be able to defeat both of the two patrician candidates Torquatus and P. Sulla. Since under Roman law, one of the two consuls had to be a plebeian, a patrician candidate for consul had to out poll any other patrician candidate for consul as well as surpassing any plebeian candidate but one. Crassus may have supported Sulla, and without Crassus' support, Catiline would have had no real chance of election.

On the other hand, Catiline may not have returned from Africa in time to profess his candidacy for the first election. His return could have been delayed by the failure of the senate to send a successor upon the expiration of Catiline's term as *pro praetor* or by other events such as inclement weather. In all events, the voiding of the first election seemed to have provided Catiline with an opportunity to run for consul and achieve his life-long ambition. He may have thought that it would be easy to defeat the patrician Torquatus who did not have the financial resources of Sulla. He may have concluded that, given the threat of prosecution for extortion, it was important to attain the consulship at this time and thus gain immunity from prosecution.

In all events, when Catiline applied to run in the second election (which was probably set for November),[19] the consul, L. Volcatius Tullus, after consulting the *princeps civitatis* or *clarissimi* (the most famous leaders of the state which meant a *consilium* consisting of *consulares* (ex-consuls) and close associates who were in effect the consul's cabinet)[20] refused to accept Catiline's candidacy.[21] Sallust gives two reasons for this action. First, he says that Catiline had been charged with extortion. Second, he says that Catiline had not submitted his name within the prescribed number of days. Most scholars interpret this statement as indicating that, since Catiline had not submitted his name for the first election within the prescribed period of time, he was not eligible to run in the second, which was intended to be a rerun of the first without the two candidates who had been convicted of bribery.[22] Woodman makes the unlikely contention that when the consuls announced that a second election would be held, Catiline failed to file within the prescribed number of days.[23] Asconius says that Catiline was disqualified solely because he had been accused of extortion.[24] Now, it seems that a criminal prosecution which reached a certain stage would preclude a candidacy for office.[25] It also seems that Catiline's prosecution had not reached such a stage.[26] If Catiline had been disqualified as a matter of law –either because of extortion prosecution or because he missed the filing deadline for the second election, there would have been no need for Volcatius to consult with the *clarissimi*. It was the novelty of the situation that led to such consultation.[27]

Based on the advice of the *consulares*, Volcatius refused to accept Catiline's candidacy,[28] thus torpedoing Catiline's hopes and insuring the election of Torquatus. Volcatius' decision was probably influenced by the *optimates*' support for Torquatus. It may also have reflected pressure from Q. Metellus Pius, one of the foremost *optimates*, who did not want Catiline to obtain the consulship and thus immunity from the anticipated prosecution for extortion. Certainly, Pius was a major witness against

Catiline when Catiline was tried for extortion in the following year.²⁹ One would have thought, however, that any opposition from Pius would have been neutralized by Catulus' support for Catiline.

Surprisingly enough, Catiline seemed to have accepted this decision with good grace.³⁰ In theory, a rejected candidate could still pursue his candidacy. However, such an action would have been foolhardy since the consul could refuse to accept the candidate's election if he managed to win.³¹ Catiline was no fool. Moreover, it is probable that Torquatus promised Catiline that if he acquiesced in Volcatius' decision, Catiline would receive optimate assistance in his trial in the following year. In addition, Catulus may have urged caution on Catiline. Perhaps Catiline had seen his attempt to profess his candidacy as a long shot and thus was not terribly disappointed by Volcatius' decision.

At this point occurs the 'First Catilinarian Conspiracy' – a fiction which was invented by Cicero in his *In Toga Candida* and refurbished in in the *First Catilinarian, Pro Murena* and *Pro Sulla*.³² Significantly, Cicero's original version of the story only accused Catiline and Piso of plotting to murder the senators.³³ In the *First Catilinarian*³⁴ he expanded the story to include the murder of the consuls as well as the leaders of the Republic and claimed that Catiline had appeared armed on the *comitium* (assembly place) on 31 December 66 for this purpose. However, in the *Pro Murena*, Cicero referred only to the planned murder of the senators.³⁵ It was not until the *Pro Sulla* that Cicero alleged that the plan was to kill the consul designates and install Autronius and Catiline as consuls in their place.³⁶

This tall tale was then picked up by Sallust,³⁷ who claims that on 5 December 66, Catiline met with Autronius, and Gn. Calpurnius Piso,³⁸ a *quaestor* elect whom Sallust describes as being 'a noble of the utmost daring, destitute and factious, who was spurred on by need and wicked habits to overthrow the Republic'. The object of the meeting was the formation of a conspiracy to kill the consuls designate on 1 January before they assumed office. Then the conspirators would seize the fasces, claiming the consular offices for Autronius and Catiline, while Piso with an army would seize the two Spanish provinces and one P. Sittius would take control of the province of Africa. After the initial conspiracy was discovered, they postponed the *coup d'etat* to 5 February and added to their original plans a plot to murder many senators as well. Allegedly the plot fell through because on 5 February 65, Catiline gave the signal too soon and accordingly the attack had to be called off.³⁹

Another version of the story given by Torquatus the Younger in his prosecution of P. Sulla in 62 was that the leaders of this conspiracy were Sulla and apparently Autronius, who were trying to take by force the consulship which they had lost in the courts.[40] Suetonius[41] alters this version of the story to make the leaders of this conspiracy Crassus and Caesar, who planned to reinstate Autronius and Sulla as consuls. Suetonius also mentions Piso and the Spanish expedition, but omits any reference to Catiline. In addition, he attributes the failure of the conspiracy to the failure of anyone to give the signal. Dio Cassius basically adopts Torquatus the Younger's version but adds Catiline and Piso to the list of plotters.[42] Livy indicates that it was Sulla and Autronius who planned to kill the consuls designate and take their places.[43]

The absurdities in any of the classical versions are self-evident. What government would discover a conspiracy to kill the heads of state and, rather than taking action, let the conspirators assemble for a second effort? Why would Catiline join in such a conspiracy when he had high hopes of being elected consul? Why would Piso who was a *quaestor*-elect (and an ally of Crassus) join such a conspiracy? Why would Crassus and Caesar embark on such a risky venture? Moreover, even if the conspirators (whoever they were) succeeded in this attempt, how were they to maintain themselves in power? They had no army. In all events nothing untoward occurred on the *Kalends* (1) of January 65. Torquatus, the consul, when questioned about the alleged plot a year later, indicated that he had heard something of the story but refused to give credence to a groundless rumour.[44] Torquatus even testified in Catiline's defence at his trial for extortion.[45] He hardly would have done so if Catiline had been plotting his murder a few months before.

Due to the inherent implausibility of this story and the different variants which appear in ancient sources, almost every modern historian has regarded it as a fiction.[46] However, some have been taken in by the tale,[47] despite Asconius' wise comment that this story was an *opinio* – (a rumour)[48] to which he did not attach any credibility.

Syme suggests that the story of the First Catilinarian Conspiracy grew out of rumours that the adherents of Autronius and Sulla planned some kind of demonstration at the inauguration of the *optimate* consuls.[49] Rumour of an alleged plot became so prevalent that the senate panicked and voted the consuls-elect a bodyguard.[50] It is of course possible that Catiline, who was relying on Torquatus' support for his upcoming trial, may have appeared armed in the *comitium* to help protect Torquatus from possible threats. All preparations against violence proved unnecessary. After the inauguration had passed without incident, one senator proposed to appoint a committee to investigate this matter, but the proposal was vetoed by a tribune. This action may have been prompted by the tribune's fear that the investigation might develop into a political witch hunt with Crassus as a potential victim.[51]

A more likely origin of the fable is an incident at the end of December 66 which disrupted the trial of the ex-tribune, Manilius for bribery. Manilius had been the sponsor of the law which gave Pompey command of the war against Mithridates.[52] Manilius was prosecuted for extortion by one of the *optimates* following the expiration of his tribuneship on 10 December; the case was initiated before Cicero who was the *praetor* in charge of the extortion court.[53] Manilius may also have been threatened with prosecution for *maiestas* (treason).[54]

According to Dio Cassius, Manilius was seeking to delay the extortion trial so that Cicero would defend him as a favour to Pompey. Cicero, however, did not want to offend the *optimates* by defending Manilius. Accordingly, the orator scheduled the case for trial while he was *praetor*; Cicero gave Manilius only one day to prepare for a trial rather than the normal ten.[55] This ruling provoked a popular uproar and the next day the tribunes summoned a *contio* (meeting) of the people to address the matter.[56] Cicero justified his conduct on the grounds that he had only one day left to preside over the trial and that fairness to Manilius required that he be tried before Cicero rather than before another *praetor* in the following year.[57] Although this excuse appears to have been accepted by the crowd, Cicero was forced to agree to defend Manilius from a charge of *maiestas*.[58] At this point Cicero allegedly ascended the Rostrum and made a speech attacking Pompey's enemies, whom he indicated were behind the prosecution of Manilius.[59] The next day, Cicero resumed the extortion trial only to have it disrupted by mob violence.[60]

Asconius wrote that in *Pro Cornelio*, Cicero said the following about a disturbance associated with Manilius' trial. *Aliis ille in illum furorem magnis hominibus auctoribus impulsus est qui aliquod institui exemplum disturbandorum iudiciorum reip. perniciosissimum, temporibus suis accommodatissimum.*[61] (Manilius was driven to violent behaviour at the instigation of powerful men who wanted to create a significant disruption of the courts which was highly damaging to the state, since the times were well suited for this purpose.) Asconius identifies the *magni homines* as Catiline and Piso.[62]

This identification is certainly consistent with Cicero's reference in the *First Catilinarian* to Catiline as a disrupter of trials as well as his claim that Catiline stood armed in the *comitium* on 31 December 66.[63]

Gruen[64] challenges Asconius' identification of the *magni homines* with Catiline and Piso on two grounds: they were not *magni homines* at that time and they were not Pompeian sympathizers. Gruen does not, however, advance any alternative hypothesis as to the identity of these *magni homines*. Phillips points out two flaws in Gruen' analysis.[65] One, Catiline and Piso were well known politicians at that point; Catiline was an ex-*praetor* and Piso was a *quaestor* elect. Two, the fact that Catiline and Piso were not Pompeian adherents does not mean that all their activities were directed against Pompey or his supporters. Gruen's rejection of Asconius' claim is not persuasive.

There are several reasons why Catiline and Piso may have disrupted the trial. First, they may have had some ties to Manilius as an individual and so disrupted the trial to help him. Second, Catulus was a major opponent of Pompey and had stood out almost alone among the *optimates* in opposition to the Manilian law.[66] Afraid that Cicero would ensure Manilius' acquittal to win favour with Pompey, Catulus may have wanted to insure that Manilius was not tried before Cicero and used Catiline to disrupt the trial. Third, Crassus may have instigated the disruption for the same reason.[67] Catiline seems to have been counting on the support of Torquatus in his trial in the next year and he may have taken action at the request of Torquatus, who was a Pompeian and wanted a postponement of the trial so that Cicero would be forced to take on Manilius' defence.[68] Certainly, anyone like Catiline planning to run for the consulship did well to convey favours and pacify enemies and he may have been willing to honour Torquatus' request and do a favour to Pompey.[69] However, despite the views of some scholars,[70] this isolated incident does not constitute convincing evidence of a longstanding connection between Catiline and Pompey.

One thing is clear from this miasma. We will never know the truth of this matter.

Catiline did not run for consul in the election of 65. Probably, his failure to run was due to the fact that his prosecution had reached the stage at which he was barred from running in the consular elections for 65.[71] On the other hand, since the election of L. Iulus Caesar to the only consulship which could be held by a patrician was considered almost certain,[72] it is likely that Catiline, even if legally eligible to run, may have determined to wait out the next year. Certainly, the fact that L. Caesar was Catulus' first cousin[73] may have influenced Catiline's decision to be remain quiescent since Catulus was bound by family ties to support L. Caesar.

Catiline's prosecutor in his trial for extortion was P. Appius Claudius Pulcher (Clodius).[74] At the age of 29 and well known, Clodius' motive in bringing the prosecution was not to make a name for himself. It is possible that he was driven by *inimicitia*.[75] It is also possible that he was acting at the behest of Q. Metellus Pius who seems to have been the moving force behind the prosecution.[76] However, neither theory seems consistent with Cicero's statement to Atticus that Clodius had permitted the selection of a jury which was favourable to Catiline.[77] It is unlikely that Cicero would have misled Atticus with respect to this matter, although it is possible that he may have been mistaken in his belief about Clodius' attitude. Under both Roman law and Anglo-Saxon criminal law, both the prosecution and the defence had an opportunity participate in picking a jury. However, under Roman law the jurors were selected from the senatorial class, the equestrian order and another group of wealthy citizens who did not have enough wealth to classify as *equites*. Accordingly, a prosecutor could easily ensure a defence verdict by permitting the selection of jurors favourable to the defendant. Although Clodius was a friend of Cicero's at that time,[78] he was clearly not acting on Cicero's behalf, since a possible effect of his prosecution was to force Catiline to postpone his run for the consulship until 64, which is the year in which Cicero hoped to win this office.

The chief prosecuting witness at Catiline's trial was Q. Metellus Pius.[79] Defended by the consul, Torquatus,[80] and supported by other *consulares* (former consuls) including, presumably Catulus,[81] Catiline was acquitted.[82] Asconius claims that Catiline was convicted by the senatorial members of the jury, but acquitted by the *equites* and the *tribuni aerarii* members.[83] Cicero claimed that the acquittal was due to Clodius' *praevaricatio* (collusion) with Catiline; Asconius was not so sure.[84] In all events, the acquittal left Catiline free to run for the consulship in 64.

This trial demonstrates another major difference between Roman law and Anglo-Saxon law. Under Roman criminal law, the character of the defendant was put on trial. Romans assumed that character did not change in time so evidence about someone's character at one point in time was probative of his character at another. Someone of good character had almost automatically to be wealthy so he would have no financial interest in violating the law. Accordingly, if a defence advocate could convince the jury that the defendant had good character, a verdict of not guilty would normally follow.[85] Of course, under the Anglo-Saxon system, evidence of character is generally not admissible except under some special circumstances.[86] It is this fundamental difference between Roman law and Anglo-Saxon law which accounts for the parade of character witnesses which appeared at Catiline's extortion trial.

Chapter V

Catiline and Cicero: 65–63

A. Enter Cicero: 65–64

M. Tullius Cicero, an *eques* and *novus homo* from Arpinum (the home of Marius and an Italian town about seventy-five miles southeast of Rome), had a brilliant intellect. He and Demosthenes were the greatest orators of the ancient world when oratory was the key ingredient for political success.[1] He became the leader of the Roman bar after his successful prosecution of Verres (the corrupt governor of Sicily), displacing Q. Hortensius (Verres' advocate) in this position.[2] Unlike Demosthenes, Cicero was both an extremely accomplished writer and philosopher. He was also a successful politician. He was generally personally honest and individually moral.[3]

Cicero had a consistent political objective, which was to unite the senatorial class and the equestrian order into a *concordia ordinum* (union of the upper classes) in order to defeat any *popularis* attempts at reform or any effort to undermine the privileged position of the upper classes.[4] The two orders frequently clashed over privileges as well as over the *equites'* economic interests in making favourable business deals in the provinces and the senators' sometime interests in protecting the provinces from exploitation. Cicero had the common sense to recognize that the quarrels between the orders endangered their joint rule. His political position was a result of his oratorical skills and his identification with the interests and ambitions of the *equites*, particularly those who were members of the Italian municipalities and who saw Cicero as one of their own.[5] His main political weakness was his failure to create an organized *factio* (faction) to support him; he was forced to rely on stronger leaders like Pompey and Caesar. His legal career following his recall from exile was characterized by his defence of obviously guilty politicians as a result of his obligations to his masters.

Cicero's virtues were sometimes outweighed by his weaknesses. Vanity often consumed the whole man.[6] While all politicians have swelled egos, Cicero's was constantly on display. On almost every occasion after the end of his consulship, he spoke about his accomplishment in suppressing

Catiline's conspiracy. Compounding the dislike resulting from his constant prattling about his accomplishments was the resentment caused by a number of his 'humorous' remarks. Like many intellectuals, Cicero was fond of poking fun at those less clever than himself and made more than his fair share of enemies by his love of a *bon mot*.[7] Although fundamentally a principled conservative, there were too many times that he concluded that the end justified the means, or placed too much emphasis on being (temporarily) on the winning side.[8] Conscious of his status as a *novus homo* Cicero was ever seeking, but never achieving, acceptance from a large part of the nobility, particularly the Claudii but also the Metelli,[9] who regarded him as a parvenu.[10] His conservative nature and social ambitions led him to become a toady of the oligarchy and the mouthpiece of reaction.[11]

In addition, Cicero was less than brave, which is one reason that he chose exile rather than trial when Clodius enacted legislation directed at him, making it illegal to put Roman citizens to death without a trial.[12] In exile, the low point of his career, he gave way to despondency and moaned about his plight.[13] However, at the end of his career he fought for the Republic against Anthony, Augustus and Lepidus and was murdered by them as a consequence. He faced death with unflinching courage.[14]

In the last analysis, however, Cicero, like Catulus, failed the Republic for the same reason. Neither of them could move beyond doctrinaire conservatism[15] – admittedly very principled in Catulus' case if not always in Cicero's – and face the need for fundamental changes if the Republic was to survive. Cicero, despite his intellectual brilliance, was unable to use his ability to deal with the basic problems which confronted the Republic. At no point in his career did he even try to tackle any of the many problems facing the Republic. Of course, any kind of reform would have come at the expense of the wealthy classes whose interests he represented. He might have become the saviour of the Republic; instead he became one of its gravediggers. Cicero exemplified the failure of the governing class to make sacrifices for the common good. This failure led to the fall of the Republic and the creation of the Principate/Empire.

Having been elected *quaestor* and *praetor* in due course, Cicero was first eligible to run for the consulship in 64. Long before then, he had begun preparations for his campaign and realized that one of his formidable opponents would be Catiline. Thus, in July 65, before the consular elections that year, Cicero cattily wrote to his banker friend, T. Atticus, that Catiline would stand for consul in 64 if the jury in his trial for extortion in Africa found that 'night was day'.[16] A few days later, however, Cicero wrote again to Atticus, saying that he was considering defending Catiline in the hopes that the latter would form a *coitio* with him. Entrance into a *coitio* was a legal, albeit frowned upon, campaign strategy.[17] Cicero explained to Atticus that Clodius, the prosecutor, had permitted the selection of a favourable jury.[18] Neither Cicero's idea of defending Catiline nor his idea of entering into a *coitio* with him ever came to fruition.[19]

There is no evidence to indicate that Cicero ever offered to defend Catiline or to enter into a *coitio* with him.[20] Such an alliance would have had obvious advantages to both candidates. Because of his contempt for a non-military *novus homo* such as Cicero,[21] Catiline would not have proposed such an alliance and would probably have rejected any overture from Cicero in that direction. If Catiline had rejected such a *coitio* proposal he would have made a bad mistake, placing too much credence on his ancestry and military reputation and not enough on Cicero's oratorical skills and great following. The fact that Cicero contemplated such a *coitio* is significant since it indicates that Catiline, in 65, was considered a respectable politician with a considerable following.

B. Round I: 64

In 65, Cicero had envisioned eight individuals besides himself as potential candidates for the consulship in 64. The potential candidates were Catiline, Antonius, Galba and Cornificius, along with M. Caesoninus, C. Aquilius Gallus, T. Aufidius and M. Lollius Palicanus. Cicero indicated that he considered that the last four had no realistic chance of winning.[22] Galba was the first to throw his hat into the ring, but his early canvassing met with no success; many voters said that they were already pledged to Cicero, and others resented his jumping the gun.[23] By spring 64, the last four had dropped out, recognizing that their defeat was inevitable; three of them did not even come of praetorian stock and the fourth, C. Aquilius Gallus, who did, suffered from ill health and was absorbed in his legal practice.[24]

The remaining candidates in the election in 64 included two patricians, P. Sulpicius Galba and Catiline, two plebeian nobles, C. Antonius Hybrida and L. Cassius Longinus, and three plebeian *novi homines*: C. Cornificius, C. Licinius Sacerdos and Cicero.[25] Asconius notes that L. Cassius Longinus was a man *quamvis stolidus tum magis quam improbus videretur* (more an idiot than a villain), who was not a serious contender.[26] Although Cornificius and Sacerdos seem to have been respectable politicians, despite the fact that Cornificius had escaped the criminal charges that were brought against him by his enemies,[27] the only viable candidates were Cicero, Catiline and Antonius.[28] Antonius' father, M. Antonius Hybrida (cos. 99. cen. 97), had been a brilliant orator who was much admired by Cicero.[29] His son betrayed his father's reputation and had been expelled from the senate in 70,[30] but he had begun the *concursus honorum* again and had been elected *praetor* in 68, possibly with Cicero's help.[31] Plutarch described him as a 'man unfit to lead in either a good cause or a bad one'.[32] Catiline formed a *coitio* with C. Antonius Hybrida.[33]

The election campaign was dirty, even by Roman standards. Asconius alleges that the blatant efforts of Catiline and Antonius at bribery led the senate to propose a law increasing the penalty for this crime. This proposal may have been specifically directed against Catiline;[34] it was vetoed by the tribune, Q. Mucius Orestinus, a relative of Aurelia Orestilla. Orestinus may have been acting out of family loyalty;[35] it is more likely, however, that he was acting on the behalf of Crassus who, along with Caesar,[36] was supporting Catiline. Orestinus (whom Cicero had once defended in a criminal proceeding) also declared that Cicero was not worthy of the consulship because he was a *novus homo*.[37] Orestinus' veto led Cicero to denounce his opponents before the senate a few days before the election in a no longer extant speech that became known as *In Toga Candida*.

In this speech, Cicero claimed that Catline, Antonius and their *sequestres* (bribery agents) had met with a figure well known for his political expenditures at the latter's mansion the previous night in order to obtain additional funds for bribery.[38] Asconius says this is a reference to Crassus or Caesar.[39] Given Caesar's financial situation at this time, the source of the money must have been Crassus, who financed both Catiline and Caesar. It is possible, however, that Crassus may have been using Caesar's house as a meeting place.[40] Asconius' suggestion that the reference could have been to Caesar reflects his anachronistic view of Caesar's political significance in 64. This veiled comment is the first written evidence that Caesar had allied himself with Crassus, although the alliance may have begun the year earlier.[41] Caesar's interest in a connection with Crassus was the same as Catiline's; he needed a political backer with sufficient funds to achieve his ambitions. Crassus' interest in Caesar was the same as his interest in Catiline. He wanted to make alliances with politicians who had a future ahead of them so that he could strengthen his political position in the Republic.

In the *Toga Candida*, Cicero went on to make bitter personal attacks on both of his opponents, although he focused his attention on Catiline, whom he apparently considered to be the easier of the two to defeat. He dredged up the old rumours about Catiline's activities in the Sullan proscriptions and made repeated references to his execution of Gratidianus. Given Cicero's views of Gratidianus' policies as well as the hostility between the Tullii and Gratidiani, Cicero's attacks on Catiline's execution of Gratidianus seem particularly hypocritical. He predicted that Catiline would face prosecution for his role in the proscriptions as had several others. He alluded (cautiously) to Catiline's involvement with a Vestal Virgin, but did not dwell on this claim given that the Vestal Virgin in question was Cicero's wife's (Terentia's) sister. Cicero claimed that Catiline was an adulterer who subsequently married his own illegitimate daughter.[42] He stated that Catiline had been guilty of extortion in Africa and that his acquittal was due to collusion.[43] Cicero attacked Catiline for his *coitio* with Antonius even though he himself had contemplated a similar *coitio* with Catiline. He also claimed that Catiline had induced some unidentified person to sponsor a gladiatorial show which he was not obligated to sponsor in an effort to help Catiline's candidacy.[44] Finally, in a desperate effort to defeat his opponent, he invented part of the story of the First Catilinarian conspiracy – i.e. the supposed plot to murder members of the senate on 1 January 65.[45] Cicero also alleged that when he and Antonius had run for the eight praetorships in 68, Antonius had impudently asked Cicero to let him finish ahead of Cicero and first of all the elected *praetors*.[46]

Catiline and Antonius responded in kind, emphasizing Cicero's lack of noble status.[47] Catiline called Cicero the *inquilinus* who lived in a house which was not his own, since Cicero's real home was in Arpinum and he lived in Rome in rental quarters. It is likely that Catiline argued that his long and successful military career justified his election as consul over a mere civilian. Antonius denigrated Cicero's status, declaring: 'But I do not fear Cicero as an accuser, for I am innocent; I do not dread him as a rival candidate, for I am Antonius; I do not expect to see him consul, for he is Cicero.'[48] Other members of the nobility wrote similar attacks on Cicero's background which were issued under Catiline's and Antonius' names.[49]

There is no evidence that Catiline espoused any of the *popularis* programs during this campaign. It seems probable that he ran a traditional campaign based on his ancestry and military record. Catulus, as Catiline's friend and brother-in-law, Hortensius, Cicero's rival at the bar and general enemy[50] probably supported Catiline along with most of the nobility. *Optimate* support of Catiline is evidenced not only by the various attacks by *optimates* on Cicero's status as a *novus homo* as noted by Asconius,[51] but by the appearance of many *optimates* as character witnesses for Catiline in his trials for extortion in 64 and murder 63.[52] *Novi homines* such as Cicero were always treated with *inimicitia* by members of the nobility.[53] Catiline also had the backing of Crassus and Caesar.[54]

Cicero's *equites* supporters from all over Italy flocked to Rome to vote for one of their own[55] and, with the support of some of the nobility,[56] he won handily.[57] This victory reflected the fact that he had run an effective campaign, maximizing his great strengths which are pointed out in the *Commentariolum Petitionis*:

> For you have such as few *novi homines* have had – all the *publicani*, nearly the whole equestrian order, many municipal towns specially devoted to you, many persons who have been defended by you, men of every order, many *collegia* and, besides these, a large number of the rising generation who have become attached to you in their enthusiasm for rhetoric, and, finally, your friends who visit you daily in large numbers and with such constant regularity.[58]

However, it is likely that Cicero received support from many Pompeians given his efforts on behalf of Pompey and his supporters, although Pompey himself did not make an effort to support any candidate.[59]

Antonius, due to his father's reputation, came in a few *centuriae* ahead of Catiline.[60] Catiline had suffered a major, but not necessarily fatal, setback. Many politicians had failed in their first run at the consulship.[61] However, the failure of Catulus and Hortensius to carry the election for Catiline suggested that their political influence was declining. This conclusion is consistent with the events of the next year when Catulus was defeated in the election for *pontifex maximus* (chief priest).[62]

Sallust claims that Cicero's victory was due to support from the oligarchy, who turned to him through fear of Catiline's dangerous character and revolutionary ideas.[63] Sallust's claim stems from his view of Catiline as a lifelong revolutionary. Levick accepts Sallust's theory that Cicero won with the support of the old nobility, but suggests that Cicero's friend Atticus helped him overcome the hostility of the nobility by brokering a Faustian bargain whereby Cicero surrendered his *popularis* principles in exchange for the support of many of the older *optimates*.[64] However, Cicero had no need of such a deal to adopt a conservative policy. He had no *popularis* principles to surrender; his guiding principle was always the *concordia ordinum*.[65]

There is no evidence to support the theory that the *optimates* won the election for Cicero.[66] Cicero had devoted a good deal of political effort over the past several years to obtaining the support of Pompey – or rather of Pompey' friends – through his defence of the Pompeiians, Manilius and Cornelius, as well as through his support of the Manilian law which gave Pompey command of the War against Mithridates.[67] The *optimates* were opposed to the creation of special commands for Pompey and had no reason to favour Cicero, who was an ardent Pompeian and a *novus homo*. Indeed, Cicero had recognized the *optimate* hostility to Cicero which occasioned Cicero's plea to Atticus to help him gain the support of, or at least neutralize, the oligarchs.[68] Q. Cicero[69] recognized this point when he wrote:

Iam in populo quam multi invidi sint, quam multi consuetudine horum annorum ab hominibus novis alienati, venire tibi in mentem certo scio; esse etiam non nullos tibi iratos ex iis causis quas egisti necesse est. Iam illud tute circumspicito, quod ad Cn. Pompei gloriam augendam tanto studio te dedisti, num quos tibi putes ob eam causam esse non amicos

(I know very well that there are many others who despise you...And take a close look at those supposed friends of yours who might be secretly furious that you have so zealously supported Pompey.)

One exception to the oligarchs' hostility to Cicero was L. Domitius Ahenobarbus, who was one of the richest men in Rome. His wealth, connections, influence and assistance were invaluable to Cicero.[70] Cicero acknowledged the aid of L. Domitius Ahenobarbus in a speech delivered during his consulship when he went out of his way to praise his backer's father.[71] Ahenobarbus may have supported Cicero because he was one of the young nobles who served in Sicily when Verres was governor; they were accused of cowardice by Verres and defended by Cicero.[72] Cicero may have been supported by Q. Caecilius Metellus Pius, Catiline's bitter enemy. Gruen suggests that Cicero may have been supported by the *optimate* C. Calpurnius Piso (the governor of Cisalpine Gaul which was the part of

Italy north of the Apennines)⁷³ because he wrote to Atticus saying that he intended to see Piso when campaigning in Cisalpine Gaul and implied that he would solicit his support. Contrary to Gruen, there is no evidence to indicate Piso supported the orator. His few *optimate* supporters did not carry the day for Cicero.

C. Round II: 63

In either late 64 or early 63, L. Lucceius commenced a prosecution of Catiline for the latter's actions during the Sullan proscriptions.⁷⁴ The prosecution was probably brought under the *Lex Cornelia de siccaris et uneficis* (the Cornelian law dealing with murderers and poisoners). Prosecutions of some participants in the Sullan proscriptions had begun before the summer of 64. Prior to the 64 consular election, L. Lucius, a former centurion in Sulla's army who had acquired a vast fortune during the Sullan proscriptions, had been convicted along with L. Bellienus, Catiline's uncle, who had executed L. Ofella, a Sullan who stood for the consulship against Sulla's order.⁷⁵

Why Lucceius undertook the prosecution is unknown. A former *praetor*, Lucceius could have been attempting to increase his standing with the public since he was to run for the consulship in 60. However, prosecution was usually the tool of the young and inexperienced, something which Lucceius was not. Since Lucceius was Cicero's close friend,⁷⁶ it seems likely that he undertook the prosecution at Cicero's behest. However, Lucceius was also Pompey's close friend and Lucceius' prosecution of Catiline may have been partially motivated by his desire to attack a leading ally of Crassus.⁷⁷ In addition, it is possible that Lucceius, who formed a *coitio* with Caesar to run for the consulship for 59, was acting at Caesar's behest. However, this is unlikely in view of the Crassus-Caesar-Catiline connections.

Nothing is known about the specific charges brought by Lucceius beyond the obvious fact that they involved murder during the Sullan proscriptions. In his speech to the jury, Lucceius repeated the charge made by Cicero *In Toga Candida* that Catiline had committed adultery with a woman and then married his daughter by her.⁷⁸ Apart from Torquatus, the *consulares* who had supported Catiline in the extortion trial also appeared in his defence in this case.⁷⁹ Catiline emerged unscathed from the trial, which took place in early 63.⁸⁰ However the trial, along with the preparations for his defence, diverted some of Catiline's time, energy, and resources from campaigning.

This result may have been Cicero's intent. Lucceius afterwards published his speech against Catiline.⁸¹

Marshall has translated Suetonius, *Divus Iulus*,¹¹ *atque in exercenda sicariis questione eos quoque sicariorum numero habuit* (and in working in the court dealing with murderers, he also had a number of those murderers convicted) as stating that Caesar, as a *curule aedile*, was the judge in these cases; Marshall suggests that Caesar was the judge in Catiline's case as well and was responsible for his acquittal.⁸² Certainly, it was not unusual for former *curule aediles* to be pressed into service as judges.⁸³ However, this sentence in Suetonius could be translated as saying that Caesar was a prosecutor in these cases. Cicero himself suggests that Caesar was the prosecutor and not the judge.⁸⁴ Dio Cassius indicates that Caesar was either the prosecutor or behind these prosecutions.⁸⁵ Accordingly, there seems to be no evidence for Marshall's theory that Caesar was the judge in Catiline's case and was therefore responsible for his acquittal.

After his acquittal, Catiline returned to the campaign trail. Often, a candidate would make a tour of the towns of Italy to gather support before returning to Rome and focusing his campaign there.⁸⁶ Catiline could have made such a tour of Italy in the year before.⁸⁷ After his initial defeat, Catiline may have recognized that he needed to increase the number of his supporters outside Rome if he was to succeed in his final bid. In 63 Catiline seems to have spent more time in seeking votes throughout Italy, particularly in Etruria, whose residents were close enough to Rome to travel to the city and vote. Etruria was important for another reason; its residents were distributed among fourteen rural tribes.⁸⁸ A large turnout from Etruria could carry the large number of *centuriae* assigned to these tribes, since normally few voters in the rural tribes would travel to Rome to vote.⁸⁹ Since Catiline had lost in 64 by only a few *centuriae*, he could have concluded that significant support from Etruria would put him over the top.

In the course of one of these trips, he may have encountered C. Manlius, a former centurion who had served with distinction under Sulla and had then settled in the Sullan colony near Faesulae.⁹⁰ Manlius, whom Catiline may have known in the days when they both served Sulla, probably remonstrated to Catiline about the condition of the Sullan soldiers who had been settled in Etruria. According to Cicero and Sallust (who seems to have followed Cicero on this point), many of these men had wasted their resources in riotous and lavish living and fallen into debt. They hoped for new proscriptions in order to revive their finances.⁹¹ P.A. Brunt suggests more plausibly that some of the Sullan veterans fell into trouble because they had been given public lands that were not suited for farming while others, who had been given good farms, saw them damaged by the devastations accompanying the revolt of Lepidus and the slave uprising under Spartacus.⁹² In addition, many of the Sullan small famers could not compete economically with crops raised by slave labour on *latifundia* or with cheap grain which was imported from abroad.⁹³ Others of the Sullan veterans lacked experience in farming and others had lost their taste for it.⁹⁴ In any event, many of these former soldiers had fallen into debt.⁹⁵ They constituted a significant class of disaffected citizens. Ironically, aligned with them were the Marians who had lost all or part of their farms to the veterans as a result of the Sullan land settlements and accordingly opposed the government which supported the Sullan settlement.⁹⁶

One of the major questions about the Roman economy in the late second and early first century was the extent to which small farmers had been forced off their lands (and into Rome) because of their inability to compete with the product of the *latifundia* or with cheap grain imported from abroad. The older view is that these factors resulted in a depopulated countryside and a loss of the yeomanry who manned the Roman legions in time of war.⁹⁷ It is generally recognized that this view is overstated. Indeed, S. Hin has calculated that the number of yeomanry in Italy increased in the first century.⁹⁸ Similarly, J.W. Rich claims that Rome did not suffer from a military manpower shortage in the latter half of the second century.⁹⁹

On the other hand, however, there is considerable evidence that the ancient picture was accurate with respect to some parts of Italy. Thus, Luuk de Ligt¹⁰⁰ notes that the rise of the *latifundia* and the decrease in small farmers characterized coastal Etruria and parts of central Italy, but did not impact most other areas of the country. Certainly, the failure of both the Gracchian and Sullan efforts to resettle Etruria with new colonists suggest that small farmers could not successfully compete with the *latifundia* in one of the most fertile and productive areas of Italy.

This trip marked a turning point in Catiline's life. Until this time he had been an *optimate* to the extent that he had any political philosophy; he had never made any attempt to exploit social or economic discontent. Certainly, he had been an agent for Crassus, but no one ever suggested that the richest man in Rome was a true *popularis* (if such an individual actually existed). There is no evidence that Catiline was involved in tribunicial legislation, which was the main focus of traditional *popularis* politicians. Although many historians see the year 63 as being dominated by *popularis* legislative and judicial efforts – often instigated by Crassus and/or Caesar and repelled by Cicero –[101] Catiline does not seem to have been involved in these matters. Catiline had always sought office by the same means employed by most members of the nobility: use of his friends and family, the *amicitia* of other politicians, and expenditure of funds for bribery. Now, he apparently realized that these means would not enable him to achieve his ambition; there were too many rivals with more connections and more money. In the 63 elections a number of the leading *optimates* were backing Murena, Lucullus' subordinate and friend, and Cato and other *optimates* were supporting Silanus, Cato's brother-in-law.[102] The *optimates* would be of little help to Catiline in 63.

The Roman economy in 63 was buffeted by a monetary crisis. Gold fell in such a short supply that Cicero sponsored legislation to prevent its export from Rome.[103] Interest rates seemed to have been quite high since Cicero, writing on 1 January 61, stated that rates were 12%,[104] whereas the more normal interest rate would have been 8.33%.[105] The monetary crisis may have been the indirect result of Pompey's victory in the Mithridatic War and the reopening of the Asian provinces for investment, since this development would have drained capital from Italy.[106] Debtors found it difficult to borrow money, and property values began to decline.

Given the economic situation, there were only three 'solutions'. One was to let the crisis run its course in the belief that ultimately supply, demand and money supply would come into equilibrium – at considerable cost to the debtor class and economic losses to society in general. Cicero basically favoured this approach, although he did make some effort to drive down interest rates.[107] Another was to increase the money supply – as was done in the Great Depression, the Great Recession and the Covid recession – and force interest rates lower, thereby enabling debtors to refinance and to pay off debts with inflated coin. This approach was to shift much of the financial losses from the debtor class to the creditor class. A third approach would be to debase the coinage by permitting debtors to pay off debt with debased coinage or, looking at it another way, require creditors to accept payment of debt at x percent of the amount due.

Driven by some sympathy for his former comrades in arms, as well as by ambition, Catiline decided to appeal to those in economic distress.[108] Like many of his contemporaries, Catiline recognized that the Gracchian injection of socio/economic politics into the Roman political arena resembled the firing of a pistol at a concert. The noise was loud and vulgar, but it was impossible to ignore. As the campaign went on, Catiline would become the leading advocate of debt reform. Cicero claimed that Catiline proposed *tabulae novae* (literally new slates).[109] Sallust echoes this claim.[110]

What is meant by *tabulae novae*? Some scholars have interpreted this term as referring to the cancellation of all debts.[111] Giovannini[112] explains the literal meaning of the term; Roman loan instruments were printed on clay tablets which contained the names of the lender and borrower, the amount loaned, the date due and the rate of interest. Any modification of these terms required the creation of a new tablet. Cancellation of all debts would have led to complete economic collapse. It would also discourage all future creditors from lending money to anyone.[113] *Tabulae novae* in the sense of abolishing all debt was a bogeyman created by Cicero to scare the voters. Giovannini contends that Catiline meant by *tabulae novae* only a reduction in interest rates, a delay in due dates and more favourable conditions for debtors, not the cancellation of all, or even part of, debts. Such measures were not revolutionary; even Cicero had established *tabulae novae* when he arranged for the citizens of Salamis, Cyprus to repay loans to Brutus (Caesar's later assassin) at the rate of 12% rather than 48%.[114] Similarly, a few months later Q. Considius sought to defuse the popular support for Catiline's insurgency by extending the time for payment of debts and waiving interest for the extension period.[115]

However, such a limited program would have been of little help to most of Catiline's supporters, whose debts were so great that they could never be repaid. Contrary to Giovannani,[116] it is likely that Catiline supported a partial cancellation of debt by one means or another. Such partial abolition would have required *tabulae novae*. Certainly, this theory is supported by Sallust's rendering of an oral message from Manlius to M. Rex in October 63 stating that the Catilinarians sought a partial cancellation of debts by letting debtors pay off their debts with debased currency.[117]

Cicero was to admit that the pressure for debt reform was never greater than in 63.[118] According to Dio, a tribune had introduced legislation in 63 to cancel some, or perhaps all, debts.[119] Many members of the propertied class, whose votes were counted first in the election, were in debt or had major economic concerns that made them sympathetic to Catiline's proposals.[120] Many of the Sullan veterans had been adversely impacted by the shortage of both cash and credit as well as by other problems.[121]

Catiline's debt policy was designed to appeal to those relatively well-off Romans who were encumbered by debt or concerned by general economic conditions, not to the urban poor who had little electoral power.[122] However, Yavetz, contradicting past historical thinking which believed that the poor could not have incurred debt because no one would extend credit to them, noted that abolition of debt 'would have lightened the burden of shopkeepers who often found themselves in debt because of a lack of working capital.'[123] Cicero's biased, albeit generally accurate, description of the groups supporting Catiline in the *Second Catilinarian* demonstrates that Catiline's supporters included many debtors.[124] To the extent that when Catiline ran on a platform in 63 it was one which called for partial elimination of debt.

Going to the election, as in the prior year, Catiline had the assistance of his own friends and the *amicitia* of Catulus and his coterie. Catiline may have hoped for some help from Antonius and his connections.[125] He was supported by many younger members of the aristocracy, such as M. Caelius Rufus, who felt the spell of his charisma.[126] With his advocacy of debt reform, Catiline had obtained the support of all of those who would benefit from such a proposal.[127] In addition, Catiline may have endorsed some kind of agrarian legislation but that was not a significant part of his platform.[128] He was probably again backed by Crassus and Caesar, as Crassus' ally and dependent.[129] Since Crassus supported Murena in his post-election trial for bribery, Crassus may have supported Murena (his kinsman) in the election as well; however, such support for Murena for one consulship would not have precluded Crassus' support for Catiline for the other.[130] We know from one Roman inscription on a campaign bowl, *Cassius Longinus quei Catilinae sue suffragatur* (Cassius Longinus supports the candidature of Catiline) that Cassius Longinus supported Catiline.[131]

Catiline also obtained the assistance of many prominent women whose political influence in Rome should not be understated.[132] Among them was the wife of D. Junius Brutus (cos. 77), Sempronia, whom Sallust caustically describes as a woman...

> who had often performed many deeds of masculine audacity. This woman was quite fortunate in her lineage and figure as well as in her prominent husband and children. She was learned in both Greek and Latin literature, she played the lyre and danced more elegantly than was appropriate for an honest woman, and had many other belongings

that were embodiments of luxury. But nothing was less dear to her than decorum and modesty. It was hard to tell whether she was less sparing of money or reputation. So great was her lust that she sought men more often than she was sought by them. But often before now she had repudiated her debts, and been privy to murder. Now, poverty and extravagance combined to drive her headlong. By no means did she lack intelligence; she could write a verse, tell a joke, engage in conversation that in turn was tender, modest, or wanton; in short, she had made many witty remarks and had great charm.[133]

While women could not vote in Rome, they could influence husbands, sons and lovers.

The overall result of Catiline's efforts was to broaden the basis of his support.[134] With a greater political base, Catiline had high hopes of attaining the consulship. However, there was a downside to his endorsement of debt reform and agrarian legislation. Some of the *optimates*, who had been his supporters in the past, undoubtedly abandoned his cause this time around.

The other candidates in 63 were the plebeians D. Junius Silanus and L. Licinius Murena and the patrician, Ser. Sulpicius Rufus.[135] None of these was a particularly strong candidate, but the first two had significant political backing: Silanus had the support of his brother-in-law Cato and his allies[136] and Murena had the support of Lucullus and his *optimate* friends.[137] Cicero claimed that Lucullus' soldiers who attended the election advocated effectively on behalf of their former officer.[138] In addition, Murena has the support of Lucullus' major enemy, Clodius.[139] Sulpicius was a personal friend of Cicero who supported him.[140]

A major problem faced by this historian is that much of the information that we have about the campaign in 63 and the ensuing election comes from Cicero's *Pro Murena*,[141] which is a brilliant and amusing oration made on behalf of an obviously guilty politician who had won the consulship by bribery. The oration is characterized by a series of attempts to draw the jury's attention away from the evidence of bribery by making fun of the prosecutors, praising Murena both for his own and his father's military activities, denigrating Sulpicius individually, and barristers in general, and playing up the threat posed by Catiline. All of Cicero's speeches must be taken with a pinch of salt; *Pro Murena* requires as full shaker.[142]

A good example of Cicero's tactics in the *Pro Murena* is his claim that Sulpicius lost support because he had given up active campaigning and commenced preparation for the prosecution of the successful candidates. According to Cicero, Sulpicius spent his days keeping the other candidates under surveillance, talking to witnesses, taking down sworn statements, making excited charges of electoral malpractices, and issuing demands for new legislation to increase the penalties against bribery.[143] Cicero undoubtedly exaggerated the extent of Sulpicius' 'prosecutorial' activities. Sulpicius was no political novice; he ultimately attained the consulship in 51.[144] It is unlikely that Sulpicius ran as poor a campaign as Cicero claims. On the other hand, *Pro Murena* was delivered only a few weeks after the elections and Cicero's arguments would not have seemed credible to the jury if Sulpicius had engaged in none of the behaviour which Cicero attributed to him.

Prior to the election, there was a good deal of legislation, instigated by Sulpicius, directed at curbing *ambitus* (bribery). Cicero proposed a *lex Tullia de ambitus* which added ten years' banishment to the punishment for electoral bribery.[145] Catiline saw the measure as being directed at himself,[146] as it in fact was. Cicero was terrified that if Catiline was defeated but remained in Rome, he would retaliate against Cicero. The law also prohibited candidates from giving gladiatorial games in the year in which they were running unless required to do so by a will and it precluded defendants from avoiding trial by pleading illness through the provision of a trial in absentia for a defendant who made such an excuse.[147] The gladiatorial games aspect of the legislation may have been due to the fact that in the previous year a Catilinarian supporter provided gladiatorial contests in an effort to gain popular support for Catiline's candidacy.[148] Cicero in *Pro Murena* falsely alleged that Sulpicius pressured him to bring in the *lex Tullia*, insinuating that Sulpicius was being vindictive to Murena by increasing the penalties for bribery.[149] It is somewhat surprising that Crassus did not have a tribune veto this bill, as had happened in the prior year. Possibly, however, he considered such a veto would have backfired in view of the protests the prior year when Q. Mucius Orestinus had vetoed a bill aimed at preventing bribery.[150]

Cicero led the successful opposition to Sulpicius' further proposals (which may have been made as proposed amendments to Cicero's bill).[151] These proposals would have eliminated the practice of choosing in advance one *centuria* to vote before all others.[152] Many Romans believed that the results from the first *centuria* reflected the wishes of the gods; accordingly, the vote of this *centuria* had more of an impact than the votes of the others either because of superstition or the bandwagon effect. Great efforts were spent to secure the vote of this *centuria* by bribery.[153] If the *centuria* to vote first was not selected until election day, politicians would not know whom to bribe.[154] In the absence of such foreknowledge, bribery would probably diminish, since it would be unfeasible to bribe everyone. Another of Sulpicius' proposals was to have the order in which *centuriae* voted by lot also chosen by lot, as opposed to the system where the richer *centuriae* voted first. This proposal would have given the poorer classes a little more say in elections, which were often decided before the *centuriae* in which they were enrolled were called upon to vote. Cicero also successfully defeated Sulpicius' final proposal to give the prosecutor the authority to first select 125 members of a jury panel with the defence then being permitted to reject 75 of the 125.[155] This proposal would have improved the chances that a jury would be impartial.

In opposing Sulpicius' general reform proposals Cicero could have been motivated by several different things. In opposing the jury proposal, he may have been motivated by economic self-interest. Trial lawyers do not want impartial juries. They want juries which they can sway by their rhetoric and misleading tactics. In opposing the other reform proposals, Cicero may have been motivated by his natural conservatism. However, the fact that these measures threatened the political control which the *optimates* generally exercised furnished a major reason for his opposition. Cicero had no interest in creating a more honest electoral system.

As the campaign went on, Cicero claims that he became alarmed as he saw Catiline, confident and cheerful, entering the forum every day in search of support, closely followed by a band of young men, surrounded by *clientes* and henchmen, and accompanied by Sullan colonists from Faesulae and Arretium led by Manlius.[156] Cicero feared that Catiline would emerge victorious as one of the two consuls.[157] Ignoring the *inimicitia* between the two men, Cicero was terrified by Catiline's proposal for debt relief which threatened the financial status of members of Cicero's power base – the *equites*. Similarly, to the extent that Catiline had called for agrarian reform, he threatened the interests of the senatorial class as well as the *equites*. Cicero began to pull out all the stops to defeat Catiline. Although Cicero contends that he supported Sulpicius throughout the contest, it seems probable that he switched his support to Murena after concluding that Sulpicius could not win.[158]

Catiline, on the other hand, became increasingly bitter about the tactics of Cicero and Cato. When Cato declared in the Senate that he would prosecute any successful candidate other than Silanus for bribery and specifically threatened Catiline with prosecution, Catiline lost his temper.[159] His face flushed with rage, his dark eyes flashing, he bitterly retorted, *iudicium minitanti ac denuntianti respondisset, si quod esset in suas fortunas incendium excitatum, id se non aqua sed ruina restincturum* (If a fire is kindled against me, I will extinguish it not with water but with general ruin).[160] As the elections grew closer, Cicero probably announced that he would join Cato in a prosecution of Catiline if the latter won, in the hopes of voiding the election results and forcing Catiline's banishment from the city under the new bribery law. On the other hand, if Catiline lost, Cicero planned to defend the successful candidates from prosecution for bribery, regardless of their guilt.

Traditionally, elections were scheduled for the middle or end of July.[161] Ramsey has demonstrated, however, that half of the time the consular elections took place after July, which meant that elections were either frequently scheduled for dates after July and/or were postponed beyond July.[162] Two days before the date set for the consular elections in 63, Catiline allegedly declared in a meeting at his home that 'it would be possible to find a trustworthy defender of the poor only in one who himself was poor; those who were poor and downtrodden should not trust in the promises of the rich and the fortunate; that those who wished to replace what they had spent or recover what had been taken from them should look at what Catiline owed, what he owned, and what he dared; it was necessary for one who was to be leader and standard bearer of the downtrodden to be the least timid and the most desperate among them.'[163] Cicero presumably heard of this statement from an informer who may have exaggerated it in the telling; on the other hand, the consul was quite capable of rephrasing the statement in an inflammatory manner.

After Cicero learned of this statement, he persuaded the senate to postpone the election which was scheduled for the next day in order that Catiline's remarks could be discussed.[164] On the next day Cicero called upon Catiline to arise and explain his remarks to the assembled senators; allegedly the latter did not deny them but rather declared, *duo corpora esse rei publicae, unum debile infirmo capite, alterum firmum sine capite; huic, si ita de se meritum esset, caput se vivo non defuturum* (There are two bodies in the Republic: one weak with a frail head, the other strong but without a head, and the second body would not lack a head as long as he lived.)[165] Cicero claimed that the senators groaned at this remark but took no action because some senators did not fear Catiline's 'threats' and other feared antagonizing him.[166] On the other hand, the senate's lack of reaction may have been due to the fact that many in the senate sympathized with Catiline's views[167] and that other senators dismissed these remarks as campaign talk. In Cicero's later opinion, Catiline should not have been allowed to leave the senate alive;[168] however, the timorous consul did not call on his supporters to murder Catiline as both Tib. and C. Gracchus had been murdered.[169]

Following this remark, Cicero proposed the adoption of various unspecified measures against Catiline. The senate declined to adopt any of these proposals, refusing to give in to the wave of hysteria that Cicero was trying to create.[170] After this debate and the senate's inaction, Cicero pretended to be even more terrified of Catiline and refused to attend the popular assemblies unless accompanied by a bodyguard,[171] which was made up of young *equites* who were more than willing to kill Cicero's opponents.[172]

The length of time for which the elections were postponed is unknown.[173] Cicero's *Pro Murena* moves from describing Catiline's remarks in the senate to describing Cicero's arrival on the election field, which may suggest that the postponement was not long.[174] Plutarch states that Crassus's receipt in mid-October of letters warning him about the Catilinarian conspiracy occurred 'not long after' the election.[175] This statement suggests that the election was postponed until early autumn.

Postponing elections was a tactic that Roman politicians used to deprive their opponents of supporters who were forced by economic or personal circumstances to leave Rome following the postponement, or to enable their own supporters, who would not have been able to come to Rome in time for the originally scheduled election date, to get there for the rescheduled date.[176] Cicero was well aware that Catiline depended on the support of many of the Etrurians who had come to Rome to vote[177] and presumably knew that these men could not stay in Rome indefinitely, both because they could not afford the expense and because their farms needed their attention. It is 150 miles from Faesulae to Rome by road. Assuming a man walked twenty-five miles a day, the round trip would take twelve days. If he went on horseback the round trip would take at least six days and probably closer to eight. If someone came to Rome to vote and returned to Faesulae because the election had been postponed, he might not be able to make a second trip to the city. If Cicero managed to delay the elections until mid-September, even those Etrurian farmers who had the financial resources to stay in Rome from late July onwards would have needed to return to Etruria to harvest grapes.¹⁷⁸ It seems likely that Cicero did manage to delay the election until harvest time.¹⁷⁹ Assuming that he succeeded in delaying the elections for six or seven weeks, it is likely that many of the Etrurian farmers and other Italian supporters of Catiline had left Rome by the time the election occurred.¹⁸⁰

In another effort to defeat Catiline Cicero made sure that soldiers from the army of L. Lucullus, who was waiting to make a triumphal entry into the city, were brought to the election field to demonstrate their affection for Murena, their former comrade in arms. They may have influenced some voters.¹⁸¹ (They could also have voted, but their votes would not have been significant because they were enrolled in the lower classes.) However, Cicero may have magnified the significance of Lucullus' soldiers in his *Pro Murena* in an effort to distract attention from the evidence of Murena's bribery. Probably more significant that the presence of the soldiers were the efforts of Clodius, a former officer of Murena, who organized and directed the vast bribery scheme which led to Murena's success.¹⁸²

On the election day Cicero dressed in a cuirass (as he had been doing for several weeks as he paraded around the city) and, accompanied by a strong bodyguard, fearlessly approached the election grounds, where he marched about, purposely letting his tunic slip on occasion to alert the onlookers to the steps had had to take to save his life from Catiline's murderous designs.¹⁸³ Cicero later claimed that Catiline and Autronius (the convicted *popularis* candidate from 66) had planned to kill him on the election grounds.¹⁸⁴ Of course, no attempt was made on Cicero's life and no disturbances occurred. None had been planned. Cicero later admitted that he had no fear of a murderous attack, but was trying to scare the voters with his tactics.¹⁸⁵ Indeed, Cicero admitted that he had not seen Catiline on the field; the only 'conspirator' whom he saw on the election grounds was Autronius.¹⁸⁶ Cicero's contrived ploys during the campaign and on the election day may have persuaded a sufficient number of swing voters to support Murena and cause Catiline's defeat.

Cicero's opposition to Catiline seems as much personal as political. Why he carried on an *inimicitia* against Catiline is not clear.¹⁸⁷ It may be that he had indeed offered to join Catiline in a *coitio* in 65 and had then been humiliated by Catiline's rejection of this offer. It may have been that Catiline's attacks on Cicero in the 63 consular campaign as a 'boarder' created eternal enmity between the two. However, the vehemence of Cicero's latter attacks on Clodius and Mark Anthony suggests that Cicero tended to convince himself that his political opponents were evil men whom he should oppose by any means, fair or foul.[188] Cicero had his own 'enemies list'.

Chapter VI

Catiline: Rebel: Autumn 63

A. The Conspiracy: September 63

Catiline's second defeat meant the end of his political career. He was now four years past the age at which the most successful politicians reached the consulship.[1] He was bankrupt politically, distressed financially,[2] and turbulent emotionally. Catiline blamed Cicero above all others for his misfortune, but he also saw the hands of the *optimates* in his defeat for an office that he felt was his by both birth and ability. Enraged beyond measure, he decided to seize by force what he could not obtain peacefully. Sallust suggests that conditions were ripe for such an effort since *In Italia nullus exercitus, Cn. Pompeius in extremis terris bellum gerebat; ipsi consulatum petenti magna spes, senatus nihil sane intentus: tutae tranquillaeque res omnes* (there was no army in Italy, Gn. Pompeius was waging war in far-away lands …the senate was distracted and conditions on all fronts were safe and calm.)[3] Catiline's alleged inflammatory remarks during the course of the campaign suggested that he would not accept defeat quietly. It is inconceivable that he did not recognize the possibility of defeat and had not begun preparations for an insurgency although he did not make the decision to take action until after the election.[4] Indeed, the fact that Manlius took the field at the end of October is a clear indication that some preparations for the insurgency had been made prior to the September elections, but not much earlier. Had the insurgents started earlier, they would not have faced the problem of lack of arms which confronted them in the autumn of 63.

Sallust ascribes the beginning of the conspiracy to a 1 June 64 meeting.[5] The historian antedated the beginning of the conspiracy and the meeting by a year. Sallust pictures the various Catilinarians furtively approaching Catiline's mansion and entering the doors to be led by slaves through the confines of the house to a dark room lit only by the glare of flickering torches and the gleam in the eye of the tall dark man who was both their host and their leader. Probably among the first to arrive were Catiline's chief lieutenants, the lethargic P. Cornelius Lentulus Sura and the impetuous C. Cethegus. Lentulus has been consul in 71, but had been expelled from the senate by the censors in 70, leaving him to retrace the *concursus honorum* (the course of offices necessary to becoming consul), becoming *praetor* in 63. He had an imposing presence, a graceful carriage, and a powerful and pleasing voice, all of which concealed a slow wit, a lame delivery and lethargy. He believed in a prophecy that three Cornelii would rule Rome and that he, after Cinna and Sulla, would be the third and that his ascension would occur in 63, since that was the twentieth anniversary of the burning of the Capitol.[6] Cethegus is described by Sallust as the opposite of Lentulus; he was one who was…

> Forever complaining of the sluggishness of his associates, claiming that by their hesitations and procrastinations they were squandering great opportunities. Actions not words were what the situation called for. Give him a few helpers and while others held back, he would storm the senate house. A wild and forceful man, he held that speed was everything.[7]

Following them came that torpid fat man, L. Cassius Longinus, whose figure belied a nature that was as quick as it was tortuous.[8] Then came Q. Curius, a former *quaestor* who had been expelled from the senate for immorality. Curius was as untrustworthy as he was reckless, utterly regardless of what he said or did, and incapable of concealing his own misdeeds, let alone those of others.[9] Along with him came P. Autronius, the *popularis* candidate in 66. Cicero was later to describe Autronius as:

> audacious, intemperate and lustful; when he defended his immoral practices, he used foul language, as well as his fists and feet; it was his practice to evict men from their properties, murder his neighbours, break up court trials by force of arms and the assistance of his retainers; in prosperity to disregard all and in adversity to fight for evil against the good, not bowing to the republic or succumbing to fortune.[10]

Next to arrive was L. Vargunteius, a resident of Cortona in Etruria, who had become an *eques* when he lost his senatorial rank upon his conviction for bribery.[11] Other members of the senate were in attendance also: P. Sulla[12] and Ser. Sulla, (the sons of Ser. Sulla), M. Porcius Laeca, Q.

Annius Chilo and L. Calpurnius Bestia. From the equestrian order came M. Fulvius Nobilior, L. Statilius, P. Gabinus Capito[13] and C. Cornelius. In addition, many nobles from the Italian towns and municipalities also attended the meeting.[14] They probably included L. Sergius, a cousin of Catiline, who allegedly was his bodyguard.[15] Now, Cicero's and Sallust's description of the conspirators was perhaps a trifle exaggerated. Nevertheless, one would not find members of the Rotary club conspiring to overthrow the government.

Sallust further claims that there were many other nobles who secretly supported the conspiracy, not from lack of resources, but from desire for power. The historian indicates that the majority of young nobles supported the scheme.[16] As usual, Sallust overstates his case; if a majority of the younger members of the nobility had supported Catiline, he would have won the election. Finally, Sallust notes that many believed that Crassus was aware of the scheme and hoped to become chief among them if the conspirators were successful and thus thwart the schemes of his rival, Pompey.[17] Crassus, regardless of his knowledge of the conspiracy, would not have become involved in such a reckless enterprise.[18] Similarly, Caesar, who had grown in public stature since his election as *pontifex maximus*,[19] would have avoided involvement in the conspiracy.[20]

When the group assembled, Catiline addressed them. The speech attributed to Catiline is a Sallustian creation since Sallust, like all ancient historians, invented the speeches which he attributed to historical figures.[21] Why did they do this? With minor exceptions (in the case of the speeches in the senate on 5 December 63) the exact words of speeches were not recorded. Making a virtue out of necessity, historians began to invent or recreate speeches for the protagonists. In some ways they rejoiced in this situation since it gave them a great opportunity to exercise their artistic sensibilities and outshine other historians. Some historians, such as Dio, delighted in writing such speeches because he was influenced by the Second Sophistic movement, which placed a major emphasis on rhetoric.[22] Historians who had been public figures had a particular advantage in knowing how public figures would address an audience. Although speeches were the main vehicle for historians' imagination, in some circumstances letters and dispatches would serve the same purpose.[23]

There are three possible approaches one could follow (or combine to some degree) in composing a speech. One could create speeches which, on a high level of abstraction, dealt with recurring issues and which could be inserted in a text and used whenever this issue seemed to appear. These speeches seemed often to be rhetorical exercises following fixed conventions; a good example of this is the speech that a general would give to soldiers before battle. Another approach would be to create speeches which reflected the historian's own political and moral views.[24] A third approach would be to create speeches which embodied what one believed that speaker probably would have said on that occasion. Thucydides explained this approach which many ancient historians followed:

> In this history I have made use of set speeches some of which were delivered just before and others during the war. I have found it difficult to remember the precise words used in the speeches which I listened to myself and my various informants have experienced the same difficulty; so my method has been, while keeping as closely as possible to the general sense of the words that were actually used, to make the speakers say what, in my opinion, was called for by each situation.[25]

It is likely, however, that the substance of the Sallust/Catiline speech resembled speeches that Catiline did give before the election, as well as what he did give after his defeat.[26] It is logical to assume that at the beginning of such a speech, Catiline commended his hearers on their loyalty to him, criticized the oligarchy and promised great rewards if he was successful in the election, declaring *at nobis est domi inopia, foris aes alienum, mala res, spes multo asperior* (we have only destitution at home, a load of debts abroad, bad times at the present and worse time in the offing,) He promised *tantum modo incepto opus est, cetera res expediet.* It is only necessary to make a beginning; the rest will be easy).[27] He stated that the main thing he hoped to accomplish was debt reform.[28] After Catiline had finished, he was besieged with questions. He probably did not divulge any of the detailed plans for the conspiracy, but stated that the major goal was debt reform. He also probably claimed that the conspirators would have support both at Rome but also abroad with P. Sittius of Nuceria, who had armed forces in Mauretania.[29] Dio Cassius states that Catiline also listed agrarian reform as a second goal of the conspiracy.[30] Upon the conclusion of the meeting, he summoned each to swear an oath of fidelity in accordance with Roman custom.[31]

Following the election, Catiline did not delay an instant (which suggests that he had Plan B at hand.) He ordered C. Manlius, who had remained in

Rome for the postponed election, to go to Faesulae and the adjoining part of Etruria to prepare the Sullan colonists for an armed struggle; he sent a certain Septimus of Camerinum to rouse Picenum; and he dispatched C. Iulus to Apulia and others to other areas such as Umbria on similar missions.[32] He contacted the Marcelli (father and son) in Paelignum and instructed them to prepare for an insurrection there.[33]

Meanwhile, according to Sallust's somewhat melodramatic description, Catiline was busy at Rome; his dark figure with bloodshot eyes and a pallid complexion walked, with a gait that alternated between fast and slow, throughout very sector of Rome as he sought to recruit more supporters. He sought out, one by one, those whom he thought likely to be willing to join the plot, pointing out the weakness of the government, the strength of the conspirators, and the great rewards which all would receive should they succeed in their audacious design. He selected as potential conspirators only those who had the greatest need or the greatest daring.

What were the aims of the conspiracy and who were the Catilinarians? The basic aim of the conspiracy was to carry out the program for which Catiline had campaigned – debt relief including partial cancellation of debt through one measure or another. Many, if not most, of the conspirators would benefit from this scheme. Another aim of the insurgency was to restore civic rights (and possibility some property rights as well) to the descendants of Marians, whose fathers had lost their property in the proscriptions and whose civic rights had been abolished by the Sullan legislation.[34] A third aim of the insurgency was to grant Roman citizenship to the inhabitants of Transpadana, which was the one region in Cisalpine Gaul whose citizens had not been granted this privilege.[35] A final aim of the insurgency may have been the old *popularis* goal of agrarian reform.[36]

A number of the conspirators were disappointed office seekers who thought that their political fortunes would do better under a new regime.[37] There were certainly some former *Sullani* who had profited from the confiscations during the proscriptions and hoped to improve their fortunes through the same methods.[38] Some members of the urban poor probably saw in the insurgency some possibility of improving their lot. Sallust, in his normal jaundiced fashion, states that these people supported the conspiracy did so

> ...out of a general desire for revolutionary change. They would act in this manner as rabble are always wont to do since in every state

those who lack wealth always envy the prosperous, praise the wicked, hate the old and admire the new, and from general disgust with their own lot, hope for general upheaval. Capable of thriving amid trouble and turmoil, these men always survive and never suffer by reason of any change.[39]

The reality is that the conditions in some parts of Italy had become so disheartening for decades that tens of thousands of farmers had left their ancestral homes and immigrated to the city where they often found some work and also benefited from the public dole of grain.[40] The urban proletariat while eking out a miserable existence was ready to support any action which might improve their condition. They owed no allegiance to the Republic, which showed no loyalty to them.[41]

One of the major disputes about the Catilinarian conspiracy involves the date of its inception. As noted earlier, Sallust dates the beginning of the conspiracy to 1 June 64.[42] Sallust's dating is followed by Plutarch and Appian,[43] but not by Dio Cassius, who dates the beginning of the plot to the aftermath of the 63 consular elections.[44] Most modern historians have followed Dio Cassius.[45] Sallust's dating has been staunchly defended by A. M. Stone[46] and A.J. Woodman.[47] They are wrong. The obvious flaw in Sallust's chronology is that, in the summer of 64, Catiline had no reason to organize a conspiracy to overthrow the Roman government which he hoped to head up as consul in 63. The second major flaw is the omission in any of Cicero's contemporaneous writings of a claim that the conspiracy began in 64. Had the conspiracy begun in 64 and its existence been betrayed to Cicero by Q. Curius in early 63 as Sallust alleges,[48] Cicero would have so claimed in the original Catilinarian orations or in their revision three years later. Finally, had the conspiracy begun a year earlier, the conspirators would have used that time to gather large stores of weapons to arm their followers; in reality, the absence of sufficient arms was one of the main reasons that prevented the conspirators from making effective use of the large number of men who flocked to Catiline's standard.[49]

Why the inaccurate dating?[50] Sallust's acceptance of an early date for the beginning of the second Catilinarian conspiracy (like his acceptance of the fable of the First Catilinarian conspiracy) reflected his basic thesis that, starting with the dictatorship of Sulla, Catiline was driven by a desire to seize the supreme power in the Republic indifferent to the means by which he achieved such result.[51] It would have been inconsistent with

Sallust's artistic characterization of Catiline to examine his evolution from *optimate* to a *popularis* leader to a revolutionary. Why does Woodman follow Sallust? In the last analysis, he accepts Sallust's picture of Catiline as the devil incarnate. Thus in his conclusion, Woodman compares Catiline's personality to that of Hitler.[52]

In the days following this election, Catiline redoubled his efforts, sending both money and arms to Manlius in Etruria, who proceeded to put both to work as he began to train some two thousand Sullan veterans to take to the field.[53] Manlius did his recruiting not only among the Sullan veterans, but also among descendants of the Marians who had lost the larger part of their lands in the Sullan settlement; in addition he may have recruited some of the brigands who were infesting the countryside.[54] Manlius' success in recruitment reflected his abilities as a commander as well as the desperate straits of his recruits.

B. Betrayal: October 63

Coup d'états are seldom successful. As Sallust pointed out, any success by Catiline and his followers would be but temporary; the real power in the Republic lay in the hands of Pompey, who could take advantage of the situation and use the actions of the conspirators as justification for seizing control of the Republic as Sulla had done some decades before.[55] Catiline's decision to attempt to overthrow the government reflected far less a rational calculation of his chances of success and far more a desperate effort to restore his fortunes. He was clearly aware of how Marius and his supporters seized power when Sulla was away in Asia only to be ousted by the returning Sulla. Catiline may have believed that he could make a deal with Pompey when he returned, or he may simply have decided to leave the problem of Pompey to the future and focus his energies on seizing power in Rome.[56] B. Levick has speculated that Catiline had been in contact with Pompey during 63 and that both Catiline's electoral and conspiratorial activities were coordinated with the dominant figure in the Roman political scene who would take advantage of success by Catiline to put himself as the head of the Catilinarian movement.[57] If this speculation is correct, and there is no evidence that supports it, Catiline had a plan for dealing with Pompey and vice versa.

As the conspirators increased their activities, their former allies, Crassus and Caesar, became anxious. They were pessimistic about the conspirators' chances of success and feared that the failure of the conspiracy would result in their downfall as well as that of the conspirators. Moreover, they realized that, in the unlikely event that the conspiracy succeeded, Pompey would return with his army to restore order in the Republic and possibly engage in a proscription of his political opponents. Accordingly, they determined to protect themselves by turning over to Cicero information about the conspiracy without revealing the extent of their connections with the Catilinarians. They may have entered into an explicit understanding with the consul that he would protect them from the *optimates* in exchange for their help against the Catilinarians. On the other hand, they may have concluded that by helping Cicero against the Catilinarians, they would protect themselves from any attacks by the *optimates*. Caesar gave the consul information about the conspiracy, an act which Cicero acknowledged in the senate.[58] Crassus chose to act in a more melodramatic fashion.[59] On the evening of 19 October, Crassus went to the homes of Q. Metellus Pius and M. Marcellus[60] and requested that they accompany him to Cicero's house on a mission which he told them was of great importance to the Republic. These distinguished citizens then went to Cicero's home, demanded admittance from an overawed doorkeeper, who was induced to summon the consul.[61] Cicero was probably not overjoyed at being disturbed by these nocturnal visitors, but rose from his couch to greet his unexpected guests.

Without giving the consul time to catch his breath, Crassus explained that, earlier that evening, his doorkeeper had come in and given him some letters which had been left by an unknown stranger. Upon examining the letters, he found one addressed him and others to various prominent citizens. Opening the letter addressed to him, Crassus found an anonymous warning to leave the city lest he die at the hands of Catiline, who was planning a bloody uprising. Not daring to open the other letters, Crassus immediately rushed off to see the consul, collecting the other two along the way. (Probably the other two were among the addressees of the mysterious letters.) Crassus then turned all the letters over to the consul. The nature of the consul's reaction to this story is not known. Concealing his own thoughts, however, Cicero probably thanked Crassus for the warning and promised the visitors that he would take suitable precautions to protect the city.

There are several theories about the authorship of these letters.[62] The most likely one is that Crassus had arranged the charade to alert the government to the danger posed by Catiline (and thus disassociate himself from the conspiracy) without acting so openly as to incur the wrath of his former allies. Another theory is that Cicero forged the letters himself with the plan that if Crassus revealed the letters to the senate, Crassus would thus sever any ties with the conspirators and if Crassus did not reveal the letters, Cicero would arrange for their discovery and implicate Crassus in the plot. The second theory seems improbable, since Crassus could have escaped the trap by burning the letters. Another even less likely theory[63] is that one of the young aristocratic followers of Catiline may have written these letters, wishing to warn friends of the dangers they faced. A letter to one friend is barely possible; to three or more is unbelievable, since that number of letters were certain to come to the public eye and reveal the existence of a conspiracy. It is likely that while Crassus and Caesar publicly disavowed involvement in the conspiracy, they may have stayed on the edges of it in hopes of improving their positions if the conspirators were successful.

On the morning of 20 October, the consul assembled the senate, which was already apprehensive because of the rumours about a conspiracy, and related the events of the previous night. He then delivered the remaining letters to their intended recipients, bidding each man in turn to read his letter to the senate. Each letter contained a warning similar to that given to Crassus. At that point, Q. Arrius, an ex-*praetor*, arose and read a letter from an Etrurian friend advising that Manlius was recruiting forces in Etruria and was awaiting a signal from Rome to take the field.[64] Arrius' announcement was too timely to be coincidental; Arrius was probably acting in concert with Cicero and/or Crassus to whom he had been allied for his entire career.[65] The revelation of this design for a rising convinced the senate that Cicero was not crying wolf this time and it decreed that a state of *tumultus* (insurrection) existed in Italy.[66]

The problem with conspiracies is that someone almost always spills the beans. In this case it was Q. Curius. Curius was addicted to gambling and lost most of his fortune in this manner.[67] For some period of time Curius had been carrying on an affair with a noble lady[68] named Fulvia on whom he lavished expensive presents. As his wealth decreased, so did her ardour. Attempting to impress Fulvia, he alternatively promised her the stars and threatened her with his dagger. His unusual behaviour aroused her suspicions and she wormed out of him the existence of the conspiracy which she promptly revealed to Cicero without identifying her source; probably she used the consul's wife, Terentia, as an intermediary since it would have been easier for her to contact Terentia than Cicero.[69]

Ultimately, Terentia or Cicero induced Fulvia to identify Curius as the source of the information and persuaded the latter to become a mole by promising the couple immunity from prosecution[70] (and probably a large amount of money as well).[71] The result was that Cicero was forewarned about all of the conspirators' plans.

When Curius and Fulvia first came into contact with Cicero is not known.[72] However, it is likely that it occurred on 20 October because on the next day (21 October), Cicero arose in the senate to lay bare some of the details of the conspiracy, to predict that Manlius would take the field on 27 October and to claim that Catiline had postponed the murder of the *optimates* until 28 October.[73] Clearly, Cicero had much more specific information than had been in his possession the previous day; the source of such information was probably Curius and Fulvia. As a result of Cicero's revelations, the senate passed the *senatus consultum ultimum*.[74]

The senate may have expected Cicero to use the decree to take some forceful action against the Catilinarians. Cicero, however, had no intention of emulating some of his *optimate* predecessors by using the cover of the *senatus consultum ultimum* to murder his opponents. Aware that he had barely convinced the senate of the dangers posed by Catiline and conscious of the public support for the latter,[75] he knew that to take drastic action against the conspirators on the dubious authority of the *senatus consultum ultimum* would lead to his own destruction.[76] He decided to foil the conspirators' designs by stationing guards (commanded by the minor magistrates) throughout the city.[77] According to Cicero, many of the *optimates* fled the city, ostensibly to preserve the Republic from the loss of their precious lives, while others who remained were protected by Cicero's guards.[78] Meanwhile Cicero refused to enter the forum without his bodyguard.[79] When 28 October had come and gone without a wholesale massacre of the *optimates*, many began to claim that Cicero had falsely accused Catiline.[80]

Catiline, however, was aware that time was running out and that Manlius had taken the field on 27 October. Catiline may have made plans to seize Praeneste on the night of 1 November, but called off the attempt after Cicero had placed a guard around the walls of Praeneste.[81] Praeneste would have been a logical town for the conspirators to seize because not only was it the site of a Sullan colony of veterans, but also included a large number of Marians who had been dispossessed to make room for them.[82] As in Etruria, both groups were discontented and fodder for the insurgency.

Praeneste, being much closer to Rome than Faesulae, would have been a better headquarters for the insurgents.

On or about 1 November, L. Saenius rose in the senate to read a letter he had received from an Etrurian associate advising that Manlius had unfurled his standard on 27 October and taken the field with a large force. At the same time other senators reported the occurrence of ominous portents and omens; others more practically minded brought in reports of servile insurrections near Capua and in Apulia.[83] This news dispelled all doubt about the enormity of the danger threatening the Republic.[84]

The senate acted at once, ordering the *praetor* Q. Metellus Celer to raise levies in Picenum and Cisalpine Gaul and after dealing with the insurgents in these areas, to proceed to attack Manlius' forces. It sent another *praetor*, Q. Pompeius Rufus, to raise forces in Capua and crush the Catilinarians in that city. Then it ordered Q. Metellus Creticus, who was waiting with his army to enter the city in triumph to take his forces and stamp out the rebels in Apulia. Finally, it sent Q. Marcius Rex who, like Metellus Creticus, had been awaiting his triumph (which was being delayed for political reasons) to Etruria to hold Manlius in check until Celer came to support him.[85] Celer seems to have been given some sort of overall command of the various forces.[86] Rewards were offered to any who would betray the conspirators, and the gladiator bands, which might be subverted by the conspirators, were sent out of the city to Capua and other towns in Italy.[87] Sallust makes the exaggerated claim that these precautions changed the entire atmosphere of the city, filling the community with terror with each citizen measuring the danger by his own fears.[88] This claim, of course, is inconsistent with his assertion that the urban plebeians favoured the designs of Catiline.[89]

Meanwhile, Manlius was not idle in Etruria; he trained the men who had rallied to his standard Marcius recruited others. According to Sallust, he sent representatives to Marcius Rex to convey a message along the following lines.

> We swear before gods and men, general, that we have taken up arms to harm neither our country nor our fellow citizens but merely to protect ourselves from being sold into slavery. We are all wretched; most of us have lost both reputation and patrimony while the severity of the usurers and the weakness of the magistrates have rendered ineffectual the law which forbids the sale of bankrupt debtors such as ourselves into slavery. Often your ancestors, taking pity on the common people,

assisted them by the passage of laws which relieved their poverty-stricken condition. Even in our memory, the senate, moved by the prevalence of debt, decreed that debts contracted in gold could be paid in copper. Often in the past the common people, actuated by a desire for power and resentment at the haughtiness of the magistrates, have taken arms and seceded from the Republic. We are following their example, not because we want either power or wealth which are the causes of all wars and contention between men, but because we seek liberty, the loss of which no good man can endure. We beseech you and the senate to concern yourselves for your fellow citizens and restore to us the protection of the law which the unfairness of the magistrates has taken away. Do not force us to decide in what manner we can sell our lives most dearly.[90]

The above passage is Sallust's rendering of Manlius' message,[91] just as the speeches of Catiline set forth in the *Bellum Catilinae* are Sallustian creations. Now, it may reflect the substance of Manlius' message to Marcius Rex or it may not.[92] Marcius Rex responded by telling the insurgents to lay down their arms and petition the senate for relief, which was certain to be granted by a body which was so compassionate and merciful that no one had ever appealed to it in vain.[93] At this point both sides abandoned the propaganda war and prepared for armed conflict.[94]

Back in Rome, Cicero still hesitated to take action against Catiline or the other conspirators. The consul may have induced the young L. Aemilius Paulus Lepidus (cos. 50) to charge Catiline with breach of the peace in violation of the *Lex Plautia de Vi*.[95] Paulus was an *optimate* and a close supporter of Cicero,[96] even though he was the son of the *popularis* consul of 78, M. Aemilius Paulus Lepidus, whose insurgency had been crushed by Catulus. In prosecuting Catiline as his first public act, he was following the traditional career path of ambitious young men – prosecution of a prominent political figure. In addition, by prosecuting a friend of Catulus, he was avenging his father, whose plot to overthrow the government had been thwarted by Catulus. Lepidus filed the charge shortly after the news of the rising in Etruria reached Rome.[97]

Catiline managed to turn the tables on his enemies by proclaiming his innocence and audaciously offering to surrender to the custody of the *consulare*, Manius Aemilius Lepidus, next of Cicero himself, and finally of the Q. Caecilius Metellus Celer (who had not yet departed the city to raise forces in Picenum). All of those distinguished gentlemen refused Catiline their hospitality. At this point Catiline persuaded his boon companion, M. Marcellus or Metellus (a fellow conspirator) to receive him as his honoured guest.[98] In the *First Catilinarian,* Cicero sarcastically suggested that Catiline had selected Marcellus because *quem tu videlicet et ad custodiendum diligentissimum et ad suspicandum sagacissimum et ad vindicandum fortissimum fore putasti* (you thought that he would be most diligent in guarding you, most astute in suspecting you and most energetic in punishing you).[99]

Despite the success of this manoeuvre, Catiline recognized that at some point Cicero might nerve himself to take action, or some *optimates,* following the example of their ancestors, would summon a mob to end Catiline's career.[100] In all events, Catiline yearned to take the field. Accordingly, he decided to abandon his role as head of the city conspirators for the more congenial one as leader of the insurgent army.[101] On the night of 6 November, Catiline summoned the conspirators to meet at the house of M. Porcius Laeca in the street of the scythe-makers.[102] When all had arrived, he rebuked them for their timorousness and failure to further his plans. Catiline pointed out that Manlius was in the field and that others whom he had sent to various parts of Italy had commenced hostilities, but that the city conspirators had accomplished nothing. He declared his eagerness to leave for Etruria but was unwilling to do so as long as Cicero posed a threat to the insurgency. He then asked for volunteers to assassinate the consul.[103]

Although many of the conspirators shrank from taking any drastic action, C. Cornelius and L. Vargunteius proposed to gather a group of armed men who, disguised as Cicero's *clientes,* would appear at the consul's house the next morning and, having gained admittance, would assassinate the defenceless consul.[104] After approving this scheme, Catiline announced he would depart the city following the assassination of Cicero. He instructed some of the conspirators to go with him, others to go to various parts of Italy and incite the populace, and still others, to remain at Rome and prepare to set fire to parts of the city at the appointed time so that he and his army could enter in the ensuing confusion and seize control.[105]

As soon as the meeting ended, Curius rushed to inform Fulvia of the assassination plot. She immediately alerted Cicero to the impending attack. The latter strengthened his guard and instructed its members to refuse admittance to Cornelius and Vargunteius and their friends when they appeared at his house on the morning of 7 November.[106] The would-be attackers were accordingly denied entrance and left, although not without creating some kind of a disturbance which was quelled by the guards.[107]

The conspirators immediately reported their failure to Catiline who postponed his plans to depart – possibly out of unwillingness to leave the city as long as Cicero lived, possibly out of a desire to discover who among the conspirators had betrayed the plans to the consul, who had obviously been alerted to the plot. Catiline held another meeting with the conspirators that night – 7 November – in which he probably began inquiries about the leak. Curius apparently reported the events of this meeting to Cicero.[108] Meanwhile, Cicero probably spent the day of 7 November consulting, as was his custom, with the *consulares* like Torquatus[109] and preparing a denunciation of Catline.

The next day, 8 November,[110] Cicero convened a meeting of the senate in the temple of Jupiter Stator, which he had surrounded with guards.[111] Catiline attended in an effort to brazen out the attack which he knew was coming.[112] Cicero arose from his seat when the session began and commenced his greatest oration,[113] crying out, *Quo usque Catilina tandem abutere patienti nostra.* (How long, O Catiline, will you abuse our patience?)[114]

C. Cicero's First Catilinarian Oration: 8 November 63

In the *First Catilinarian*, Cicero revealed his knowledge of the intimate details of the conspiracy, including Catiline's plans to have Vargunteius and Cornelius murder him earlier the previous morning.[115] He claimed that when Catiline entered the senate that day, no one greeted him and that everyone in the area in which Catiline seated himself moved away from him.[116] Cicero went on to repeat every charge ever levelled against Catiline's personal life. He declared: *exire ex urbe jubet consul hostes* (the consul orders an enemy to leave the city.)[117] As Cicero continued, Catiline became more and more alarmed. He determined to break the spell cast by the consul's oratory. Accordingly, Catiline rose and interrupted Cicero's speech to declare that he would not go into exile voluntarily and demanded that the consul propose a motion to send him into exile, if Cicero believed that he was such a threat to the Republic.[118]

The consul, overcome by the effect of his own oratory, fell into Catiline's trap and moved that Catiline be sent into exile. The still timid senate greeted this proposal with dead silence. Recovering quickly, Cicero then moved that Catulus be sent into exile. The amazed senators began to shout their opposition to this outrageous suggestion. Cicero then declared that the silence of the senate with respect to a motion to send Catiline into exile, when contrasted with its open derision of a similar proposal with respect to Catulus, indicated clearly its sentiments in this matter.[119] Thus, the consul extracted himself from the pit into which he had fallen.

Cicero went on to justify his failure to put Catiline to death immediately, on the grounds that not everyone had been convinced of Catiline's guilt. He claimed that Catiline, if left unimpeded, would depart Rome with all his followers, who could then be hunted down and eliminated.[120] Cicero concluded his oration with a pious invocation of Jupiter as the protector of the city.

Critics have pointed out that the *First Catilinarian* is inconsistent. From an intellectual standpoint, Cicero alternates between saying on the one hand that the safety of the Republic justifies Catiline's execution and citing a number of historical examples where 'rebels' had been forcibly repressed by the oligarchs[121] and saying on the other hand that he will not take such action against Catiline and between stating that Catiline should leave Rome, and then claiming that he is not ordering Catiline to go into exile.[122] Cicero, however, was not trying to create a model of intellectual consistency.

What was Cicero attempting to accomplish with the *First Catilinarian*? First and foremost, he was trying to convince his sceptical audience that there was a real conspiracy afoot. He was in the position of the boy who had cried wolf too often, and his fellow senators were dubious about his claims of conspiracy; they were unwilling to send Catiline into exile, let alone support his execution. Secondly, like any criminal prosecutor, by claiming that the government knew everything that the Catilinarians were doing and was closing in on them, he was trying to scare those involved in the conspiracy into turning state's evidence. Thirdly, he was trying to convince Catiline to leave the city without forcing him to do so. Cicero believed that his own life was not safe until the city wall stood between him and Catiline.[123]

According to Sallust, Catiline then arose to defend himself. Shaken by the revelation of his plans, perturbed by Cicero's oratory, Catiline, for perhaps the only time in his life, was cowed. His eyes downcast, as though conscious of his guilt, he stammered out a few feeble remarks, asking the senate not to believe the unfounded charges against him, given the reputation of his family and the patriotism of his ancestors. Gradually, regaining some of his nerve, he began to argue that it was inconceivable either that a man of his rank would plot against the Republic, or that a 'lodger' like Cicero would seek to preserve it. The last argument was too much for the enraged senate. Catiline's speech was interrupted by cries of 'traitor' and 'assassin'. An enraged Catiline allegedly retorted angrily: *Tum ille furibundus: Quoniam quidem circumventus inquit, ab inimicis praeceps agor, incendium meum ruina restinguam* (Because I am beset by enemies and driven headlong, I will put out this fire with destruction.) With that, he rushed out of the senate house and returned to his mansion.[124] The credibility of Sallust's account is undercut by the fact that he transfers Catiline's remarks, allegedly made during the election campaign, to this occasion – presumably for artistic purposes. Like many other parts of the *Bellum Catilinae*, this dramatic account is unreal.

Plutarch more credibly states that when Catiline arose to respond, he was shouted down, and Cicero rose and ordered him to depart from the city, saying that, since one of them did his work with words and the other with arms, the city wall must lie between them.[125] Plutarch's account is subject to scrutiny since he takes a portion of Cicero' *First Catilinarian* – *magno me metu liberaveris, mod inter me atque te murus intersit*[126] (You will free me from a great fear once a wall stands between us) and transposes it to the events following Catiline's attempted rebuttal. Diodorius Siculus gives a far less dramatic, but probably more realistic, account when he writes that at the conclusion of Cicero's speech, Catiline left the senate without attempting to respond.[127]

Had Cicero have given the signal, Catiline might have been killed that day by the consul's bodyguard.[128] Catiline knew his man and was not worried that Cicero would steel himself to take such drastic action. No such signal was given. Nevertheless, Catiline concluded that there was little he could accomplish in the city and resolved to leave that night. Before departing, he called together the remaining conspirators (headed by Lentulus and Cethegus) to his home and ordered them to assassinate Cicero if given the opportunity, but to concentrate on recruiting supporters in preparation for a rising when Catiline arrived outside the city gate at the head of Manlius' army.[129] He instructed them to prepare to start fires at various parts of the city in order to distract the authorities when he made his attack.[130] The attack was planned for the night of the Saturnalia (17 December), when the city guards would be enjoying a drunken holiday and ill prepared to meet an attack.[131] At the conclusion of this meeting, Catiline mounted his horse and, in the company of Publius, Tongilius, Mincacius, and perhaps three hundred others, rode through the darkened Via Aurelia, out of the city gates, and headed north.[132] The guards, presumably under instructions from Cicero, took no steps to oppose their departure.

What Catiline thought as he heard the hooves of his followers' horses ringing on the cobblestones of the empty streets is unknown. It is probable, however, that he was happier with the prospect of open warfare than secret conspiracy and that Cicero was equally happy, since his life was now safe and he was relieved of pressure from the *optimates* to take drastic action against Catiline.[133] The next morning Catiline's supporters began to spread the rumour that Catiline had left the city to go into exile in Marseilles[134] (which was the favourite home of Roman exiles.)[135] Over the next several days, they also delivered to some of the *optimates* letters which Catiline had written en route, saying that false accusations and private intrigues by his enemies had driven him to exile, a step he had taken not out of consciousness of guilt, but solely out of a desire to save the Republic from further dissension.[136] In addition, Catiline sent a letter to his old friend Catulus, which Sallust quotes as follows:

> Your extraordinary loyalty known and pleasing to me in great dangers gives me confidence in your approval. For that reason, I resolved not to make any defence of my new course of action. I have decided to explain it- not from any consciousness of guilt but because-so help me god – you will recognize it as true. Aroused by injuries and insults, deprived of the fruit of my industry and labour, I have not obtained the position due my rank. I have taken upon myself, in accordance with my custom, the cause of an unhappy people, not because I am incapable to paying the debts that I have contracted under my name with my own property (while the generosity of Orestilla and her daughter could have paid the debts that I have incurred under the names of others) but because I have seen unworthy men in a place of honour which I believe was denied me because of false suspicions. For this reason I am following a course which is honourable enough in light of my situation in the hope that it may preserve the remnants of my reputation. I wish to write more but it is reported to me that a hostile force is being prepared against me. Now, I commend and entrust Orestilla to your loyalty. Defend her from injury as your children have requested. Farewell.[137]

Catulus read this letter to the Senate without comment. The letter certainly revealed how Catiline, resentful of his treatment by the *optimates* and Cicero, and moved by the plight of the people, had undertaken the path of rebellion.[138]

On the evening of 9 November, Cicero convened a *contio* (assembly of the people) and delivered extemporaneously the *Second Catilinarian*, in which he informed the people of the departure of Catiline from the city. It is always questionable how many people in this or any other *contio* (which were held in the open) actually heard the speaker's remarks, although it is possible that much of the substance of the speech may have been relayed by those standing in front to those standing behind them and so on. Cicero declared that the departure of Catiline constituted a great victory, since Catiline had been far more dangerous in the city than out of it. However, he claimed that he had not forced Catiline to leave, but that the latter had done so of his own accord. Based on information probably supplied by Curius and Fulvia, Cicero predicted that Catiline, instead of going into exile in Marseilles, would assume consular insignia and take command of Manlius' forces outside of Faesulae.[139] He defended his decision to let Catiline leave unscathed and invited all of Catiline's followers to follow their leader's example and leave the city.

Cicero, like a prosecutor addressing a grand jury, then enumerated in somewhat prejudicial fashion the six groups who, he claimed, supported Catiline:

(1) Wealthy men with significant debts but with resources to pay them, who hoped to escape them through a partial or total cancellation of debts.
(2) Men who had great debts, but who sought power by a revolution.
(3) Sullan veterans who needed new proscriptions to replenish their coffers.[140]
(4) Other men who had financial problems and hoped for a partial or total cancellation of debt.
(5) The criminal element in society.
(6) Dissolute aristocratic youth.[141]

The consul closed, once again, by invoking the gods' help in defeating the enemies of the Republic.[142]

Did Cicero delude himself and his audience in claiming that Catiline was a greater threat in Rome than he would be in Etruria? Certainly, the conspirators in Rome, bereft of Catiline's leadership, bungled the planned coup d'état, and with it, the insurgency. However, it is not certain that they would have done any better with Catiline's leadership, given Curius' treachery. The conspirators were allegedly unbalanced men, who seldom met together without overindulging in both women and wine.[143] Their record up until the time of Catiline's departure was nothing to boast about. Thus, Catiline might not have been as effective in the city, had he remained there, as Cicero believed, while in Etruria he proved to be a most effective leader of Manlius' forces. In the last analysis, however, the fate of the insurgency would be decided in Rome and not in Etruria and Cicero's claim that Catiline's departure was a victory for the government was prescient.

On his way north, Catiline stopped at Arretium where he stayed in the home of his lieutenant, C. Flaminius. The two spent several days in this town, distributing arms to the populace, which had already been aroused by other agitators.[144] Fulfilling Cicero's prediction, Catiline assumed the *fasces* and other consular insignia to emphasize his claim that he had been cheated of that office by the machinations of his enemies.[145] He then proceeded to the camp of Manlius. There he found only two thousand men, whom he organized into two legions.[146] By vigorous recruiting, he increased the number to between 12,000 and 20,000 whom he distributed equally between the two legions; however, only a quarter of these men were well armed.[147] Many of his forces just had spears or lances and some had only sharpened stakes.[148]

While the date that the news of Catiline's activities reached Rome is not known, Ramsey has convincingly demonstrated, based on his analysis of how long Catiline took to get to Manlius' camp and how long information of his arrival would have taken to reach Rome, that the news probably reached Rome on or about 16 or 17 November.[149] The next day the senate formally declared that both Catiline and Manlius were *hostes* (enemies). It decreed that C. Antonius should raise forces and pursue Catiline, while Cicero was to remain in the city and guard against any uprising there.[150] (Antonius probably left the city as soon as possible, which means he departed on either 18 or 19 November.)[151] The senate then offered amnesty to all insurgents except those who had already been convicted of a capital offense, provided that they laid down their arms by a certain day. Of all involved in the insurgency, not one accepted the senate's offer, or claimed the previously offered reward for betraying the uprising.[152] Whatever may be said against the insurgents, they were men of courage and determination.

Meanwhile many men, hitherto uninvolved in the insurgency, treated the senate's offer as a call to arms and set off from all parts of Italy to rally to Catiline's side. Among these was Aulus Fulvius, the talented, personable and studious son of a senator, who was captured on his way to Catiline's camp, brought back to Rome, and handed over to his father, who ordered that he be put to death. The father allegedly said that he had raised his son to fight for the Republic against Catiline and not to fight for Catiline against the Republic.[153] Asconius relates a story that Clodius also set out to join Catiline in Faesulae, but turned back when he thought the better of it.[154] Certainly in later years, after Cicero and Clodius had become bitter enemies, Cicero frequently taunted Clodius with his alleged involvement in Catiline's conspiracy. Whether there is any truth in Cicero's charges is questionable. Clodius was a close friend and supporter of Murena and probably had no involvement in the conspiracy.[155]

Back at Rome, P. Autronius and the other conspirators were making desperate efforts to send arms to the ill-equipped forces in Etruria.[156] At the same time, another conspirator, C. Marcellus, attempted to tamper with one of the gladiator bands which had been sent from Rome to Capua. He was aided in this scheme by M. Aulanus, a military tribune under Antonius. Aulanus had been intriguing for the conspirators in Pisaurum, and other parts of the Gallic territory.[157] Unfortunately for these conspirators, Cicero had assigned the energetic *quaestor* P. Sestius, to Antonius' staff, since Cicero distrusted his fellow consul. When learning of the situation in Capua, Sestius showed commendable initiative and, leaving Antonius to his own devices, rushed to Capua with an armed force, expelling the Catilinarians from the city.[158]

These incidents were not isolated. The Catilinarians were active throughout Italy. There were disturbances in Apulia, in Bruttium, and in Picenum, as well as in the northern provinces of Cisalpine and Transalpine Gaul caused by those whom Catiline had sent to these districts. Sallust questionably claims that the conspirators in these areas acted so imprudently that their conduct seemed almost insane. Allegedly, their mysterious nocturnal meetings and their ceaseless activity caused more apprehension than actual damage. Their activity served only to expose them to government officials who were quick to react. Q. Metellus Celer, relying on the *senatus consultum ultimum*, imprisoned several conspirators in Picenum and C. Murena (the official responsible for Cisalpine Gaul) did the same for this province, effectively suppressing the insurgency in these areas.[159] Thus, from much agitation, nothing came. It is likely that the disturbances throughout Italy reflected Catilinarian attempts to exploit differences between the Italians and Roman colonists, which resulted from disputes about land tenure.[160] To the extent that there were servile insurrections at this time, they were not instigated by, or related to the Catilinarian movement.[161]

Cicero's biggest problem in the second half of November came not from the Catilinarians, but from his erstwhile friend, the indefatigable Cato.[162] Cato, making good on his threat from the prior summer to prosecute the successful consular candidates (other than Silanus), joined with the disappointed Sulpicius to prosecute Murena for his extensive bribery.[163] The exact date of this trial is not known, but it must have occurred after Antonius had left the city (18/19 November),[164] and before the seizure of the Gauls on the nights of 2 and 3 December. The *optimate* leaders recognized that a successful prosecution of Murena would substantiate Catiline's claim that he been unjustly deprived of the consulship. In addition, a successful prosecution would prevent Murena from taking office and leave the Republic with only one consul in place. Accordingly, Cicero took on Murena's defence, with the assistance of, Q. Hortensius and Crassus.[165] The appearance of Crassus on Murena's side indicated that the rich man of Roman politics had withdrawn any support from Catiline.

In the first part of the trial, Cato and Sulpicius vigorously attacked Murena's illegal campaign tactics. Crassus and Hortensius defended the consul-elect with equal vigour.[166] Cicero, who spoke third, was determined to outshine Hortensius, his rival, whose speech had been well received. Cicero became so consumed with the rivalry that he was unable to sleep the night before and his delivery suffered accordingly.[167] However badly delivered, the speech (at least when rewritten) was a brilliant exercise in composition – and obfuscation. Mocking Cato's stoicism and Sulpicius' learnedness in the field of jurisprudence,[168] Cicero appealed blatantly to the jury's fear that a conviction of Murena would aid the insurgents' cause.[169] One of Cicero's most effective tactics as a trial lawyer was to make fun of opposing counsel and the opposing parties and *Pro Murena* is a brilliant example of Cicero's tactics at his most effective.[170] His efforts were successful and Murena was acquitted.[171]

In a less public, but perhaps more significant victory, someone, Cicero or perhaps one of the other *optimates*, persuaded the great financier, Q. Considius, to announce that he would not press any of his creditors for payment of their debts, or even payment of interest on them.[172] Cato, when he assumed the tribuneship on 10 December, also persuaded the popular assembly to expand the number of citizens permitted to buy grain at subsidized prices, thereby alleviating the economic distress of the urban masses.[173] Both of these actions had their intended effect of weakening Catiline by reducing the economic pressures on his supporters.

Chapter VII

Lentulus' Blunder: November–December 63

A. Involvement of the Gauls: Late November 63

The departure of Catiline left the conspirators in the city with Lentulus and perhaps Cethegus as their heads.¹ Neither was fitted by nature or experience for a position of leadership. Lentulus, indolent and arrogant, possessed a political record which was more distinguished in appearance than in reality.² The nature of the man is best revealed in the incident which gave him his cognomen *Sura* ('leg'). When Lentulus was *quaestor*, he was summoned by Sulla to account to the senate for his malfeasance in office. Lentulus appeared in the senate with a careless and contemptuous air and, declining to defend himself or to present his accounts, showed his *sura* to the senate as Roman boys were wont to do when they were playing and they missed a ball thrown to them.³ Further light is shed on his character by another incident which followed his acquittal for malfeasance by two votes. Lentulus did not rejoice, but rather decried the fact that he had spent money bribing an unnecessary juror.⁴ Cethegus, as rash as Lentulus was slow,⁵ had a reputation based on the sole claim that he had once gone to Spain in the 70s and made an unsuccessful attempt to assassinate its then governor, Q. Metellus Pius.⁶

Such were Catiline's successors. It is hardly shocking that the two of them botched the conspiracy. What is surprising is that Catiline gave them the opportunity to do so. Possibly, he felt that they would work well in harness because of their opposite natures. More likely, he had no one else who was more capable. By their very nature, conspiracies attract misfits – not successful men. In the days following Catiline's departure his seconds, however, showed some initial competence and busied themselves in the plans for a coup d'état. Recognizing that the *optimates* and other prominent citizens would leave their homes open on the eve of the Saturnalia (17 December) so that their *clientes* could leave their annual gifts, Catiline had probably instructed Lentulus and Cethegus to make plans for a number of the conspirators to pose as *clientes* and gain admittance to the homes of the *optimates*, whom they would murder in their beds.[7] Lentulus and Cethegus also arranged for Cethegus to lead a group to assassinate Cicero.[8] On top of that, they even made preparations to have a number of youths of prominent families dispose of their parents.[9] They were supposed to have lined up 400 conspirators to slaughter all members of the senate.[10] This latter claim seems incredible, since involvement of that number of men would have resulted in everyone knowing about the plot. Finally, they made plans to have L. Cassius Longinus, L. Statilius, and P. Gabinus set fire to twelve sections of the city.[11]

Afraid of leaks, Lentulus and Cethegus told each individual conspirator no more than what he would need to know to perform his specific task. They informed only the most prominent conspirators of the date set for the rising; the rest were instructed to act on the night after L. Calpurnius Bestia, one of the newly elected tribunes, convened a *contio*, and denounced Cicero.[12] They falsely told the main body of the conspirators that the purpose of the rising was to enable the conspirators to escape from the city and join Catiline's forces.[13] Curius promptly informed Cicero of the 'plan' as described to him by Lentulus and Cethegus. It seems obvious that the Catilinarians' real plan was simply an updated version of the earlier plan to seize the city by a rising within and an attack by Catiline's forces from without. By setting a number of fires in various parts of the city, the conspirators hoped to distract the attention of the authorities and facilitate the outside attack.[14] Catiline's goal was to seize Rome, not destroy it.

Meanwhile, Lentulus, following Catiline's instructions, continued to seek recruits from all ranks and stations of life, contacting as Catiline had done those whom he thought would, by nature or situation, be favourable to the insurgency.[15] Cethegus undercut Lentulus' efforts by constantly complaining Lentulus was moving too slowly.[16] One result of Cethegus' constant complaints may have been to pressure Lentulus to take drastic action. Upon learning that two ambassadors from the Gallic tribe of Allobroges (who lived in what is now southern France in the northern part of the Roman province of Transalpine Gaul) had come to Rome to complain about the malfeasance of the Roman officials who governed them, Lentulus determined to enlist their assistance.[17] He believed that the economic situation of the Gauls as well as their general warlike nature could make them ready allies of the Catilinarians. Accordingly, he instructed P. Umbrenus, one of the conspirators who had been a trader in Gaul and who knew many Gallic leaders, to meet with the Allobroges and sound out their willingness to join the Catilinarians.[18]

Lentulus' decision to enlist the Gauls was foolish for several reasons. He never considered the likely possibility that the Gauls would betray the conspiracy to the government. In all events, his priority should have been ensuring the success of the *coup d'etat*. Enlisting the assistance of the Gauls would do nothing to secure the success of the coup d'état, since the best that they could do would be to send cavalry to Italy months after the coup d'état had occurred. Finally, securing foreign intervention would increase opposition to the Catilinarians if and when the Gallic cavalry arrived, since the Romans historically had battled Celtic invaders. Lentulus' attempt to involve the Allobroges at this time was a gamble, the risks of which greatly outweighed any potential reward.

Pursuant to Lentulus' instructions, Umbrenus approached the Gauls in the forum and inquired about the state of their tribe. Upon their telling him of the reason for their trip, he expressed sympathy for their situation and inquired as to results of their mission. They told him that they had been unsuccessful in persuading the senate even to hear their complaint. They proclaimed that they were so desperate that they had little to hope for besides death. Umbrenus told them 'If you will prove yourselves men, I will show you a way to escape the great evils which are afflicting you.' After Umbrenus said this, the Gauls became as cheerful as they had been despondent and begged Umbrenus to rely on them. Convinced by their statements, Umbrenus led them to the home of Sempronia which was near the forum and suitable for a meeting, since Sempronia's husband (D. Junius Brutus) was away from Rome.[19]

Upon arriving there, Umbrenus sent for Gabinus whose presence he thought for some reason would give his words greater weight. Upon Gabinus' arrival, Umbrenus told the Gauls about the plot. In an effort to impress them, he named as members of the conspiracy not only men who were actually involved, but also men who were unconnected to it, in order to make the conspirators seem more powerful than they were.[20] He promised the Gauls that in exchange for their help, the insurgents would remove the officials who were oppressing them. When the Gauls promised to support the conspirators, he dismissed them.[21]

The Gauls were less naïve than the conspirators. They debated among themselves whether they would gain more by joining the conspirators or betraying them. Their desperate situation, their love of war, and the hope of booty suggested that they should choose the conspirators' side, while their desire for certain rewards as opposed to uncertain prospects pressed them to the government's side. Fortunately for the government, caution prevailed and they revealed the plot to Q. Fabius Sanga, the *patronus* (patron) of the tribe whom he considered his *clientes* and whose interests he represented in dealings with the Roman government.[22] According to Sallust, Sanga wasted no time in informing the government of these developments[23] by contacting L. Murena, the consul elect with the information that the Allobroges had given him and in turn Murena and his son-in law – L. Pinarius Natta – passed the information on to Cicero.[24]

Meanwhile, Cicero was well aware that the expulsion of Catiline had not ended the efforts of the Catilinarians in Rome. He was continually receiving reports from spies and informers concerning the conspirators' plans. When he learned of the conspirators' effort to enlist the Gauls, he realized that the conspirators had delivered themselves into his hands. He instructed Sanga to have the Gauls feign a strong interest in the conspirators' designs, to meet as many members of the conspiracy as possible and, while promising them support, gather evidence against them.[25]

Following Cicero's instructions, on 1 December, the Allobroges had Gabinus arrange a meeting with Lentulus, Cethegus, Cassius and Statilius[26] At the meeting, the Gauls told the conspirators that they were planning to return to Gaul the next evening. They requested that the four give them letters to their leaders concerning the plot and pledging to assist the Allobroges if the Allobroges would help them. Cassius Longinus refused to give them such a letter on the grounds that he was travelling to the land of the Allobroges and would speak in person to the leaders of the tribe.[27] The others were far more gullible and signed letters stating that they, along with Cassius Longinus, had requested the Allobroges to send cavalry to Italy while the conspirators would furnish sufficient infantry to seize control of the peninsula.[28] In the presence of the Allobroges, Cethegus decried the plan of waiting for the Saturnalia and declared his willingness to attack the *curia* (senate house) at once if only a few would help him.[29]

In addition to these letters, Lentulus told the ambassadors that the Sibylline oracle had predicted that he would be the third of the Cornelii to rule Rome.[30] He claimed that 63 was the tenth year after the acquittal of the Vestal Virgins and the twentieth after the burning of the Capitol and that it was fated to see the destruction of Rome and her empire.[31] It is likely that Cethegus' rashness and Lentulus' reliance on prophecy did nothing to increase the Allobroges' respect for the conspirators, or tempt them to side with the Catilinarians. Lentulus then asked the Gauls to visit Catiline's camp on their way home and to exchange pledges of fidelity with Catiline himself. Lentulus instructed T. Volturcius of Cortona[32] to go with them as a guide to Catiline's camp.[33] After the meeting, the Gauls immediately reported to Cicero what had transpired.[34]

The next day Cicero began his preparations to thwart the conspirators' plans. Accordingly, he called two *praetors* whom he considered good *optimates* to his house. When L. Valerius Flaccus and C. Pomptinus arrived, he explained the situation to them. He ordered them to take a group of men from his bodyguard and arrest the Allobroges when they left Rome that evening. He gave them directions as to where and how they were to accomplish this mission. As it was growing dark, they set out at once to surround the Mulvian Bridge over the Tiber on the road north from Rome, planning to seize the Allobroges once they were on the bridge.[35]

Early that evening, before the *praetors* had placed guards around the bridge, L. Cassius Longinus left the city and thus escaped arrest the next day.[36] Lentulus allegedly stayed up late at night writing a letter to Catiline which he entrusted to Titus Volturcius to deliver when he and the Gauls arrived at Catiline's camp.[37] In addition, Volturcius was allegedly instructed by Lentulus to tell Catiline that he should rally slaves to his banner and march on Rome as soon as possible.[38] Volturcius joined the Gauls who departed from the city in the early morning hours of 3 December. They reached the Mulvian bridge at about 3am that morning.

Once they entered the bridge, the *praetors* sprung their trap and, amid loud shouts, rushed at the Gauls from both ends of the bridge. Both sides drew swords. Although Cicero had not informed the Gauls of the plan (possibly because he did not trust them completely), the Gauls quickly realized what was going on and surrendered without further resistance. Recognizing Volturcius called upon the Gauls to resist and with his back to the bridge, defended himself for a few minutes against the *praetors'* forces. Recognizing Pomptinus as an acquaintance, called upon the latter to guarantee his life if he surrendered. Having received assurance from Pomptinus, Volturcius ceased his struggle.[39]

The *praetors* immediately sent a messenger to Cicero to inform him of the seizure of the Gauls and Volturcius, and most importantly, to give him the letters from the conspirators. The messenger sped back to the city, aroused Cicero's doorkeeper, and relayed the news to the anxious consul. Cicero was relieved because his plan had succeeded, but troubled because he was now faced with the problem of confronting the conspirators.[40] He believed that if he took extra legal steps, he could face subsequent prosecution; yet, if he did not move against them, the Republic would be endangered. Accordingly, he steeled himself for action.[41] The *praetors* brought the Gauls and Volturcius back to Cicero's home as the dawn was breaking.

Later that morning Cicero summoned first Gabinus, then Statilius, then Cethegus, next Lentulus and finally Caeparius to meet with him at his home. Why these five? Presumably these men (1) were believed to be in the city and (2) had been specifically named as conspirators by the Gauls.[42] The unsuspecting conspirators appeared as ordered except for Caeparius, who had been instructed to go to Apulia to stir up the enslaved shepherds there. Caeparius was not in his house when the summons came and later, learning of the seizure of the Gauls, he attempted to flee.[43] Gabinus was the first to arrive, followed in short order by Statilius and Cethegus; Lentulus, as usual, was last because he had stayed up the night before composing the three sentence letter to Catiline.[44] The first three were seized by Cicero's bodyguard; in recognition of Lentulus' status as *praetor*, the consul forbade his seizure, but took him by the arm and informed him of his detention.[45]

The timing ascribed to these events by Cicero seems contrived. Why would the Gauls start off on a trip which would last for weeks in the early hours of the morning? If the Gauls and Volturcius reached the Mulvian bridge around 3am, as Cicero claims, and arrived at Cicero's home as the dawn was breaking, how did Cicero have a chance to examine them before summoning the conspirators and calling for a meeting of the senate? Did Cicero really put on his case, so to speak, in the senate without conferring with his witnesses? It seems probable that the events in question occurred early in the evening of 2 December (not early in the morning of the next day) and that Cicero spent several hours in the early morning interviewing the Gauls and Volturcius and rehearsing their testimony – something he could not have done had his chronology of events been accurate. Certainly, the events of the next day show Cicero as an extremely able prosecutor presenting a compelling case to a jury. The consul's careful stage management of the ensuing senate proceedings makes his account resemble a Perry Mason novel or a communist show trial, complete, of course, with informers, admissions of guilt while on the stand, and acceptance of punishment as being due. All of this could not have been done without preparation. Cicero was too experienced a trial attorney to have put witnesses on the stand without thoroughly rehearsing their testimony.[46] His false chronology was designed to conceal his activities in preparing the testimony of the Gauls and Volturcius.

B. Discovery – 3 December 63

News of the arrests spread quickly and many senators gathered at Cicero's mansion. They urged him to open the letters and to make sure that they contained treasonable content before he summoned the senate lest he be accused of rumour mongering in the event that the letters contained nothing incriminating. Cicero refused to do so because he wanted to open the letters in view of the full senate and avoid any charge of having altered the contents of the letters. (Of course, Cicero had no need to open the letters since he knew their incriminating contents from the statements of the Gauls.) Cicero then sent messengers out summoning the various senators to an emergency meeting of the senate to be held at the shrine of Concordia. While waiting for the senate to assemble, on the basis of information supplied by the Allobroges, Cicero sent another *optimate praetor*, C. Sulpicius, to search Cethegus' house for a supply of weapons.[47] Cicero then had his bodyguards take the three conspirators to the shrine while he led Lentulus there accompanied by Flaccus, who carried the conspirators' letters.[48] Cicero made arrangements for four men, G. Cosconius, another *praetor*, M. Messala, P. Nigidius and Appius Claudius, to make a record of the senate's proceeding.[49] It is likely that these men served as relay team whose members recorded a portion of each speech a few minutes after the remarks had been delivered.[50]

When enough members of the senate had assembled, Cicero opened the meeting by relating to the anxious senators the events which had led to the arrest of the conspirators. He then proceeded to call his witnesses as though he was presenting a case to a jury. First was Volturcius whom he questioned without the Gauls. When Volturcius came in, he appeared terrified and feigned innocence to make sure that he received the guarantee of immunity that Cicero presumably had promised him earlier. At Cicero's motion, the senate offered Volturcius immunity if he would reveal what he knew about the conspiracy.[51] Recovering from his fear and trembling without apparent difficulty, Volturcius admitted that he bore instructions from Lentulus to Catiline as well as a letter urging Catiline to enlist slaves into his army and to march on Rome as soon as possible. Upon Catiline's approach, Volturcius explained, the conspirators would set the city ablaze and massacre the entire citizen body, leaving Catiline to intercept and kill any fugitives and then to join his fellows in the city.[52] Volturcius claimed that he had only been enlisted (by Gabinus and Caeparius) into the conspiracy a few days before and knew nothing more about the conspirators' plans.[53] Volturcius' story may have reflected Cicero's embellishments designed to inflame public opinion against the Catilinarians and reduce the chance of a rising in the city.

At this point, Cicero staged another theatrical intervention: he had sent the *praetor* Sulpicius (not the candidate for consul) to search for arms at Cethegus' house. Sulpicius, or someone sent by him, came running in to Cicero and the senate and announced the discovery of a large supply of swords and knives at Cethegus' house. Cethegus boldly but unconvincingly retorted that the discovery was not surprising, since he was well known as a connoisseur of fine weapons and these were part of his personal collection.[54]

Cicero then proceeded to lead in the Gauls, who had been off stage like actors waiting for their cue.[55] They dutifully related the story of their involvement in the conspiracy, of the letters that they had obtained from the conspirators and of the conspirators' requests that the Allobroges send cavalry to Italy. They gave an account of Lentulus' recitations of the Sibylline prophecies and they described the quarrel between Cethegus and the others about the advisability of taking action before the Saturnalia.[56] The Gauls then identified the conspirators with whom they had met.

After the Gauls finished their testimony, D. Junius Silanus, the other consul-elect, and C. Calpurnius Piso, a *consulare*, interrupted the proceedings to declare that Cethegus was reputed to have said that three *consulares* and four *praetors* were going to come to an unfortunate demise.[57] After this interjection, the consul ordered the conspirators to be led in. Cicero then selected the letter to the Allobroges which bore Cethegus' seal and forced the latter to acknowledge it. He then broke the seal and read the letter, which stated that Cethegus would fulfil the promises he had made to their ambassadors and urged the Allobroges to fulfil the commitments made by their envoys. Cethegus was allegedly shocked by this development and fell silent. Then Cicero did the same with respect to Statilius; his letter contained much the same message as in Cethegus'.[58] Cicero then turned to Lentulus and forced him to acknowledge that his seal, which contained a portrait of his illustrious grandfather, was on the letter. Remarking that the sight of grandfather's face alone should have deterred Lentulus from committing a heinous crime, Cicero broke the seal and read the letter to the senate. Lentulus' letter to the Allobroges was to much the same effect as the others. Cicero offered Lentulus an opportunity to explain the letter which the latter declined.

However, after the remaining evidence was presented,[59] Lentulus asked the Gauls and then Volturcius why they had come to his house. The Gauls responded by sticking to their original story and asking Lentulus if he had ever mentioned the Sibylline prophecies to them. At this point, Lentulus broke down and confessed, according to Cicero, due to the emotional impact of the revelation and detection of his crime.[60] Probably in response to a signal from Cicero, Volturcius stepped forward and demanded that the letter to Catiline that Lentulus had given him be opened. Although badly shaken, Lentulus identified his seal and his handwriting. The consul then read the following letter to the senate:

Quis sim, ex ego, quem ad te misi, cognosces. Fac cogites, in quanta calamitate sis, et memineris te virum esse! Consideres, quid tuae rationes postulent! Auxilium petas ab omnibus, etiam ab infumis.

(Who I am you will know from whom I have sent to you. Consider what your situation demands. Seek aid from all, even the lowest.)[61]

It was probably that at this point L. Caesar, Lentulus' brother-in-law, declared that Lentulus should be put to death – since the letter encouraged Catiline to lead a servile rebellion.[62]

This letter raises more questions than it answers. Why an unsigned letter that does not identify the sender, but contains Lentulus' seal? What was the point of the cryptic letter? If the real message that Volturcius carried was that Catiline should enrol slaves in his army, why have a letter at all?[63] Why did Lentulus urge Catiline to enlist slaves when Catiline had steadfastly stated that his cause was that of free men?[64] One obvious answer is that he did not. Rather, Cicero replaced the real letter with a forged letter and induced Volturcius to fabricate the story about the possible enrolment of slaves to prey upon the Romans' fear of a slave rebellion such as that led by Spartacus less than ten years before.

After reading this letter, the consul had Gabinus brought in. Presumably Cicero repeated the same process with Gabinus' letter that he had done with the others. In all events, Cicero claimed that Gabinus finally confessed. Cicero is less than clear as to what Gabinus confessed to. He claimed that at this point all of the conspirators appeared dazed and furtive glances at each other, admitting their guilt by their appearance. The consul turned to the senate to request it to take action to protect the Republic. The senior *consulares* (prompted by Cicero?) successfully sponsored the following resolutions:

(1) That M. Tullius Cicero be thanked for his courage, prudence and foresight in saving the Republic for the greatest danger.
(2) That L. Flaccus and C. Pomptinus, the *praetors*, be praised for their courageous and loyal assistance to the consul.
(3) That C. Antonius Hybrida be thanked for avoiding involvement in the conspiracy.
(4) That P. Lentulus should resign his praetorship since he had forfeited his rights to that office as well as his rights as a citizen by his actions.
(5) That P. Lentulus, C. Cethegus, L. Statilius and P. Gabinus be kept in custody.
(6) That L. Cassius Longinus, M. Caeparius, P. Furius (a Sullan colonist from Faesulae), Q. Annius Chilo and P. Umbrenus also be taken into custody.
(7) That a public thanksgiving be declared to the immortal gods in honour of Cicero because 'he had saved Rome from burning, the citizen from massacre and Italy from war.' This was the first time such an honour had been bestowed on a civilian.[65]

Lentulus (having first resigned office), was given over to the custody of P. Lentulus Spinther, Cethegus into the custody of Q. Cornificius (who had been a candidate for consul in the 64 election), Statilius into the custody of Caesar, Gabinus into the custody of Crassus, and Caeparius (who had been captured outside the city and brought back to the shrine) into the custody of Gn. Terentius (who is not otherwise known.)[66] That fact that two of the conspirators were handed over to the *popularis* leaders may indicate that the consul was giving Crassus and Caesar the Hobson's choice between letting their prisoners escape, thus revealing their involvement in the conspiracy, or holding the prisoners and participating in Cicero's efforts to suppress the conspiracy, making it harder for them to attack Cicero's actions later on.[67]

On the other hand, Crassus and Caesar may have volunteered for this duty as a means of demonstrating that they were not involved in the conspiracy.[68]

On the evening of 3 December, Cicero delivered his *Third Catilinarian* to the people. Commencing with an extended eulogy of his own efforts, Cicero related in dramatic fashion the events of the preceding two days.[69] He then claimed credit for driving Catiline from the city and stated, accurately, that Catiline had been a far greater threat in the city than in Etruria, since he would not have bungled in the way that the remaining conspirators had. Cicero accused the conspirators of planning to burn the city.[70] He implied that he had done as much to save the Republic from internal enemies as Pompey had done from external foes. Cicero invoked the statute of Jupiter, which he had carefully moved that morning so that it was pointing at him, as indicating that Jupiter would help uncover plots against the Republic and preserve Rome. He urged all citizens to join in the public holiday declared by the senate to celebrate Cicero's efforts. He closed with a second eulogy to himself for his efforts to save the city despite whatever political dangers he might face in the future for his action in exposing the conspiracy.[71] He promised that he would continue to be active to preserve the fortunes, lives and homes of his fellow citizens.

According to Sallust, Cicero's speech had its desired effect and the urban poor who had generally favoured the cause of insurgents, became frightened at the measures which the consul told them the conspirators were planning. Sallust claimed that although they would profit rather than lose by the normal activities of war, they knew that any firing of the city would be calamitous because it might destroy their only possessions – their homes, their clothing and their food supplies. Consequently, they began to denounce Catiline and to praise Cicero as a man who had rescued them from a fate worse than slavery.[72] While Sallust's description of the urban poor's reactions seems to reflect his customary jaundiced views of the common people, it is likely that the consul's rumour mongering did produce a shift in public opinion away from support of the Catilinarians. However, Drummond, citing several factors, such as the recall of Sestius and his force from Capua to help maintain order in Rome,[73] argues that there was still a strong undercurrent of support for the conspirators.[74]

Chapter VIII

The End of the Conspiracy: December 63

A. Cicero's Dilemma: 4 December 63

Following the delivery of the *Third Catilinarian,* Cicero left the forum to spend the night at the home of a friend, P. Nigidus Figulus, because Cicero's own home was being utilized for the winter festival of the *Bona Dea* (the good goddess of chastity and fertility). This festival was celebrated each December at the home of one of the two consuls; only women were permitted in attendance at this celebration. As Cicero walked through the dark streets, surrounded by his bodyguard and escorted by a large group of cheering citizens, many of them bearing torches whose flickers lit the dark night, it is likely that the consul must have felt a wave of inner exultation which pushed to the back of his mind his foreboding about the future.[1]

Once at Nigidus' home, however, he began to consider what action he should take with respect to the conspirators. Throughout the autumn he had frequently declared that the Catilinarians should be put to death as the Gracchians and others had been killed.[2] However, he had justified his failure to act because he had not convinced everyone that Catiline and his followers presented a threat to the Republic. Instead, he had followed a course of watchful waiting, hoping that the conspirators, given enough rope, would hang themselves. They had more than fulfilled his expectations. They had done such a thorough job of botching the conspiracy that they had removed the necessity for drastic action at the same time that they had made it politically feasible. In the hysteria of the moment, Cicero did not realize that the discovery of the plot had rendered the conspirators harmless. He believed that they still posed a threat to the Republic.[3] Cicero concluded that he had only two alternatives; both bad from his standpoint. One was to put the conspirators to death – a death for which he would be held responsible. Long term imprisonment was not an option. Rome did not have any prisons other than the Tullianum which was used solely for executions.[4] Confinement under guard in private homes was customary to prevent a defendant from escaping before trial.[5] It was not a long-term solution. The only viable alternative to putting the conspirators to death was to keep them under guard until such point as the insurrection had been crushed and then to try them, believing that they would be convicted and go into exile. This approach was unprecedented and certainly posed logistical difficulties – particularly if the conspirators' friends decided to rescue them. If, however, the conspirators were imprisoned and then tried after Catiline's inevitable defeat and acquitted or subject only to a fine, they would be free to seek revenge on Cicero and his family. Cicero was terrified by this last possibility. His exaggeration of this concern led to his ultimate downfall.[6]

Even with this analysis, however, Cicero was in no hurry to put the conspirators to death. A man whose general indecisiveness became legendary,[7] Cicero had a typical intellectual's reluctance to use force.[8] Nor did the *senatus consultum ultimum* really offer any justification for execution of the conspirators. Under the unwritten Roman constitution, only the *comitia tributa* could enact a law.[9] The senate did not have that power.[10] Thus, the *senatus consultum ultimum* did not have the force of law.[11] Moreover, in the past the *senatus consultum ultimum* had been invoked against those who were openly in arms against the Republic. Here, however, the conspirators had been captured before they could take up arms.[12] Cicero knew that the inapplicable historical precedents which he had recited in the *First Catilinarian* were of dubious legality. He was well aware of how Caesar had attacked the legality of actions taken under the *senatus consultum ultimum* a few months earlier when he arranged for T. Labienus to prosecute C. Rabirius for his participation in the extra judicial murder of L. Saturninus in 100.[13]

Surprisingly for a people who were inured to cruelty, the Romans viewed capital punishment of a Roman citizen (but not of slaves and non-Romans) with a horror which arose from their recognition that its imposition made every citizen a participant in cold blooded murder. The *Leges Valeriae, Semproniae* and *Porciae* had established the right of any Roman citizen sentenced to death by a magistrate to appeal (*provocatio*) to the *comitia centuria* (the electoral assembly). The accused could voluntarily go into exile as long as the last *centuria* in the *comitia centuria* had not voted.[14] As a practical matter, these laws had eliminated capital punishment for offences against the Republic since those obviously guilty of capital offences would go off into exile before being convicted.[15]

Nevertheless, Cicero was desirous of senate endorsement for any executions.[16] His approach was essentially political, not legal, since the senate was not a court and had no power to condemn the conspirators or to authorize the consul to put them to death. However, its approval of the execution would hopefully offer the consul some political protection. In the last analysis, one's assessment of the execution depends on the extent to which one sees *salus civitatis lex suprema est* (the safety of the state is the supreme law) as well as to the extent one sees the detained conspirators as presenting a real threat to the Republic.[17]

Cicero was torn between his concern about the legality of his action (and the possible legal and political consequences thereof) and his conviction that the execution of the conspirators was necessary for the safety of the Republic. Carried away by the drama of the moment that he had done much to create, Cicero believed that execution of the conspirators was necessary for the public safety. He was wrong. His execution of the conspirators was worse than a crime; it was a blunder.

Cicero began discussing the possible courses of action with his host, P. Nigidus, Q. Cicero and a few other[18] members of his *consilium*, including L. Manlius Torquatus and L. Lucceius.[19] This discussion probably went on for a good part of the evening until it was interrupted by the sudden arrival of Cicero's wife, Terentia. She informed the men that while she and the other noble women of Rome had been celebrating the festival of the *Bona Dea*, the fire which the women had lit as part of the festivities had gone out. A few seconds later, however it suddenly burst forth with a great flame. Although the other women were terrified by this event, the Vestal Virgins were not and declared to Terentia that this was a sign from the gods that the consul should adopt whatever measure he was considering as the course of action which would lead him to glory and safety. They then instructed Terentia to leave the ceremony immediately and inform the consul of what had transpired.[20] It is less than clear whether this 'miracle' was a result of Terentia's plotting or whether it was someone else's hand behind the curtain. Terentia's intervention led Nigidus and Q. Cicero to renew their arguments in favour of putting the conspirators to death. According to Plutarch, Terentia, a woman as eager to govern the Republic as to run her home, advocated the same course of action in view of the 'miracle'.[21]

Cicero summoned a meeting of the senate on the next day (4 December). This meeting was interrupted by the guards, who reported that a man had been captured outside the city walls in the early morning hours. When this

L. Tarquinus was brought before the senate, he promised to tell all that he knew if he was assured of immunity.[22] Upon such immunity having been conferred by the senate, the consul ordered him make a full confession. Tarquinus proceeded to relate the same story that Volturcius had told about the plan for fires, the murder plot and Catiline's march on the city. He then shockingly declared that he had been sent by Crassus to advise Catiline not to be worried by the arrest of Lentulus, Cethegus and the rest but to hasten his march in order to encourage the rest of the conspirators and rescue them all from danger.[23]

All who heard this story were taken aback in amazement; an uproar arose with some declaring the story incredible,[24] while others crediting Tarquinus nevertheless believed that the government would to be better to propitiate Crassus than drive him to unite openly with the conspirators. Still others had no opinion but, desiring to curry favour with their major creditor, they angrily denounced the accusation as false. Cicero, sensing the mood of the senate and perhaps mindful of his agreement with Crassus and Caesar, moved that Tarquinus' testimony be considered false and that he be held under guard and denied further hearing until he revealed the names of those who instigated his story. The senate adopted the motion with alacrity.[25] Crassus was obviously feared because he was known to take vengeance when his ox was gored.[26]

No one ever discovered who was behind Tarquinus, although there was much speculation about this matter. Some at the time thought that P. Autronius had been behind the story in an effort to force Crassus to use his influence to protect not only himself but the conspirators as well. Still others thought that Cicero himself had been behind the accusation in an effort to prevent Crassus from using his influence to protect the Catilinarians; this theory is improbable because Crassus had already allied himself with the government. It is, of course, possible that Tarquinus was an agent for one of Crassus' opponents. However, the most likely explanation for Tarquinus' action is that he was a government informer on the make who saw an opportunity to collect a reward for false denunciations.

Sallust wrote that years later (after Cicero and Crassus had become enemies) Crassus told him that he believed that Cicero was responsible for the smear.[27] Dio Cassius states that Cicero in *Expositio Consuliorum Suorum*[28] claimed that both Crassus and Caesar were involved in the second Catilinarian conspiracy.[29]

Asconius notes that Cicero in his *Expositio Consiliorum Suorum* claimed that Crassus was behind the First Catilinarian Conspiracy.[30]

The reality is that in 63, Cicero made no efforts to attack Crassus and indeed protected Caesar.[31] However, Crassus clearly believed the contrary and thought that Cicero's suspicions were based on the incident on 19 October when Crassus had delivered the mysterious letters.[32] Cicero's latter charges concerning Crassus' and Caesar's complicity with the Catilinarians were probably the result of the enmity which arose between Crassus and Cicero when Crassus supported Clodius' efforts to send Cicero into exile, and between Cicero and Caesar when Caesar destroyed the Republic.[33]

Sallust states that the *optimates* made at least one effort to bring down Caesar. According to Sallust on 4 December, Catulus and C. Calpurnius Piso endeavoured to persuade Cicero to implicate Caesar in the conspiracy by offering him bribes or political favours. Sallust claims that Catulus was smarting over his loss to Caesar in the race for *pontifex maximus* earlier in the year and Piso was bitter because, also earlier in the year, Caesar had prosecuted him for extortion allegedly committed while he had been governor of Transalpine Gaul. The two approached the consul and suggested that he have either the Allobroges or Volturcius denounce Caesar as a conspirator. They pointed out that such a charge would be credible given that Caesar's great debts would make him a logical adherent of Catiline. The consul was unmoved by their entreaties, influence, or bribes and refused to cooperate with their scheme. Nothing daunted, Catulus and Piso took matters into their own hands and began to spread rumours that Volturcius and the Allobroges had implicated Caesar in hopes of arousing public hostility towards him.[34]

Sallust, a major partisan of Caesar, is the sole source for this story. It rings false. For one thing, Catulus had a reputation of being one of the most honourable Romans. When Catulus was opposing the *lex Gabina*, which was to give command of the war against the pirates to Pompey, he pointed out the dangers which would occur if Pompey died and rhetorically asked, 'who should be able to take his place?' Whereupon, the assembly replied, 'You.'[35] Catulus' alleged action seems completely out of character.[36] In addition, Syme believed that one of Sallust's motivations in writing the *Bellum Catilinae* was to glorify Caesar and absolve him of any role in the conspiracy.[37] Without necessarily crediting Syme's theory, the creation of a false story about *optimate* efforts to condemn Caesar would have been consistent with Sallust's Caesarian sympathies and hatred of the oligarchs.

On the other hand, it was clear that an *inimicitia* existed between Catulus and Caesar and between Piso and Caesar; in Roman society an *inimicitia* would justify almost any kind of action against a foe.[38] Accordingly, this story is not inherently incredible.

While the senate was occupied with voting rewards to Volturcius and the Allobroges, Cethegus managed to send a message to his freedmen and slaves, a picked body of men trained for violent deeds, urging them to assemble and rescue him. At the same time the freedmen of Lentulus began scouring the streets, attempting to rouse the artisans and slaves to rescue their master. Others of Lentulus' dependents made efforts to contact the leaders of the armed *collegia* (unions) in order to secure their assistance in a rescue attempt.[39]

Learning of these actions on the night of 4 December, Cicero took steps to foil these plans by increasing the guards around the homes in which the conspirators were imprisoned, filling the forum and the Capital with soldiers, and ordering the *praetors* to enlist all the veterans in the city into temporary service.[40] Despite Cicero's precautions, an unsuccessful effort seems to have been made to rescue Lentulus and Cethegus.[41] This abortive attempt may have sealed the fate of the conspirators by demonstrating the difficulty of keeping them confined. On the morning of 5 December, Cicero convened the senate and referred the question of what should be done with the conspirators to it for its advice.[42] He again surrounded the senate's meeting place with armed guards[43] under the command of Atticus,[44] whose unprecedented involvement in public affairs emphasized the gravity of the situation.

B. The Senate Debate: 5 December

Cicero presumably arranged for the four men who took down the proceedings on 3 December to do the same for 5 December.[45] The first order of business was the passage of a resolution declaring that the conspirators were *hostes* who had accordingly lost their rights as citizens.[46] There was, of course, no basis for such a resolution, since the senate was not a court and could not terminate the conspirators' civic rights.[47] Then Cicero submitted the question of what should be done with the conspirators.[48] Following the customary practice of calling upon various senators in order of their rank and seniority, he first called upon the consul elect, Decimus Silanus to give his opinion.[49] Consuls elect were called upon first because they would be responsible upon entering office to enforce the senate's decisions.[50] Silanus, probably by pre-arrangement, declared that the prisoners should be put to death and that the same punishment should be accorded to L. Cassius Longinus, P. Furius,[51] P. Umbrenus and Q. Annius Chilo when they were captured.[52] According to normal practice, Cicero then called upon the other consul elect, followed by the *consulares*, the *praetors*-elect then the ex-*praetors* until everyone in the senate had been given an opportunity although it was rare that a junior senator said anything.[53] Silanus' proposal was endorsed by Silanus' co-consul, Murena and all the *consulares*: Catulus, P. Servilius Vatia, M. and L. Licinius Lucullus, Curio Senior, L. Manlius Torquatus, M. Aemilius Lepidus, L. Gellius Poplicola, L. Volcacius Tullus, C. Marcius Figulus, L. Aurelius Cotta, L. Iulus Caesar, Cn. Calpurnius Piso and M. Acilius Glabro.[54] Two *consulares* were missing: Hortensius and Crassus. It is surprising that Hortensius did not attend the senate since he was a leading *optimate* and active in politics; however, the absence of Crassus about which Cicero later commented is hardly surprising. Crassus did not wish to condone the execution of the conspirators or to oppose it openly (particularly given Tarquinus' accusations) and thus prudently stayed at home.[55]

After the *consulares* has spoken, Cicero called upon Caesar, one of the *praetors* elect.[56] Cicero was surprised and a little puzzled by Caesar's attendance at this meeting in view of Crassus' absence. Cicero probably regarded Caesar as an up and coming *popularis* politician who had won some attention by the lavish games he had given as *curule aedile* and by the bribes he had paid to win election as *pontifex maximus*.[57] Until 3 December Caesar had done little to stand out from his rivals despite his family connections, personality, and political sense.[58] This day, however, was to make his reputation and the reputation of his greatest opponent, M. Porcius Cato.

Now Caesar became a general without an equal; he never lost a battle.[59] He became a tremendous writer. He was a good orator. Probably the most able man produced by the last generation of the Republic, it is perhaps fitting that his greatest success was the destruction of the Republic. Unlike Sulla, he had no idea as to what should replace the Republican constitution. He was consumed by his own ambition and ultimately paid the price for it. No one, however, has ever questioned his courage. His appearance, let alone his speech on that December day, could easily have cost him his life. On the other hand, his speech did lead to his elevation to the front rank of Roman politics. He saw that Cicero had presented him with a great opportunity if he was willing to run a risk, as he had when he borrowed huge sums to bribe his way to the position of *pontifex maximus*.[60]

In Sallust's version of his speech, Caesar reasonably pointed out that there was no need to put the conspirators to death in violation of the *Lex Porcia* and the *Lex Sempronia* (which forbade the execution of Roman citizens without a trial) since they did not pose an imminent danger to the Republic. He proposed that they be sent to various municipalities in Italy where they could be kept under guard. He also moved that their property should be confiscated and that no one should be permitted in the future to make any motion to pardon them.[61] Cicero states that Caesar's proposal called for lifetime imprisonment.[62] This claim is improbable because there was no provision in Roman law for life imprisonment and no prisons to place anyone in for any period of time.[63] It is far more probable that Caesar was calling for temporary imprisonment until Catiline had been crushed at which point the conspirators could have been tried and would presumably have gone into exile to avoid the death penalty.[64]

Caesar' speech caused many of the senators to lose their nerve[65] and led to some backtracking, which Cicero tried to stem with his *Fourth Catilinarian*. Years later, Cicero claimed that he had resolved before the senate meeting that the conspirators should be put to death; however, he did not claim that he made any effort to persuade the senate to adopt this view.[66] This claim is consistent with the text of the *Fourth Catilinarian* which says that Cicero will take whatever action the senate advised.[67] Indeed, an endorsement of any of the proposals before the senate would have undermined Cicero's main purpose in referring the matter to the senate, shifting responsibility from his shoulders to theirs. Moreover, Roman political tradition required the consuls to refrain from endorsing or opposing specific proposals before the senate although they could call to the attention of the senate matters which were relevant to the discussion in question.[68]

An examination of the text of the *Fourth Catilinarian* seems to indicate that it may be a combination of two different sets of remarks. The first six paragraphs seem to be a rewritten, elaborate version of *exordium* (beginning) in which the consul would at the very beginning of the session describe the matter at hand before the senate.[69] The second part of the speech sounds like it was a summary of proposals made by various senators which the consul would present at the end of a debate. D.L. Stockton suggests that the final part of this speech was delivered at the conclusion of the debate.[70] However his theory is unconvincing because it is inconsistent with the lack of reference in the *Fourth Catilinarian* to Cato's speech and its reference to a proposal which was withdrawn by Silanus before the conclusion of the debate.

It seems more likely that the second part of the *Fourth Catilinarian* was delivered quite soon after Caesar's speech and probably before Ti. Claudius Nero made his proposal to postpone any decisive action until the defeat of the conspirators, since Cicero makes no reference to Nero's proposal or to Silanus' subsequent retreat from his initial proposal. Cicero begins the second part of the speech by describing each of the proposals by Silanus and Caesar in some detail. He then argues that the *Lex Sempronia* did not protect the conspirators because they had been declared *hostes* although this argument made a nullity of the *Lex Sempronia* since it enabled the senate to take away citizenship without trial. He then describes the wickedness of the conspirators and says that the whole populace supported their execution. Finally, he declared that he was willing to make any necessary sacrifice for the public good. He declared that he would be willing to execute either proposal. While he did not openly endorse Silanus' proposal, any listener would conclude that Cicero supported it.

That Sallust makes no reference to the *Fourth Catilinarian* in relating the debate is not surprising, since he makes no reference in the *Bellum Catilinae* to any of the *Catilinarians* other than the first. Moreover, Sallust wanted to focus on Caesar's and Cato's role in the debate[71] by attributing to them extremely philosophical and abstract arguments that reflect Sallust's and not their thinking.[72] To treat Sallust fairly, it is unlikely that the *Fourth Catilinarian* made much of an impression on the senate. It is the shortest of the four speeches about the conspiracy. In addition, it was probably subject to the most revision as the political situation turned against Cicero in later years and Cicero tried to shore up his position by emphasizing the wickedness of the conspirators and the extent to which the whole populace supported their execution. One particular passage seems to be a later edition after Clodius had forced Cicero into exile[73]: *Quod si aliquando alicuius furore et scelere concitata manus ista plus valuerit quam vestra ac rei publicae dignitas, me tamen meorum factorum atque consiliorum numquamm, patres conscripti, paenitebit.* (But if at some later time this band [of evil doers] is aroused by another's madness and evil and overcomes your authority and the authority of the Republic, nevertheless I shall not repent, conscript fathers, of my advice and my deeds today.)[74] Another likely addition was the maudlin section towards the end of speech when Cicero asks the senators to protect his baby son if he should later succumb to attacks by opponents.[75]

Not long after Cicero had spoken, Nero proposed that the number of guards around the conspirators be increased and that the senate consider what should be done at some later point in time.[76] Nero's proposal was in substance the same as Caesar's. Among those speaking in favour of Caesar's proposal was Q. Cicero, who was a *praetor*-elect.[77] At some point Silanus withdrew his own proposal and said that he agreed with Nero's approach.[78] Silanus may have even made the specious claim that in proposing the supreme penalty, he meant not death but life imprisonment.[79]

Catulus was the first to speak in direct opposition to Caesar and tried in vain to rally the senators to support Silanus' original proposal.[80] The debate dragged on with succeeding senators speaking in favour of one proposal or another without one side or the other gaining momentum.[81] Cato, the tribune elect, however, stiffened the backs of the *optimates*. He pointed out the grave dangers presented by the conspiracy to the Republic and to the property of the senators. He argued that executing the conspirators would dishearten Catiline's forces, whereas letting them live would encourage others to join the conspiracy. He contended that the danger of the conspirators being rescued would be as great in other cities as it was in Rome, hinting that those who had opposed the death penalty secretly hoped for the escape of the conspirators.[82] Cato then praised Cicero in fulsome terms.[83]

In the course of the debate Cato saw Caesar furtively receiving a note. Cato interrupted his speech to call the attention of the senate to the incident, insinuating that Caesar had just received a message from those sympathetic to the conspirators. Caesar did not deign to reply, but handed the note to Cato. The tribune elect read the note and realized it was an illicit love message to Caesar from Cato's half-sister, Servilia. Somewhat red-faced, he hurled it back at Caesar, crying 'Take it you sot.'[84] One has to question the veracity of this story. Why would Servilia send a love note to Caesar during this vital session of the senate? Why did Cato refer to Caesar as a 'sot' when it was Cato – not Caesar – who had a reputation for drinking?[85]

Regaining control and resuming his speech, Cato pointed out that Romans in the past had been willing to execute even their own children for treason to the Republic; he declared that the conspirators should be executed and their property confiscated given the threat that they posed to the lives and property of the senators.⁸⁶ Cato's appeal to the purse strings of the senators carried the day; all of the *consulares* and the majority of the other senators praised Cato's proposal as that of a 'great' and 'distinguished' statesman.⁸⁷ Although the ensuing debate still saw some division and the labelling of supporters of Caesar's opinion 'cowards', Cato had turned the tide.⁸⁸

Caesar did not give up the fight. Leaping to his feet before the senate voted, he complained that Cato had acted unfairly in combining in one proposal the harshest penalty proposed by Silanus with the harshest penalty Caesar had proposed. He probably asked Cato to amend his motion to delete the provision for forfeiture of property; however, Cato stood steadfast and the other senators were not moved. Caesar then appealed to the other tribunes, but in vain.⁸⁹ Cicero, however, acting on his own initiative, scrapped the proposals of Silanus, Nero and Caesar, and then put Cato's motion, minus the provision for the confiscation of the conspirators' property, to a vote.⁹⁰ Cicero explained to his friend Atticus that he had taken this course of action because it seemed that Cato's motion was the best expression of the views of the senate.⁹¹ This motion was adopted by the senate which then adjourned.⁹² Even Cethegus' brother voted in its favour.⁹³

Meanwhile the course of the debate was being reported to the crowd which waited outside the meeting place. Among them were the consul's bodyguards. This group, already suspicious of Caesar, possibly due to the rumours that Catulus and Piso had spread, became enraged at Caesar's opposition to the imposition of the death penalty. Seeing him approaching on his way out of the meeting, they drew their swords and threatened him. C. Scribonius Curio (a senator and friend of Caesar) placed his cloak over Caesar to protect him. Fortunately, Cicero arrived at this moment and when the guards looked to him for a signal to continue the attack, the consul, possibly to his later regret, honoured his promise to Caesar and shook his head.⁹⁴ Piso and Catulus are alleged in later years to have criticized Cicero for saving Caesar.⁹⁵ Caesar prudently absented himself from the senate for the rest of the month.⁹⁶

C. The Execution: 5 December 63

Upon the adjournment of the senate, Cicero resolved to act at once lest another attempt be made to rescue the conspirators. Going to the Tullianum,

Cicero ordered the officials there to prepare to put the conspirators to death. Having stationed guards around that place, he then went, accompanied by many senators, to the home where Lentulus had been imprisoned and took the latter, still under guard, to the Tullianum. The *praetors* performed the same office for the other prisoners.[97]

As Cicero led Lentulus down from the Palatine Hill, along the Via Sacra and through the middle of the forum, the people who lined the streets shuddered as the procession passed by. According to Plutarch's colourful description, especially affected were the young men who thought that the procession initiated them into the mysteries of the oligarchical regime.[98] Finally, the group reached the Tullianum, which contained an underground room as a death chamber. This room was little more than a pit dug some twelve feet below the surface of the earth, surrounded on four sides by wall and on top by a vaulted roof of stone. Neglect, stench and darkness made this chamber horrible to behold. Once Cicero and his party reached the building, the officials lowered the executioners into the lower chamber of the Tullianum through a hole in the floor. Then Cicero and his party entered the upper chamber and handed over the prisoners to the officials who then lowered them one by one into the pit where each was strangled to death with a noose. In this manner perished first Lentulus, then Cethegus, then Statilius, then Gabinus and finally Caeparius.[99] In 44, Anthony claimed that Cicero refused to hand over the bodies of the conspirators to their family for burial.[100]

When the deed was done, Cicero left the prison. Seeing among the crowd waiting outside the prison some who were friends of the conspirators and who might still entertain hopes of rescuing them, Cicero cried out in a loud voice, *vixerunt* (they have lived) thus dispelling their hopes without violating the Roman custom of avoiding all direct references to death.[101] The consul then turned his steps homeward. Plutarch wrote:

> The citizenry did not view his progress with silent decorum but rather greeted him with cries and clapping of hands, calling him *parens patriae* (the father of his country). Men and women who lived along the route he traversed filled their hours with lamps and torches to illuminate his programs and enable them to see the great man, going home, escorted by the noblest citizens of the Republic- generals who had brought to a successful conclusion great wars and had been accorded triumphs and soldiers who had added to the Roman dominion on land and sea but

who freely admitted that while the Roman people were indebted to them for wealth, spoils and power, they were so much more indebted to the consul for their very preservation.[102]

This was Cicero's finest hour – and the hour of his downfall.

The populace would not remain favourably disposed for long – partly because Cicero could not stop boasting about his suppression of the conspiracy.[103] However, the period of public hysteria continued for a while enabling Cicero and the *optimates* to investigate any whom they suspected of involvement with or sympathy for the conspirators.[104] Cicero allegedly summoned for interrogation not only those against whom he had specific information, but also many whom he only suspected of involvement. Many of these interrogations were conducted in his own home, a fact which later gave rise to the rumour that he used these investigations to extort large sums of money from many indiscreet citizens.[105]

It was during this period that Caesar went to the senate to defend himself against charges that he was involved in the conspiracy. His defence provoked uproar. As the senate deliberations continued longer than usual that day, Caesar' supporters outside the senate became alarmed that the meeting would end in Caesar's death. They descended on the senate house and demanded, successfully, that Caesar be permitted to depart.[106] Such was the spirit of the times.

Almost immediately following the execution of the conspirators, opposition began to arise to the dominance of Cicero. Leading this opposition was the new tribune, Q. Metellus Nepos. Nepos, a capable soldier, had served under Pompey (who was married to Nepos' stepsister, Mucia) in the war with Mithridates.[107] With the end of that conflict in sight by the spring of 63, Pompey had taken thought for his political future and sent Nepos to Rome to seek election to the tribuneship, which Nepos could then use to further Pompey's interests. Nepos left Asia and took a ship to Brundisium in Apulia (the port in Italy nearest to Greece and the East) where he took the road north to Rome. On the way, his baggage train encountered Cato, who was traveling south to his estate in Lucania. Cato had recently declined to run for the tribuneship on the grounds that a great office, like a strong medicine, should not be taken on unless needed. Upon learning of Nepos' plans, Cato stopped without a word, thought for a while, and then announced to his astounded companions that he must return to the city and seek the tribuneship in order to oppose Nepos. Cato believed that Pompey had sent Nepos to assist Pompey in overthrowing the Republic. He told his companions 'There is no time for rest for we must defeat Pompey or die in the attempt.' Pausing only to spend the night at his estate, Cato returned to Rome where he sought the tribuneship, much to the unhappiness of Nepos, who realized that Cato as a tribune could negate all of his proposals. However, Nepos could no more prevent Cato's election than Cato his: both entered into their offices on 10 December 63.[108]

Nepos, an astute politician, realized that the Catilinarian fiasco had weakened the *popularis* leaders like Crassus and Caesar, while the witch hunt was creating a backlash against Cicero and the *optimates*. He determined to use the judicial murder of the conspirators as a means to neutralize the *optimates* in much the same way as the *optimates* had used the Catilinarian conspiracy to neutralize Crassus and Caesar. Nepos hoped to leave the Republic virtually leaderless so that the returning Pompey would dominate it. When Nepos began to attack Cicero for his unlawful execution of the conspirators, the latter asked Mucia, Pompey's wife and Nepos's stepsister and Claudia, Nepos' sister-in-law, to use their influence (or their husbands' influence) with Nepos to call off these attacks.[109] Nepos, however, remained obdurate. Cicero also recalled Sestius (and his force from Capua) to maintain order in the city.[110] However, any disorder in the city must have been rapidly suppressed because Sestius could not have spent more than a day or two there before being sent on to join Antonius and his army.[111]

On 31 December, when Cicero, in accordance with custom, tried to give his final speech in the *comitia tributa*, Nepos and Bestia refused to permit him to address the crowd. They did allow him to take the traditional oath that he had faithfully discharged his duties while in office. Ascending the rostrum, Cicero gave the traditional oath, but then swore that he had saved the city, a statement which, according to Cicero, was met with approbation by his audience.[112] The fact that Nepos and Bestia stopped Cicero from making the traditional speech indicates, however, that some portion of the population was dissatisfied with Cicero's execution of the conspirators. Indeed, Cicero's statement may have earned him even more *odium* (enmity).[113]

The next day Nepos attacked Cicero in the senate for executing Roman citizens without a trial. He seems to have repeated this attack two days later. Cicero made scathing responses to both attacks. His reply to Nepos prompted the latter's brother, Q. Metellus Celer, the *praetor* in charge of one[114] of the armies seeking out Catiline, to send Cicero a bitter letter complaining about Cicero's remarks concerning his brother. Cicero replied in a placating fashion, contending that he was only defending himself against Nepos' unprovoked attacks.[115] In an effort to protect Cicero, the senate adopted a *consultum* giving immunity to those acting to suppress the conspiracy and declaring that anyone who sought to prosecute them should be considered a *hostes*.[116] Again, this *consultum* did not have any legal effect.

On 3 January 62, Nepos unsuccessfully proposed to the Senate that Pompey be recalled to deal with the uprising headed by Catiline.[117] When Nepos (with the support of Caesar) then proposed this measure to the *comitia tributa*, Cato vetoed this proposal at which point an armed struggle ensued. Cato's forces emerged victorious.[118] The senate then passed another *senatus consultum ultimum* which resulted in a defeated Nepos finally slinking off to the camp of Pompey.[119] Cato then so praised Cicero in a speech that the *comitia tributa* voted Cicero the title of *parens patriae* (father of his country) for his decisive action against the conspirators.[120]

Chapter IX

Marius Eagle: December 63 – January 62

A. The Battle of Pistoria: January 63

Meanwhile, in Etruria Catiline had been drilling his ill-equipped forces, recruiting more soldiers, and waiting for the coming of Saturnalia. Towards the end of November, the approach of Antonius's army forced him to abandon his camp near Faesulae[1] and to march North into the Apennines from which he sometimes seemed be heading to Gaul and other times to Rome, but at no time offering Antonius any opportunity for battle. He intended to preserve his small force for the march on Rome on the eve of Saturnalia.[2] Although desperate for recruits, he refused to enrol the great number of slaves who had flocked to Manlius (and who may have temporarily joined the insurgents) because such action was inconsistent with leading the cause of free men and also because he was confident in the strength of his own forces.[3]

The news of the collapse of the conspiracy and the execution of the conspirators struck Catiline's camp like a thunderbolt. Whatever chance of the success the insurgency had (and it was small) had vanished. Those of his soldiers who had taken up arms in hopes of loot or revolution deserted.[4] Only about 3,000 stayed on, although they were all well-armed.[5] Catiline resolved at this point to abandon Italy and lead his force to Transalpine Gaul[6] (and probably past the boundaries of this province) where, beyond the power of the Republic, he could find fertile land on which he could establish a military colony similar to those which Sulla had established in Etruria. He may also have had some hopes of support from the discontented Allobroges who lived in the far end of Transalpine Gaul and who in later 62 staged a revolt which was put down by C. Pomptinus, who had been sent to Gaul as a *pro praetor*.[7]

Catiline led his small army by forced marches along the Apennines until reaching the neighbourhood of Pistoria, where he probably planned to descend from the mountains, gather supplies, take the *Via Cassia* (which ran along the shores of the Mediterranean) to Genoa, and from there march on back roads to Transalpine Gaul.[8] He moved slowly both because of the difficulties involved in taking a force which included cavalry through the mountains as well as because of a lack of supplies.[9]

Unfortunately for Catiline, Metellus Celer seems to have anticipated this move. Having crushed the insurgents in Picenum, Celer turned northwards along the *Via Aemelia* (from Arminium to Placentia) and then moved west to cross the Apennines on the Remus road.[10] During this march, Celer learned of Catiline's plans from deserters of his army. Accordingly, he stationed his three legions astraddle the road which Catiline would use to descend from the mountains to reach the *Via Cassia*. Antonius, with a force even larger than Celer's, had been following at Catiline's rear, although he had chosen to march along the *Via Cassia* (where he could make good speed). Antonius' second in command, M. Petreius, a former *praetor*, was an experienced solder who had spent thirty years in the army as a tribune, prefect and *legatus*. Petreius, along with P. Sestius who had reinforced Antonius with his Capuan force, had been continually urging Antonius to act more aggressively and to attack Catiline's forces while they were on the march.[11] Antonius, for whatever reason, had disregarded their advice but had kept on Catiline's track.

Blocked from the route to Gaul, hemmed in by mountains, and lacking supplies, Catiline decided to fight. He chose to face not Celer, whose defeat would have freed the road to Gaul, but rather Antonius, whose defeat would have opened the way to Rome. Accordingly, at the very beginning of January 63 he led his army in the direction of Antonius' force which was only a few miles away from his own.[12] Catiline's decision to confront Antonius seems to have been based on the hope that the latter would not put up stiff resistance. Antonius, however, knew which way the wind was blowing and conveniently came down with an attack of arthritis or gout, which in his case may have just been cold feet.[13] He turned over command of his army to M. Petreius, recognizing that this action would permit him to escape blame if Catiline prevailed, but still claim some credit if Catiline was defeated. With Antonius claiming illness, M. Petreius eagerly took command and prepared to attack Catiline.

Recognizing that he would be attacked, Catiline selected a level area which lay between the mountains on the left and rugged rocks on the right for the battlefield.[14] It is commonly believed that the site of the battle is found in the Campo Tizzoro (formerly *Campo di Zoro*) which is a town located on the Pistoiese Mountains, in the municipality of San Marcello

Piteglio in the province of Pistoia.[15] This terrain was ideal for a small force like Catiline's, since it prevented Antonius' army from outflanking his smaller contingent. When Catiline reached the place where he intended to make his stand, he rode up and down the line of his force, shouting words of encouragement to his men.[16] He then sent away his own horse and the horses of the other officers so that everyone in the ranks would know that they all would share the same fate. On foot he then organized his forces for the battle. He put eight cohorts (probably the great bulk of his forces) in the centre, keeping the rest in reserve. From the reserve he took his centurions and the best armed of the new recruits whom he stationed in the front ranks. He ordered Manlius to lead the right and a certain Faesulan, the left. Catiline stationed himself in the centre, underneath the eagle which Marius was said to have used as his standard in the war with the Cimbri.[17] There, he could command both the centre and his reserve which was placed directly behind the centre. Surrounded by his freedmen and attendants, he awaited the approach of Petreius' forces.[18]

Meanwhile Petreius' scouts reported the location of Catiline's force. When Petreius reached the battlefield, he placed his cohorts of veterans, who had been recalled to the service because of the insurgency, in the front line. He stationed the remainder of his forces, including the praetorian cohort (which comprised his elite troops) in the rear as a reserve. He then rode his horse up and down his line, shouting encouragement to his soldiers and calling by name some of the legionnaires who had served with him before, reminding them of their past feats of arms.[19]

Sallust's detailed account of the battle follows:

Petreius, when he had completed all of his preparations, had the trumpet sounded and ordered his cohorts to advance a little. Catiline did the same with his forces. When the two armies had reached a point where they could join in battle, each side uttered a great shout, heaved its spears and rushed at the enemy. The government soldiers, remembering their reputation, attacked the insurgents with great vigour. The insurgents, not lacking in courage either, stood their ground. A great struggle ensued.

Meanwhile Catiline, with his light armed troops, was busy in the van sending reinforcements to hard pressed sections of the line and replacing wounded men with fresh soldiers, taking care of all things. On occasion, he would enter the centre of the line and participate in the fighting. At the same time he performed all the duties of a good soldier and a valiant commander.

When Petreius saw that Catiline, contrary to his expectations, was putting up a desperate struggle, he led the praetorian cohort, which he had kept in reserve, in a headlong assault against the centre of the insurgents' line. He broke through, killing all who stood in his way, and then began to swarm over the Catilinarian forces on either flank. Manlius and the Faesulan, swords in hand, were the first to fall. When Catiline saw that his army had been destroyed and that he had been left with only a few survivors, he recalled to mind his ancestry and reputation and hurled himself into the thick of the enemy where he fell fighting to the end.

After the battle was ended, it became apparent how much audacity and courage had been possessed by the Catilinarians. Almost every man had fallen on the spot he had occupied in the line of battle. A few, who had been driven behind the centre line by the attack of the praetorian cohort, lay a little distance from the rest, but these, like their fellows, had fallen with their wounds on front. Catiline, still breathing a little, was found far in advance of his men, half buried beneath a pile of dead bodies. His countenance still retained the same expression of ferocity which had characterized his appearance in life. Of the whole Catilinarian army, not a single man was taken in battle or flight; all valued their lives as little as those of their foes.[20]

Nor had the Roman army won a happy or bloodless victory. Almost all of the veteran legionnaires had fallen or suffered severe wounds. Many soldiers who afterwards out of curiosity or hope of pillage left their camp and returned to the battlefield and while turning over the bodies of their foes, recognized some who had once been guests, friends or kinsmen. Others recognized the bodies of their personal enemies. Thus, throughout the whole army soldiers experienced the varied emotions of delight, sorrow, joy and grief.[21]

Immediately following the battle, Antonius miraculously recovered from his physical problems and resumed command of the army. He did have the decency to have his soldiers wipe the blood of their fellow citizens from their swords – something they would not do in the case of foreign foes.[22] Taking credit for a victory which had been won by the bravery and skill of others, he proclaimed himself *imperator* (a general who had won a major victory in which a certain number of the enemy had been killed).[23] Antonius sent Catiline's head back to Rome where receipt of this grisly message allegedly led to a period of rejoicing in which people changed their garments to signify their deliverance from danger.[24] Meanwhile, the government had to increase the volume of coinage in 62 in order to pay for the soldiers who were called into service to suppress the insurrection.[25]

B. The Aftermath: 62–60

Cicero spent the winter and spring of 62 in prosecuting some of the remaining conspirators. Based on Cicero's testimony, M. Porcius Laeca, C. Cornelius, P. Autronius Paetus, L. Vargunteius, Ser. Sulla and P. Sulla (not the defeated candidate from 66) were all convicted for violations of the *Lex Plautia de Vi*.[26] Cicero boasted that everyone against whom he testified was convicted.[27] Metellus Nepos cracked that Cicero's evidence produced more convictions than his actions as defence counsel had produced acquittals; Cicero retorted that 'My credibility is more convincing than my eloquence.'[28]

Among others seized as suspects was one L. Vettius, who had been a member of the conspiracy.[29] In an effort to save his own skin, Vettius supplied L. Novius Niger, the *quaestor* instructed by the senate to investigate the conspiracy, with a list of alleged conspirators.[30] Later, realizing that his willingness to denounce others might prove a source of profit as well as safety, Vettius announced that his list was incomplete and requested that it be returned to him for further additions (or possible deletions). The senate, recognizing that Vettius hoped to change the list to avenge himself on some and to blackmail others, refused his request and peremptorily ordered him to reveal the names of any conspirators who had not been on the earlier list. Thoroughly shaken by the failure of his scheme, Vettius named only a few insignificant citizens as additional conspirators.[31] Vettius may have been the same L. Vettius who was a member of Strabo's consilium at Asculum[32] and who profited enormously from the Sullan proscriptions.[33] The senate ordered the publication of the list and those named thereon were convicted either in absentia (thus letting their cases go by default) or while present in the court.[34] Vettius may have been more successful in his denunciation and the subsequent conviction of the Marcelli who were convicted of starting an uprising by the Paeligni.[35]

Suetonius states that that Vettius (presumably encouraged by some of the *optimates*) included Caesar on his list and that Curius (presumably with encouragement from the same sources) also denounced Caesar as a Catilinarian, alleging before the whole senate that Catiline himself had told him of Caesar's involvement and that he had a letter written to Catiline in Caesar's own hand. Conscious of the change in the political atmosphere, Caesar boldly counterattacked. First of all, he forced the clerk of the senate to read back the portion of the senate's record from the day in the autumn when Cicero reported that Caesar had come forward to warn him about the plot. Then he persuaded the senate to rescind the reward granted to Curius on the grounds that Caesar, rather than Curius, had been the first to disclose the conspiracy. Finally, he invoked his authority as *praetor* to declare forfeit the bond posted by Vettius at the time he made his denunciations. Vettius escaped by a hair's breadth from being torn apart by Caesar's supporters. He ended up being jailed by Caesar along with Niger who had committed the unforgiveable sin of permitting a superior magistrate to be accused before his tribunal.[36] This last minute effort by the *optimates* to pull down Caesar was doomed to failure; whatever they failed to accomplish in the autumn could not be done in the spring.

Many citizens of all ranks and parties took alarm from these incidents; some feared that they would be denounced by private foes under the guise of public good while others, taking hope from the fears of honest men, prepared groundless accusations. The senate, concluding that the investigations were getting out of hand, began to clamp down. It seems to have publicized the names of all who had been secretly denounced and halted the solicitation of secret accusations. However, the prosecutions of the conspirators dragged on into the summer of 62.[37] The string of prosecutions ended in July 62 when L. Manlius Torquatus, the son of the successful *optimate* candidate for consul in 66 and a close friend of Cicero, along with G. Cornelius, who was the son of one of the alleged conspirators,[38] prosecuted P. Cornelius Sulla, the defeated *popularis* candidate in 66, for his alleged involvement in the Catilinarian conspiracy. Surprisingly, Cicero undertook Sulla's defence.[39] Normally, an advocate would not take on a case where he had to oppose a friend. One exception to this rule was when the advocate was obligated to the defendant. Cicero did not like Sulla and did not owe him any loyalty. Cicero's action reflected both political and financial reasons.[40] Following the end of the conspiracy, Cicero had sent Pompey a boastful letter, apparently claiming that his stature was equivalent to Pompey's. Needless to say, those statements were not appreciated by Pompey, who apparently sent Cicero a cool reply.[41] Concerned by Pompey's attitude, Cicero probably hoped to shore up his standing with Pompey by defending Sulla, Pompey's brother-in-law.[42] In addition, Cicero benefited from a 'loan' from Sulla which gave him sufficient money to buy a mansion on the exclusive Palatine Hill from that eminent real estate magnate, Crassus.[43]

During the course of the trial, Torquatus the Younger accused Cicero of falsifying the records of the senate from 3 December 63, which was the day on which the Gauls gave evidence against the conspirators.[44] Cicero contended that the Gauls had asked the conspirators if Sulla, like Autronius (his running mate from 66) was involved in the conspiracy and received a negative response.[45] Torquatus alleged that the Gauls had named Sulla as one of the conspirators and that Cicero later tampered with the records to delete this part of their testimony.[46] Cicero, of course, went on at great length to deny this charge.[47] Cicero's eloquence was sufficient to convince the jury and save Sulla.[48] Significantly, however, Torquatus was present with Cicero when the public records were created and would have known what the original versions stated before manipulation.[49]

Ironically, the last 'Catilinarian' to be prosecuted was C. Antonius Hybrida who, upon his return from his province of Macedonia in 59, was accused of cowardice in the face of the enemy, but was prosecuted for involvement in the conspiracy.[50] He was defended by Cicero who felt bound to defend anyone who helped him in defeating the insurgents.[51] Cicero was unsuccessful in his defence of his former colleague.[52] Antonius' conviction was celebrated by the conduct of funeral rites for Catiline, a funeral banquet, and placement of flowers on Catiline's grave.[53] Not everyone shared Cicero's and Sallust's view of Catiline.

Following the defeat of Catiline, some of the insurgents still fought on, operating half as guerillas and half as *banditti*.[54] Indeed the Catilinarians in Pelignum and Brutium seemed to have continued the struggle until the end of 62, when government forces, headed respectively by the *praetors* Q. Cicero and M. Bibulus, caught up with them and destroyed them.[55] Another band of insurgents and slaves who had once fought with Spartacus seems to have been active around Thurii until 60 when C. Octavius (the father of the future Emperor Augustus), executing a special commission from the senate, overtook them with a government force and destroyed them.[56] Still other Catilinarians seem to have been active in Greece in 58.[57] The uprising ended not with a bang, but with a whimper.

Why did the Catilinarians fail? There are three basic reasons. First is that they had made little advance preparation for the insurgency. When the insurgency began, the Catilinarians were notoriously short of arms and trained soldiers. Second is the government's prompt and effective military response.[58] When the insurgency began, two significant *optimate* generals – Q. Marcius Rex and Q. Caecilius Metellus Creticus – and their armies were waiting outside of Rome to receive a triumph which the Pompeians were denying them.[59] By taking advantage of these forces (and augmenting them with veterans recalled to the ranks), the government was able to achieve numerical superiority over the Catilinarians. In addition, government agents quickly snuffed out local uprisings by the Catilinarians before they developed any momentum. The third is Lentulus' foolish attempt to enlist the Gauls in an enterprise for which they were not needed and whose support would have been politically damaging. This action was exploited by Cicero to turn popular opinion in Rome against the conspirators and enabled him to have the conspirators' leadership in the city executed. The only chance that the insurgents had was to capture Rome through a combined attack on the city by Manlius' forces and an uprising in the city itself. Once the conspiracy in the city had been crushed, this hope disappeared and Catiline's forces began to desert, leaving him and his outnumbered army to die at Pistoria. In reality, however, the conspiracy had little chance of its success. It was simply Catiline's last desperate throw of the dice.[60] 'Some say that he is mad/ Others that lesser hate him, do call it valiant fury…'[61]

Chapter X

Historical Sources for Catiline and the Catilinarian Conspiracy

All historians and biographers are dependent on their sources. To gain a real understanding of Catiline's history, character and the goals of his conspiracy it is necessary to undertake a critical examination of the ancient sources – both primary and secondary – dealing with Catiline and his faction and thus create a more realistic picture of Catiline's nature and the goals of the conspiracy.[1] Normally, history is written from the standpoint of the victors such as Cicero: it focuses on the keys to his success and not the causes of Catiline's failures. Looking at Catiline's story from his standpoint and focusing on the causes of his initial successes and ultimate failures give us a more nuanced picture of Roman political life. In addition, examining the elements in society that provided Catiline with a broad base of support throws light on the extent to which the oligarchical domination of Roman society had more than its share of discontents. Finally, an examination of the deficiencies in the classical sources is important in determining – to the extent feasible – the motivations of the various actors in a series of events which in some ways resemble a Greek tragedy. While one may never be able to find 'objective' truth, the goal of every historian is to come as close as possible to discovering this will-o'-the-wisp.

The historian or biographer writing about Catiline and the Catilinarian conspiracy faces two basic problems. First, the major contemporary source for Catiline and the conspiracy is M. Tullius Cicero who 'demonized' Catiline in 'powerful and gaudy rhetoric'.[2] Cicero's account of Catiline was followed in the main by Sallust as well as by the non-contemporaneous ancient historians. It could be said that the entire classical tradition about Catiline and the conspiracy is essentially a series of footnotes to Cicero's account. Accordingly, a historian must be careful in analysing the contemporary and secondary sources on Catiline. Fortunately, many modern historians have recognized these issues and have approached Cicero and those who followed him with more scepticism than scholars have in the past.

Second, although Catiline was born in 106 and died in 62, almost all information we have about him deals with the period 69–62, beginning with his praetorship and ending in January 62, with his death in the Battle of Pistoria. Indeed, the only three facts that we know about his life prior to 69 was that in 89 he served on the staff of Gn. Pompeius Strabo at the siege of Asculum, that he killed M. Marius Gratidianus during the Sulla proscriptions, and that in 73 he was accused of committing adultery with a Vestal Virgin. The absence of knowledge about his early life makes it difficult to see his career in broad perspective and contributes to a teleological view of his life. That in turn has tended to preclude consideration of how Catiline was impacted by both private and public events.

There were several reasons for the heavy reliance of secondary sources on Cicero. For one thing there is the sheer volume of Cicero's writing. For example, the surviving works of Cicero take up twenty-eight of the 542 volumes in the Loeb Classical Library, far more than any other author. Had more of Cicero's works survived, his output might even constitute a greater percentage of the Loeb collection. Lost in the centuries – perhaps fortunately[3] – are the volumes of poetry that Cicero wrote. Despite the destruction of much Ciceronian material, we have more of Cicero's writings than of any other classical writer. Cicero's character: his intelligence and wit, which are evident in both his formal and informal writings, cause us to rely disproportionately on his views. Cicero was the prototype of the intellectual hero who is well beloved by later fellow intellectuals, if not his contemporaries. Moreover, Cicero did have first-hand knowledge of Catiline and the conspiracy, which makes his writings important from an evidentiary standpoint.

Another significant reason for the influence of Cicero was that during the early Principate/Empire a certain section of the nobility and the intellectuals regretted the displacement of the Republic by the Principate/Empire. While Cato was seen as the preeminent Republican, Cicero was also revered for his defence of the Republic.[4] This admiration for Cicero was partially responsible for the efforts made to cover up Augustus' role in arranging for Cicero's murder as well as to sanitize Augustus' generally bloody and duplicitous record.[5] On the other hand, however, many Augustans were critical of Cicero's public actions and moral character.[6]

Perhaps the most important factor behind Cicero's influence is the fact that classical education in the early Roman Empire was focused on Cicero's works, which were considered models for great oratory and perhaps even better writing style.⁷ Indeed, part of Cicero's motivation for publishing his speeches was his hope that they would be used in the classroom and thus ensure his immortality.⁸ Quintilian in his seminal *Institutio Oratoria* claimed that Cicero was the greatest Roman orator and used Cicero's *Pro Milone* as a model for teaching oratory.⁹ The great prose writers of the early Empire – Seneca the Younger, Tacitus, and Pliny – were greatly influenced by the Ciceronian tradition, although they attempted with some success to move beyond Cicero's style and approach.¹⁰ Cicero's philosophical works, which introduced Greek philosophical thought to Rome, became even more important in the later Empire than in the early, because, as the Eastern and Western Empires grew apart, few scholars in the West knew Greek. For example, neither of two great Western theologians – Ambrose and Augustine – were familiar with the language.¹¹ Western knowledge of Greek philosophy was based to a large degree on Cicero's rendition of the same.

The result of all these factors was the willingness of secondary ancient sources to accept with little question Cicero's account of Catiline and the conspiracy. The significance of the accounts by these secondary sources today stems from the fact that these historians had access to a number of materials that have not survived, but provided them significant information not found in Cicero's speeches and letters, or in Sallust's *Bellum Catilinae*. For example, both Asconius and Dio Cassius relied on Cicero's now-lost history of his consulship, *Expositio Consiliorum Suorum*.¹² Similarly, contemporary sources such as Hortensius' *Annales* and his orations are not extant but were available to the secondary historians.¹³ Today's scholars are more sceptical of Cicero's accounts on the one hand, but on the other are more dependent on them as source material.

The contemporaneous and primary sources of information about Catiline and his conspiracy are the writings of Cicero, Q. Tullius Cicero, Sallust, and Diodorus Siculus, as well as an inscription showing the members of the *consilium* of the Roman general Gn. Pompeius Strabo in the Social War.¹⁴ The main ancient secondary sources that were created a number of decades after Catiline's death are the works of Asconius, Plutarch, Suetonius, and Dio Cassius. In addition to these ancient secondary sources are Appian, Livy, Annius Florus, and Velleius Paterculus, all of whom basically repeat the story told by Cicero and Sallust without adding much new information. There are anecdotists such as Valerius Maximus or Aulus Gellius whose work contains nuggets of potentially useful information and authors such as Seneca who may make incidental reference to characters or incidents involved in the conspiracy in the course of writing about other topics. Finally, there are the scholiasts such as the authors of the *Commenta Bernensia* and *Adnotationes super Lucanum*, which are commentaries on ancient works containing information that the scholiasts had access to, but which have since been lost.

Cicero is the most important primary source for Catiline's career. Cicero's two letters to Atticus in the summer of 65 provide a good deal of information about the 64 consular campaign. His speech *In Toga Candida* from 64 is a source for most of the scandalous stories about Catiline as well as the invention of the First Catilinarian Conspiracy.[15] Cicero's four speeches against Catiline ('*Catilinarians*') are the major sources of information about the 'second' or 'real' conspiracy and its suppression.[16] The *Pro Murena* is the main source of information about the campaign for the 62 consulships. The *Pro Sulla* contains some important information about the records kept of the senate meeting on 3 December 63 in which Cicero produced the damning evidence against the conspirators. In addition, Cicero wrote several works that have not survived but that were used by ancient historians and commentators: (1) a prose memoir in Greek, (2) a poem entitled *de Consulatu Suo*, and (3) a poem entitled *de Temporibus Suis* and (4) the *Expositio Consiliorum Suorum*.[17]

There are several problems with Cicero as a source. One is that much of the Ciceronian material took the form of political or legal speeches. Roman political oratory at the end of the Republic was dominated by *ad hominem*, scurrilous attacks on opponents that generally had no basis in fact.[18] Cicero was a master at this tactic, which dominated his election address, *In Toga Candida*, as well as his Catilinarian orations. For example, in the *Second Catilinarian*, Cicero declared: 'What poisoner in all of Italy, what gladiator, what robber, what assassin, what parricide, what forger of wills, what cheat, what debauchee, what spendthrift, what adulterer, what infamous woman, what corrupter of youth, what crook, can be found who will not confess to have lived on the most intimate terms with Catiline?'[19]

What did the Romans make of a statement such as this? In some ways it sounds almost absurd. However, these attacks must have been taken somewhat seriously by the Romans – otherwise orators would not have used this technique. Such charges were intended to convey spiritual rather than literal truth; they characterized one's opponent as someone was morally bad no matter what he did or what reasons he had for his actions.

They were designed to energize one's supporters – not to convince the supporters of one's opponent. Think of Republicans claiming that the 2020 election was stolen despite all the evidence to the contrary.

Cicero's legal speeches were as suspect as his political speeches because the job of a Roman defence counsel was to obscure the truth and produce an acquittal of an obviously guilty defendant. For example, in *Pro Caelio* when Cicero is defending a supporter of Catiline, he declares that Catiline had the ability:

> to live strictly when in company with the morose, merrily with the cheerful, seriously with the old, courteously with the young, audaciously with the criminal, and luxuriously with the profligate. Even I myself – yes, even I, I say – he once almost deceived, as he seemed to me a virtuous citizen, and desirous of the regard of every good man, and a firm and trustworthy friend.[20]

This picture is a far cry from that of Catiline drawn in Cicero's *Catilinarians*. It does not necessarily reflect Cicero's real view of Catiline (although is contains more than a germ of truth), but it certainly reflected Cicero's need to remind the jurors of Catiline's charisma to advance his defence of Caelius.

Another problem with Cicero as a source is that he was a major participant in the events. Any participant in events has a point of view that inhibits their giving an objective account of what took place. Human nature requires any participant in an event to justify their own actions. Catiline was Cicero's most serious political opponent in the consular election in 64. Catiline was the major supporter of debt reform in 63, a proposal that was anathema to Cicero.[21] Cicero hated Catiline and vice versa. In his own mind, Cicero's major claim to fame was the rescue of Rome from Catiline's conspiracy, a claim that he repeated ad nauseam.[22] Plutarch wrote that

> Cicero made himself generally odious, not by any base action, but by continually praising and magnifying himself, which made him hateful to many. For there could be no session either of senate or assembly or court of justice in which one was not obliged to hear Catiline and Lentulus endlessly talked about.[23]

A final problem with Cicero as a source comes from the fact that he rewrote his *Catilinarian* orations and his other consular speeches three years after their delivery; thus, we have Cicero's revisions and not the originals.[24] We do not know what changes he made during these revisions. It is certain that he made stylistic changes designed to make what were great extemporaneous speeches into literary masterpieces. One also suspects that he added details about the conspiracy that he learned some time after the speeches had been delivered. Finally, it is likely that he exaggerated the dangers posed by the conspiracy to justify Cicero's action in executing five of the *Catilinarian* conspirators without trial.[25] It is likely that Cicero added passages in both the Second and the Third *Catilinarian* signifying his resolve to go ahead with the punishment of the conspirators regardless of future repercussions.[26] Thus, the *Catilinarian* speeches that we read today are different from the versions that Cicero actually delivered. The same is true with some of his other speeches; Pliny the Younger pointed out that Cicero's defence speeches – including *Pro Murena* – omitted much material when he revised the speech.[27] On the other hand, it is likely that there was basic substantive congruence between the orations which were delivered and the written version of these speeches which have survived.

Possibly even overshadowing the problem of lack of objectivity and exaggeration is Cicero's conceivable willingness to create 'alternative facts'.[28] As noted earlier in the trial of Sulla for involvement in the conspiracy, Torquatus the Younger accused Cicero of falsifying the senate records in an effort to preserve his client from conviction. The fact that a close friend of Cicero's believed him capable of falsifying public records may suggest something about Cicero's reputation for honesty.[29]

The Torquatus episode raises another essential question when dealing with ancient sources that claim to rely on public records. *What* public records were kept during the Republican period, and *where* were they kept? It seems likely that most significant public actions, including treaties, laws, and *senatus consulta*, were inscribed on stone or bronze tablets.[30] Similarly, the granting of special privileges, such as Strabo's grant of citizenship to some Spanish cavalrymen in 89, were recorded on tablets.[31] Culham suggests that the inscriptions of texts of laws and *senatus consulta* were posted in the forum and later deposited in the *aerarium* (treasury).[32] However, other written records, such as the magistrate's *commentarii* (day books) and the *tabulae publicae* (accounts of public matters), were often kept in the homes of the great nobility.[33] No official records were kept of the senate's proceedings until Caesar arranged for scribes to create daily transcripts.[34] It is not clear where these transcripts were kept. Republican Rome had no archives as such.

Cicero's letters generally constitute more reliable evidence than his public speeches, since he was not trying to shape public opinion with them. However, when his letters tried to induce the recipient to take some action or adopt a certain point of view (as they often did), the statements made in them should be regarded with more scepticism. For example, one of his letters to L. Lucceius tries to persuade the latter to write a favourable account of his consulship.[35] Another of his letters, to the venerable patrician Appius Claudius, tries to assuage the latter's pride and offence at the prominence achieved by Cicero.[36] Even when Cicero's letters were not designed to achieve specific political or personal ends, like all letters they still created, consciously or unconsciously, a favourable picture of the author and the matters that he was relating.[37] Cicero was quite candid in his letters to his chief correspondent and closest friend, Titus Atticus. These letters tended to reflect Cicero's intimate thoughts and feelings as well as his somewhat jaundiced views of his contemporaries and public affairs. For example, the first letter in the collection cheerfully predicts that Catiline would be convicted of extortion in Africa unless the sun failed to shine at midday.[38] The next letter, however, indicates that Cicero is considering forming a joint ticket with Catiline to run for consul.[39] Unfortunately, Atticus was in Rome during most of the critical period of 64–62 so we do not have correspondence between the two dealing with Catiline's campaigns for consul and the ensuing conspiracy.

Another contemporaneous work entitled *Commentariolum Petitionis* has been attributed to Q. Tullius Cicero. This work takes the form of a letter of advice to Marcus concerning campaign strategy. Karl Rove, George Bush's *eminence grise*, wrote:

> In his election advice to his brother Marcus, Quintus Cicero shows himself to be a master political strategist with a clear understanding of opposition research, organization, and turnout (though a little weak on message). Fresh, lively, and sharp, this primer provides timeless counsel and a great read for a modern political practitioner.[40]

Of course, much of the work deals with electioneering practices and procedures that are unique to the Roman political framework and even more so to the problems faced by M. Cicero as a *novus homo* campaigning for the consulship.⁴¹ However, a great deal of the advice has a broader application, as recognized by Karl Rove.

The *Commentariolum Petitionis* is significant in terms of Catiline's story in two respects. First, it describes Cicero's campaign strategy in 64, focusing on the actions he needed to take to overcome the disadvantage of being a *novus homo* without noble ancestors. Second, it contains the first version of Cicero's later claims that Catiline played a leading role in the Sullan proscriptions⁴² and that he committed malfeasance while *pro praetor* in Africa, escaping conviction only by bribing the jury.⁴³ The credibility of such charges must be judged in light of Q. Cicero's advice to Marcus in the same letter: 'By all means, if one is able to do so, call attention to any rumour of crime or wantonness or bribery on the part of your competitors that would seem consistent with their reputed way of life.'⁴⁴

Arguments have been made questioning the attribution of this work to Q. Cicero and suggesting that it was written by an Augustan writer.⁴⁵ For one thing, there would have been no need for Q. Cicero to write a lengthy letter about campaigning to his brother since not only did Marcus know a great deal about campaigning, but the two brothers were also together often enough that there would have been no need for Quintus to write Marcus.⁴⁶ Arguably, it is an example of a *suasoria*⁴⁷ which was a declamation giving advice to a famous figure in the hope that the work would gain *authoritas* by reason of the attribution.⁴⁸

On the other hand, whoever wrote the *Commentariolum Petitionis* had a profound knowledge of politics and electioneering at the end of the Roman Republic as well as of the particular circumstance of Cicero's campaign for the consulship in 63. It is unlikely that an Augustan writer would have had detailed knowledge of the problems faced by a *novus homo* or that C. Aurelius Cotta (cos. 75) was a master at campaigning.⁴⁹ In the last analysis whether the *Commentariolum Petitionis* was written by Q. Cicero or not is far less important than the fact that it is one of the few contemporary sources of information about both the 64 election and Catiline.⁵⁰

The most comprehensive of the contemporaneous sources about Catiline and his conspiracy is Sallust's *Bellum Catilinae*. Sallust knew some of the principal figures of the Catilinarian period and had the opportunity to interview others.⁵¹ For example, Sallust states that he knew both Caesar and Cato.⁵² At another point Sallust repeats a story that Crassus had told him.⁵³ However, these are the only times that Sallust makes reference to personal knowledge of the events or the personages involved. The fact that

Sallust makes specific references to these sources suggests that his work generally is not based on information that he obtained first hand from prominent political figures.

Textual consistencies between Sallust's text and some of Cicero's speeches clearly indicate that Sallust was familiar with Cicero's speeches and used them as a primary source.[54] It does not seem that Sallust was familiar with Cicero's letters since he makes no reference to Cicero' willingness to defend Catiline in the latter's extortion trial in 64 and to form a *coitio* (alliance) with Catiline for the consular elections held in 64. However, some of the information contained in the *Bellum Catilinae* must have been obtained from non-Ciceronian sources. Sallust's account of the Battle of Pistoria is so detailed that it was probably obtained from soldiers involved on both sides. Sallust's statement that Petreius won the battle by attacking the centre of Catiline's forces with his reserve seems more likely to have been based on an account from a government soldier. Sallust's description of Catiline performing both the duties of a commander and a common solder had to have been based on information from a Catilinarian refugee.

Lewis[55] points out that there is an inscription on a tomb in Sallust's hometown (Amiternum) that seems to date from near the beginning of the Second Triumvirate and that indicates that the persons buried there were 'L.1 Catilina' (meaning a person who was a freedman of L. Catilina.) and his wife. Lewis hypothesizes that Sallust may have obtained information from this freedman when he was growing up or when he returned to his hometown for a visit. At the end of the *Bellum Catilinae* Sallust wrote not that no one from the Catilinarian side escaped death but only that no *ingenua* (free born citizen as opposed to a freedman) escaped,[56] leaving open the possibility that a freedman had escaped and became the source of some of Sallust's information about the battle. Some authorities have claimed that Sallust had married Cicero's divorced wife – Terentia. If true, Sallust would have another first hand (albeit uncited) source of information. However, the general consensus of scholars is that Terentia did not marry Sallust and thus was not a source of information about the conspiracy.[57]

Now, Sallust prefaces his *Bellum Catilinae* with the following statement:

Statui res gestas Romani carptim…persscribere, eo magis quod mihi a spe metu partibus, rei publicae animus liber erat. Igitur de Catilinae coniuratione, quam verissume potero, paucis absolvam.

(I decided to write about a small part of Roman history particularly because I was free from fear, hope or partisan politics. Therefore I shall write about Catiline's conspiracy as accurately as I am able to do albeit in a few words.)[58]

Woodman has contended that Sallust and other Roman historians believed their aim was impartiality – not objective truth. History was viewed by the Romans as a species of oratory. An historian was a lawyer trying a case and presenting only those facts that fit his narrative. A work of history under this approach may contain some truths, but it is not the whole truth or nothing but the truth.[59]

A disappointed politician turned political philosopher,[60] Sallust wrote the story of Catiline's conspiracy as a morality play designed to demonstrate that the decline and fall of the Roman Republic was due to the corruption of the nobility. The *Bellum Catilinae* is a Roman version of Milton's *Paradise Lost* with Catiline as an angel whose fall was due not just to the defects in his own character but also to the corrupt state of the Republic.[61] Some portions of it are more sermon than history.[62] This defect is further complicated by Sallust's image of Catiline as an unchanging, constant personality who *Hunc post dominationem L. Sullae lubido maxima invaserat rei publicae capiundae* (after the dictatorship of L. Sulla was seized by an enormous desire to take control of the Republic)[63]

To justify his claim that Catiline had spent the twenty years between Sulla's dictatorship in the 80s and the Catilinarian conspiracy in 63 planning to overthrow the Republic, he built on the story of the First Catilinarian conspiracy invented by Cicero[64] and then has the real conspiracy begin before the consular elections of 63[65] instead of after the consular elections of 62, when Catiline's last political hopes were thwarted. Most modern historians discredit both stories although A. J. Woodman has defended their accuracy.[66] Similarly, Sallust's account of the debate on 5 December 63 over the execution of the conspirators dramatizes the clash between Cato and Caesar – the two greatest Romans of the day in Sallust's opinion – rather than recording the ebb and flow of a debate where the participants sometimes changed their mind on the issue of execution. Indeed, while Sallust had available to him copies of Caesar's and Cato's speeches,[67] he preferred to invent his own; art, not accuracy, was his objective.

Sallust's picture of Catiline was not so much the devil incarnate described by Cicero as a man with some talents and failings who fell in part due to the corrupt nature of the Roman state.[68] In that sense, his picture is more nuanced than that of Cicero because of his need for Catiline to epitomize the corrupt nature of the Roman nobility. Nevertheless, Sallust often accepted without scepticism and repeated many of those scandalous charges against Catiline that had been made by Cicero and others although, on occasion, even he questioned some of the more sensational stories. For instance, he questioned the tale that after the conspirators had their initial meeting, Catiline murdered a slave and had everyone drink from a bowl containing the slave's blood and swear an oath of allegiance to the conspiracy. Sallust wrote:

nonnulli ficta et haec et multa praeterea existumabant ab iis, qui Ciceronis invidiam quae postea orta est leniri credebant atrocitate sceleris eorum, qui poenas dederant. nobis ea res pro magnitudine parum comperta est.

(Others thought that these and many other details were invented by men who believed that the hostility that afterwards arose against Cicero would be moderated by exaggerating the guilt of the conspirators whom he had put to death. For my own part I have too little evidence for pronouncing upon a matter of such weight.)[69]

At another point, Sallust rejected a lurid story about Catiline's associates engaging in indiscriminate homosexual acts, writing *sed ex aliis rebus magis quam quod quoiquam id compertum foret haec fama valebat.* (that report became current rather for other reasons than because anyone had evidence of its truth)[70] However, these were the only sceptical caveats in the *Bellum Catilinae*. Batstone notes that Sallust omitted some of the other scurrilous charges against Catiline.[71] These gestures to objectivity, however, should not obscure the fact that Sallust's account was designed not so much to record what actually happened as to substantiate his theory about the decline and fall of the Republic.[72]

Bellum Catilinae also suffered from Sallust's own political prejudices. His accounts of the urban proletariat and its attitudes are questionable, since they reflected his aristocratic disdain for the common people.[73] Although he pays tribute to Cicero and his *First Catilinarian*,[74] Sallust boldly states that the two greatest Romans of his times were Cato and Caesar.[75] Syme's verdict on the *Bellum Catilinae* is correct: 'It was an epoch-making achievement in the literature of the Latins, creating a new style and manner. Examined as history, it exhibits manifold defects...'[76]

The final contemporary source for Catiline is Diodorus Siculus' *Universal History*. This work covered the history of the world from the Trojan War to about 60. Diodorus Siculus was, as his name implied, a Sicilian of Greek extraction. He was born in Agyrium, spent 60–56 in Egypt, and then lived in Rome from 56 to 30, during which period he did most of his writing.[77] Diodorus may have stopped his history in 60 to avoid having to relate Caesar's story, since admiration for Caesar was not politically correct in the period following his death and Augustus' rise to power.[78] Diodorus' value as a source is severely limited by two things. (1) only fragments of his last book survive. (2) given the limited social circle in which Diodorus operated, it is unlikely that he would have known or interviewed any of the participants in the events of the 60s; rather he seems to have relied on secondary sources even for events that occurred in his own lifetime.[79]

That leaves us with information provided by the non-contemporaneous or ancient historians. The traditional view of the ancient historians is that these writers focused not on uncovering new information or devising new explanations for historical events, but rather on creating artistic works of literature that were original in terms of form rather than content.[80] This 'artistic' approach was the limitation imposed by the logistics of their materials. While the ancient historians did have the benefit of using 'public' libraries, which were initially created by Asinius Pollio and Augustus,[81] they had limited ability to integrate their reading into their writings. Their basic problem came from the physical nature of the material with which they had to work: the papyrus rolls containing the ancient texts. 'These were hefty and unmanageable things; and indexing, chapter headings, and even line-and column-numbering were rudimentary or non-existent.'[82] In the absence of a way of organizing and indexing these notes (which had to be set down on other rolls of papyri), their annotations would seem to have been of somewhat limited use. Reference both to the basic source materials and to the historian's own notes was cumbersome at best.

Under the traditional view, the ancient historians sometimes relied on only one or perhaps two primary sources for a particular period because it was impractical to have more than one roll or two rolls of papyrus under inspection at a time.[83] If they had a literate slave, the slave could hold open a second source and read from it while the writer was examining another source.[84] They could also rely on their prodigious memories which sometimes led them to make mistakes with respect to details such as the number of soldiers involved in a battle.

There is a certain amount of evidence to support the traditionalist view. Certainly, most papyri were cumbersome to work with. It is obvious from reading the works of ancient historians that they generally did not cite their sources. Careful reading of some ancient historians indicates considerable artistry which reflects major efforts in the writing itself. Thus, Lushkov has demonstrated how Livy used the theme of *spolia* (spoils of battle) as well as (old architectural structures) to give several meanings to his description of historical events in which the Roman had seized the physical *spolia* or reused old architectural structures.[85] Livy himself wrote in his preface that often historians authored new histories because: *dum novi semper scriptores aut in rebus certius aliquid allaturos se aut scribendi arte rudem vetustatem superaturos credunt. utcumque erit.* (new authors always think either they have more certain knowledge to address the matter or that they believe that their writing can improve on the rough writings of their predecessors.)[86]

Despite the above, the traditional view of the limitations on ancient historians overstates the logistical difficulties from which they suffered and denigrates the quality of their historical research and analysis. Before the age of computers, semi-modern historians used note cards to records matters which they considered important and organized the note cards into in such a manner that they could locate all of the material on a given matter when they wanted to begin composing. In addition, they would sometimes write portions of a book at different times and then fit these pieces into a greater work. Ancient historians would have needed more space to contain baskets of notes on papyri or written accounts of certain episodes, but they could have followed the basic methodology of semi-modern historians. This approach certainly enabled them to capture new information and insert it into their work or to produce a new analysis of events.

It is difficult to believe that Dio Cassius, who spent ten years of research before he began writing his annalistic history,[87] did not use an approach similar to this. Otherwise, what would have been the point of his research if he simply wrote about a period based on one or two sources supplemented by what he remembered? Can any reader remember any details of a work one read ten years ago? Similarly, it seems clear that Livy must have used a similar method. As Lushkov noted, 'Source citations are ubiquitous in the *AUC*...'[88] Source citations per se are evidence of note taking. Good ancient historians were more than artists or copyists; to them the medium was not the message.

The earliest non-contemporaneous source for Catiline is Q. Asconius Pedianus (9–86 AD).[89] Little is known about Asconius' life other than that he was regarded as a distinguished historian.[90] Asconius indicates that he was writing his commentaries on five speeches of Cicero to help his sons understand the references in these speeches and thus comprehend the historical context in which they were given.[91] He was not trying to write history; his commentaries on the orations are literally a series of footnotes on Cicero's speeches as are today's commentaries on ancient works. From our standpoint, the most significant of his commentaries is on the *In Toga Candida*. Asconius did not question the basic Ciceronian/Sallustian portrait of Catiline because it was the primary material available to him.[92] Unlike many Roman historians, Asconius often cited his sources and made serious attempts to investigate and evaluate them.[93] He gives a detailed and reasoned argument for rejecting the claim of the Roman historian Fenestella that Cicero had actually defended Catiline in the latter's trial for extortion.[94] However, he did have an anachronistic view of the 60s, which has led Marshall to question his accuracy on certain matters.[95]

The next secondary ancient source of any note is Plutarch (46–120 CE). Plutarch was a Greek from Chaeroneia who was a priest at the temple of Apollo at Delphi, and both a magistrate in and ambassador for his town.[96] Plutarch was a biographer rather than an historian. His *Parallel Lives* compared famous Greeks with famous Romans whom he believed to be similar to their Greek counterparts; thus, Caesar is coupled with Alexander, Cicero with Demosthenes. Plutarch had enough practical experience in politics and diplomacy to understand the how and why of the actions of the subjects of his *Parallel Lives*. Nevertheless, the biographer was more interested in 'character' than he was in analysing historical events. Large parts of his biographies consisted of entertaining anecdotes demonstrating the character of the figure in question.[97] For example, he records the following telling story about Cicero: after making a speech praising Crassus, two days later Cicero made a speech criticizing him. When Crassus asked Cicero about the latter's change of heart, Cicero responded. 'I exercised my eloquence in declaiming on a worthless subject.'[98] Plutarch did perform extensive research and used a number of sources for his work; he was more critical of his source material than many ancient writers.⁹⁹ 'Plutarch might at times reorder, conflate, or omit events, and we must be circumspect regarding the attitudes and motivations he attributes to his subjects, but he generally did not fabricate facts.'¹⁰⁰ He did not focus on the political/historical contexts in which his subjects acted. Utterly foreign to modern readers was his interest in oracles and signs.¹⁰¹ While Plutarch was aware that these might be manipulated, he also seemed to have seen Apollo (as the god most associated with oracles) as a real entity operating on occasion in the affairs of men.¹⁰²

Plutarch spent several years in Corinth and became acquainted with some of the Corinthians who participated in the Second Sophistic movement, which emphasized oratorical skills that were frequently used to recall the glories of ancient Greece.¹⁰³ Plutarch was not a member of this movement even though he lived at its height.¹⁰⁴ However, the movement's emphasis on the accomplishments of the ancient Greeks may have provided some impetus to Plutarch *Parallel Lives*, which clearly made the point that for every famous Roman there had been an equally famous (or infamous) Greek counterpart.

For obvious reasons, Catiline and his conspiracy are dealt with most fully in Plutarch's *Cicero*. Pelling¹⁰⁵ suggests that the account of Catiline in *Cicero* falls into three divisions: (1) chapters 10–11, which deal with the background of the conspiracy and are based on Sallust; (2) chapters 12–20, which deal with Cicero's struggle with Catiline and the conspirators and are based on Cicero's secret history of this consulship; and (3) chapters 20–24 which deal with the debate in the senate and are based both on Cicero's secret history of his consulship and some other unknown source. Plutarch recorded other events relating to Catiline and his conspiracy in his *Lives* of Caesar, Cato Minor, and Crassus which are not recorded in *Cicero* because these incidents were more important to Plutarch's portrayal of these individuals than they were to Plutarch's portrayal of Cicero.¹⁰⁶

The second biographer whose work contained some information about Catiline's conspiracy was C. Suetonius Tranquillus (69 – at least 122 AD) Suetonius was trained as an attorney but instead became in effect a professional scholar who, in recognition of his scholarship, received a number of public honours.¹⁰⁷ He was in charge of the imperial archives under the emperors Trajan and Hadrian, had access to all the imperial records and thus could engage with many primary sources while writing the *Twelve Caesars*.¹⁰⁸ However, the imperial archives contained little in the way of primary materials from the Republic both because there was no formal archives from the time and because some three thousand copies of laws, treaties and grants of privilege (many of which had predated the Principate) had been destroyed in the Capitoline fire of 69–70 AD.[109]

Suetonius was careful to record his sources and often cited specific documents as evidence; unlike most ancient historians, he did not invent speeches for his subjects.[110] Suetonius devoted too much attention in the *Twelve Caesars* to the sexual activities of the emperors and too little to their policies and motivations. It may be poetic justice that Suetonius was dismissed from his position for allegedly behaving improperly with the empress Sabina while the emperor Hadrian was absent in Britain.[111] The account of his objectionable behaviour uses an unusual conjunction of Latin words, so it is difficult to determine exactly what is meant by the language.[112] It may simply be that Suetonius overstepped his bounds by reading ribald stories about Hadrian's predecessors.[113] This does not seem like a serious offence. However, the most recent scholar to study Sabina suggests that Hadrian had a 'deliberate strategy to leverage his wife's inherent prestige and latent power to the fullest.'[114] If this is the case, then it may be a partial explanation for Hadrian's action in ensuring that Sabina's good name was not besmirched. However, even if Brennan's theory is correct, abrupt dismissal of two top officials seems an overreaction, and one wonders if Hadrian was not also taking advantage of the circumstances to rid himself of men whom he no longer liked or trusted.

While Suetonius, like Plutarch was interested in character, his approach to its depiction differed considerably. Plutarch in his *Lives* wrote essays showing how a subject was dominated by a particular trait(s); his selection of events and emphasis reflected that focus. Suetonius, on the other hand, did not try to create a uniform picture of any emperor, but rather catalogued both the virtues and the vices of the emperors in light of their major responsibility of managing the great Roman Empire.

Suetonius' life of *Caesar* in his *Twelve Caesars* contains information about Caesar's involvement in three specific matters somewhat related to Catiline: the so called First Catilinarian conspiracy, the debate over the fate of the Catilinarian conspirators, and the aftermath of the suppression of the Catilinarian conspiracy. However, Suetonius' account of these events focuses on Caesar, and Catiline's name does not even appear in connection with the first matter. Suetonius' *Caesar* totally ignores the political relationship between Crassus, Caesar and Catiline during the period before

63 – presumably because he did not find it relevant to Caesar's virtues and vices. Indeed, Suetonius, far more than Plutarch, followed the ancient model of biography, which was to ignore historical background and focus on the individual's character and private life as well as his public life.[115] For all of these reasons, Suetonius' work is of obviously limited utility to a student of Catiline and the conspiracy.

It can fairly be said that Plutarch and Suetonius are the fathers of modern biography.[116] From the historian's standpoint, there are two drawbacks to the biographies of both writers (as well as to any other biography). First is the tendency of biographers to exaggerate the significance of the role played by their subjects in the early part of their subjects' career –sometimes at the expense of the more significant role played by the subject in their later career. This defect becomes apparent in Suetonius' biography of Caesar where eighteen of the eighty-nine sections deal with Caesar's career before he ran for consul; only two deal with his conquest of Gaul. Second is the tendency of biographers to assume the subject's positions and views. This was particularly true of Plutarch's account of Cicero and the Catilinarian conspiracy. This fault does not appear in some of Plutarch's other *Lives* and does not characterize Suetonius' attitude to several of the emperors.

Dio Cassius is the only secondary historian whose surviving work dealt with the Catilinarian period. This Greek historian (155– 235 AD) spent ten years researching and then another twelve years composing his *History of Rome*, which covered the history of the city from its foundation to Dio Cassius' own time.[117] Although much of his work has been lost, books 36– 40, which cover the period 67–50, have survived almost intact and provide invaluable information about Catiline and the conspiracy. Dio Cassius was a senator under Commodus; he became governor of Smyrna and then served as a suffect consul (one elected to the consulship to fill out a term not completed by the original office holder) in approximately 205 AD. Dio was also *pro consul* in Africa and Pannonia; a *pro consul* in the Empire was a civilian official who was made the governor of a province. He was finally made consul by the emperor Severus Alexander.[118] Dio was an extensive researcher.[119] His practical experience in government and politics gave him particular insight into the historical events that he related. However, Dio, like Sallust, had strong views about the fall of the Roman Republic and, unlike Sallust, he composed speeches for others which tended to focus on abstract principles of morality and statecraft and reflect his own views more than the speakers.[120] Accordingly, they are less useful to a historian.

Dio Cassius was generally hostile to Cicero,[121] noting in connection with Cicero's early career:

> Cicero, on his part, was aspiring to lead in the *res publica* and was endeavouring to make it clear to both the *populares* and the *optimates* that he was sure to make whichever side he joined preponderate. He was accustomed to play a double role and would espouse now the cause of one party and again that of the other, to the end that he might be courted by both.[122]

Millar states: 'Dio's handling of Cicero is a failure; perhaps the most complete failing of his history.'[123] Dio's antipathy for Cicero is not reflected in his treatment of the Catilinarian conspiracy because he accepts Cicero's basic story about both Catiline and his schemes.[124] Nevertheless, Dio provides detailed information about the events of the Catilinarian conspiracy which is not available elsewhere.[125] There is no reason to believe that he ever fabricated facts; his errors were generally due to discrepancies in his sources.[126]

Dio Cassius did engage in his source material in a critical way although this fact is not obvious since he says little about his sources.[127] Like many Roman historians, his work is annalistic (that is to say, it recorded what happened in each year but made little or no attempt to stand back and create a broader picture). Thus, Dio's account is reasonably accurate (to the extent that Dio's sources were accurate) but it contains little or no analysis of broader historical movements. It is often insightful in terms of analysis of character or of the motivation of individuals involved in a particular event. Levick[128] seems to diminish the significance of Dio's rather detailed account of Catiline and the conspiracy, dealing with it in only two sentences and stating that it was based on Livy, whose work for this period has not survived. Levick seems to miss both the point that, given the destruction of Livy's work for this period, Dio's work becomes more important and that Dio was a first-rate historian.

Such are the sources of our knowledge of Catiline and his conspiracy. We have more information concerning it than we do most other events in the past. Even though the information that we have comes from less than objective sources than is normal even for the classical period, there can be little dispute about the broad outlines of what happened – as opposed, for example, to *why* things happened the way that they did. The real issues with respect to Catiline and his conspiracy concern not what actually took place, but why things occurred in the way that they did and what were the motivations of the protagonists. While every historian peers through a glass darkly in an effort to illuminate the events of the past, which, given human nature, are necessarily recorded in biased accounts, an historian of Catiline and his conspiracy suffers more from this problem than most. This issue has often led to an uncritical acceptance of the classical story, or an equally uncritical rejection of the same, which makes Catiline a hero rather than a villain. The truth of the matter is that Catiline was neither. The personage that Catiline most resembled was Shakespeare's Macbeth.

Chapter XI

Catiline's Ghost in the Arts, Letters and History

The Palazzo Madama picture of Catiline illustrates how Catiline' story has inspired the imagination of artists, poets, playwrights, novelists and historians in the two millennia since his death. It presents Catiline as a solitary individual, isolated from his fellows, and head in one hand, contemplating his downfall and disgrace. This portrayal seems to be the only significant painting that features Catiline. Catiline has been portrayed in two relatively obscure operas: Ian Hamilton's *The Catiline Conspiracy* (1973) and Giambattista Casti's *Catilina* (1792), with music by Salieri.[1] It is less than clear how Catiline is portrayed in these operas. Catiline's role has been far more prominent in letters and history than in the arts.

There have been several approaches to Catiline in the letters. One approach has been to depict him as the embodiment of all evil. There are a number of references to Catiline in ancient literature epitomizing this approach. Virgil refers to him in the *Aeneid*: *et te, Catilina, minaci pendentem scopulo Furiarumque ora trementem* (and you, Catiline, hanging from a rock in hell and trembling at the menacing Furies.)[2] Juvenal writes: *quis caelum terris non misceat et mare caelo/si fur displiceat Verri, homicida Miloni, / Clodius accuset moechos, Catilina Cethegum,/in tabulam Sullae si dicant discipuli tres*? (What would not confuse heaven with earth and sea with sky if Verres was unhappy with thieves, or Milo with murders? If Clodius [who allegedly committed incest with his sister, Clodia] accuses adulterers, or Catiline, Cethegus and Clodius, Sulla's three disciples plead against proscription lists?)[3] Juvenal also wrote:

> Where is a more exalted ancestry to be found, than yours Catiline,
> Or yours Cethegus? Yet armed by night you connived to attack
> Homes and temples and set them alight, like those sons of Gaul
> In breeches, like the scions of those Senones who sacked Rome,
> An outrage punished by legal execution, in 'a coat of burning pitch'.[4]

As the Renaissance arrived, both the media and the message dealing with Catiline changed. The media was drama; the message was to picture Catiline and his opponents as abstractions reflecting broader issues, Stephen Gosson (c.1578), Robert Wilson (c. 1598) and Henry Chettle (c. 1598) wrote, now lost, plays on the Catilinarian conspiracy.[5] In 1611 the Jacobean playwright, Ben Jonson, wrote *Catiline, His Conspiracy* which basically dramatized the Ciceronian/Sallustian story; unfortunately, this work has survived. Like Sallust's *Bellum Catilinae*, the play is far more about the general decline of Rome than it is about Catiline, who is largely absent from the play after the first act. When present, however, he is painted in the darkest terms possible. The play fails as a tragedy because Jonson's Catiline is too one-sidedly evil to be a tragic hero. The only interesting – and comic – moment in the play occurs when Catiline and Cicero (separately) bemoan the fact that each is trying to soar like an eagle while leading a group of buzzards.[6]

Voltaire tried his hand at the Catiline story with his drama, *Catiline*.[7] It seems more readable than other dramas about Catiline, both before and since, because the playwright created more nuanced and therefore more interesting pictures of some of the historical characters. He noted: 'all that Cicero, Catiline Cato and Caesar do in this piece is not true, but their genius and character is faithfully represented.'[8] However, despite Voltaire's statement, the play treats Catiline as an abstract as opposed to a human figure. The dramatic focus of the play involves the conflict in Catiline between his ambition (his evil spirit) and his love of Aurelia Orestilla, his wife (his good spirit). Unfortunately, the conflict is not credible because Catiline is able, without real struggle, to ignore all Orestilla's concerns and feelings and have her beloved father murdered.

Two and a half centuries later, Henrik Ibsen, at the age of 21 wrote his first play, entitled *Catiline*.[9] Like many first-time efforts by young writers, it should have been thrown in the trash heap. Like Voltaire's play, it creates an abstract picture of a Catiline who struggles between evil (represented by the shade of a Vestal Virgin whose sister Catiline has seduced and later murdered) and good, represented by Aurelia Orestilla. Its presentation of Aurelia Orestilla as Catiline's good angel reminds a reader of Voltaire's similar depiction. This play resembles an unsophisticated version of the themes in George Lucas' *Star Wars*, in the sense of depicting a struggle between the light side of the Force and the dark side. Any resemblance between the characters in the play and the historical characters was purely coincidental. For example, Caesar appears as the conqueror of Catiline and the saviour of Rome.

Catiline has never attracted the attention of writers/musicians who produce 'musical comedies' although the figure would be amenable to the treatment of a tragic protagonist similar to that accorded Arthur in the musical *Camelot*, albeit without the light at the ending. Similarly, Catiline's story has never made it to the cinema, although he could have been shown as a hero fighting tyranny as was the protagonist in *Spartacus*.

In our own day, the medium has switched to the novel and the message has become more realistic. Stephen Saylor in his *Roma sub Rosa* mystery series has one book largely devoted to Catiline, *Catilina's Riddle: A Mystery of Ancient Rome*. In addition, he has Catiline make his first appearance in a short story in *The House of the Vestals* and includes Catiline's ghost in *Last Seen in Massalia*. Saylor is more effective than the dramatists in creating a plausible picture of Catiline as a personally charming, clever, sex-driven and shifty politician – a riddle wrapped in an enigma. Imagine Bill Clinton made of sterner stuff. *Catilina's Riddle* illustrates, however, one of the basic problems of writing historical fiction; while one can fill in gaps between known facts, one cannot deviate from them. The result is that the book is in some ways Lester Hutchinson's revisionist *The Conspiracy of Catiline*[10] put into fiction and combined with an unrelated, albeit interesting, subplot involving Gordianus the Finder (who is the main protagonist in the *Sub Rosa* series and who is the Roman equivalent of a detective).

A far less sympathetic and realistic picture of Catiline emerges in Robert Harris' *Cicero Trilogy*, three novels theoretically written by Cicero's secretary, Tiro. Harris depicts Catiline as a worse devil than even Cicero and Sallust did, since he portrays him as a physically brutal individual with an uncontrollable temper. Harris' portrayal of Catiline's opponent and his 'hero' Cicero is almost comical as it shows the latter primly rejecting Catiline's request that Cicero take on his defence in his extortion trial because Cicero believed that Catiline was guilty.[11] Not even the most devoted admirer of Cicero has ever confused him with Abe Lincoln, who refused to represent the guilty. Indeed, one could not make a living as a criminal attorney if one represented only the innocent, and Cicero became quite wealthy defending the guilty.

Ironically, the most compelling picture of Catiline from a literary standpoint is Cicero's description of him in *Pro Caelio*:

He was intimate with many thoroughly wicked men; but he pretended to be entirely devoted to the most virtuous of the citizens. He had many things about him which served to allure men to the gratification of their passions; he had also many things which acted as incentives to industry and toil. The vices of lust raged in him; but at the same time, he was conspicuous for great energy and military skill. Nor do I believe that there ever existed so strange a prodigy upon the earth, made up in such a manner of the most various, different and inconsistent studies and desires.

Who was ever more acceptable at one time to most illustrious men? Who was more intimate with the very basest? What citizen was there at times who took a better part than he did? Who was there at other times a fouler enemy to this state? Who was more debased in his pleasures? Who was more patient in undergoing labours? Who was more covetous as regards his rapacity? Who more prodigal in squandering? And besides all this, there were, O jurors, these marvellous qualities in that man, that he was able to embrace many men in his friendship, to preserve their regard by attention, to share with everyone what he had, to assist all his friends in their necessities with money, with influence, with his personal toil, even with his own crimes and audacity, if need were; to keep his nature under restraint and to guide it according to the requirements of the time, and to turn and twist it hither and thither; to live strictly when in company with the morose, merrily with the cheerful, seriously with the old, courteously with the young, audaciously with the criminal, and luxuriously with the profligate. Even I myself – yes, even I – I say – he once almost deceived, as he seemed to me a virtuous citizen, and desirous of the regard of every good man, and a firm and trustworthy friend.[12]

Only Shakespeare could have exceeded Cicero's artistry.

As shown by the chapter on the ancient sources for Catiline, the Ciceronian and Sallustian version of Catiline and his insurrection were accepted by the ancient historians and passed down like a treasured legacy to their successors, including the great German historian, Theodor Mommsen. However, the second half of the nineteenth century saw the beginning of a split between historians who basically accepted the classical account,[13] or those who have rejected it and pictured Catiline as one of a long series of *populares* who were struggling on behalf of the oppressed to right the wrongs of the *optimi/boni*.¹⁴ Inherent in all of these works is the assumption that Rome had political parties somewhat similar to nineteenth century political parties. This assumption has been thrown onto the garbage heap by modern historians, who have all recognized that Roman parties bear little or no resemblance to modern political parties.¹⁵

Until the second half of the twentieth century, however, all historians have accepted the basic Ciceronian and Sallustian account, which shows Catiline as the leader of a united conspiracy which represented a real threat to overthrow the Roman government, and which aimed to replace it with a dictatorship led by Catiline. Two modern historians, Robin Seager and K.H. Waters have rejected this entire approach by suggesting that there was no central conspiracy, but rather a collection of unrelated insurgent movements of which Catiline's was the most important. These historians see Cicero as seizing upon the situation and making Catiline a 'bogeyman' whose activities could be used to scare the senatorial and equestrian orders into a unity which could resist any attempt by Pompey to seize power upon his return from Asia.¹⁶ The difficulty with their theories is that they completely reject the major elements of the classical account, mainly by assuming that the Etrurian insurgency was unconnected to the conspiracy in the city. This assumption seems inconsistent with the fact that Catiline left Rome to go to the camp of the insurgents and that he had planned such a move before Cicero forced him to make it. Moreover, Cicero was always a Pompeian, even when it was to his disadvantage to be so. It seems improbable that Cicero was concerned that Pompey on his return would emulate Sulla and become a dictator. There is no evidence that Cicero as consul ever took any hostile steps towards Pompey. (Ironically, Pompey's return turned out to be a non-event, as he disbanded his army upon landing in Italy).¹⁷ It seems unlikely that Cicero and Sallust's story of a unitary conspiracy would have gained public acceptance if in fact there was no overall conspiracy, but rather a group of unconnected insurgent movements.

Another modern historian, Barbara Levick, does not reject the classical approach in toto, but has amended it by suggesting that Catiline had been communicating with Pompey since his return from Africa and had contemplated an alliance with Pompey when the latter returned from the East; Levick suggests that the conspiracy was designed to install a favourable regime in advance of Pompey's return.¹⁸ To her great credit, Levick has readily admitted: 'There is nothing of any connivance between

Catiline and Pompey in the sources.'[19] The difficulty with Levick's theory is that Catiline had no reason to communicate with Pompey when the former was a candidate for consul (although he may have claimed to have been Pompey's friend as many Roman politicians did).[20] After Catiline decided upon an effort to overthrow the government, he had to make some plans to deal with Pompey but he certainly did not have time to communicate with Pompey or to make any effort to coordinate activities with him. As pointed out earlier, there is no evidence of Catiline ever being allied with Pompey.

None of these three theories has any real foundation in the ancient sources. I cannot say with certainty that the arguments of Waters and Seager are unjustified, or that Levick's theory that Catiline was allied to Pompey is wrong given two unanswerable questions about Catiline and his conspiracy. The first is how much historical certainty may be attained about the matter, given the limitations of the source material. The true story of Catiline will never be known. What I have tried to do in this book is create as accurate and objective an account of Catiline's life and the conspiracy as possible, based on a critical analysis (but not a disregard) of the primary and secondary ancient sources.

There is, however, a second unanswerable question about Catiline and his conspiracy. Does this matter deserve the dominant place it has attained in the history of first century Rome? It has achieved this position in no small part due to the literary talents of Cicero and Sallust. Dio Cassius contends that Catiline 'acquired a greater name than his deeds deserved owing to the reputation of Cicero and the speeches he delivered against him'.[21] On the other hand, between the insurrection of Lepidus in 78 and Caesar's crossing the Rubicon in 49 there was no greater threat to the internal stability of the Republic than the Catilinarian conspiracy.[22]

Notes

Introduction
1. Sall. *Cat.* 5. *nobili genere natus, fuit magna vi et animi et corporis, sed ingenio malo pravoque. Huic ab adulescentia bella intestina, caedes, rapinae, discordia civilis grata fuere ibique iuventutem suam exercuit. Corpus patiens inediae, algoris, vigiliae supra quam cuiquam credibile est.4Animus audax, subdolus, varius, cuius rei lubet simulator ac dissimulator, alieni adpetens, sui profusus, ardens in cupiditatibus; satis eloquentiae, sapientiae parum. Vastus animus inmoderata, incredibilia, nimis alta semper cupiebat. Hunc post dominationem L. Sullae lubido maxuma invaserat rei publicae capiundae; neque id quibus modis adsequeretur, dum sibi regnum pararet, quicquam pensi habebat*
2. Morstein-Marx and Rosenstein (2010) 626–635.
3. The difference between the senatorial class and the equestrian order (*equites*) was not due to wealth. To belong to either class one had to have a specific amount of wealth. To belong to the senatorial class in Catiline's time, one had to possess a large amount of wealth and have been elected as a *quaestor*, which entitled one to membership of the senate and made one a member of the senatorial order. To belong to the *equites* in Catiline's time meant to have met the wealth criteria and not to have held public office. See Gelzer (1969) 1–25.
4. Paterson (1985) 38–39. However, the Social War did result in extension of citizenship to most Italians. Gruen (1974) 387–404 contends that Caesar as consul led the adoption of a moderate agrarian reform measure which, however, did not result in the resettlement on farms of any large number of the urban proletariat who (or whose ancestors) had been farmers. It was hard to keep anyone down on the farm once they had lived in Rome. As Gruen (404) points out, there was no way that the elite would permit the adoption of major reforms.
5. Brunt (1988) 68.
6. Morstein-Marx and Rosenstein (2010) 627.
7. Morstein-Marx and Rosenstein (2010) 627.
8. Morstein-Marx and Rosenstein (2010) 628.
9. Little (1934) 429–435 notes that the above form represents a modern Latinization of Cato's phrase. Plut. *Cato Maj.* 47 contends that Cato believed that Carthage constituted a real threat to Rome.
10. Sall. *Cat.* 10.
11. Dahl (2005) 315–322.
12. Conrad (2010) 168.
13. Badian (1972) 715, 722.
14. Sall. *Cat.* 29. See Chapter VIII for a fuller discussion of the *senatus consultum ultimum* and Drummond (1995) 111–113 who provides the authoritative legal analysis of this issue.

15. A noble was one whose clan included at least one individual who had reached the consular rank – a rank which was generally closed to *novi homines* (non-nobles) such as Cicero, whose clan did not include an ancestor who had attained the consulship. Gelzer (1912) 31–33. Accord: Syme (1939) 10. Some scholars have challenged this definition as too narrow. Vishnia (2012) 45. Many nobles were poor and lacked political influence or standing.
16. Dio Cass. 37.3 dates the beginning of the conspiracy to after the 64 consular election. Con. Sall. *Cat.* 17 who erroneously dates it as beginning on 1 June 64.
17. Cic. *Cat.* 2.16.

Chapter 1
1. Sall. *Cat.* 5. Each Roman belonged to a *gens*, which was somewhat akin to a clan in Scotland.
2. App. *B. Civ.* 2.2.
3. Asc. 93–94.
4. Sall. *Cat.* 13.
5. Wiseman (1985) 4; Tatum (199) 37–39.
6. Gruen (1974) 121.
7. Asc. 23. The difficulties facing a *novus homo* have been exaggerated. During the period 100 to 63, eleven *novi homines* reached the consulship. Earl (1966) 304. Con. Badian (1990) 410–412 who states that the number of *novi homines* was less than that which Earl reported. However, most of these *novi homines* had ancestors who had obtained the senatorial rank and who, in most cases, had reached the praetorship. Between 94 and 63, Cicero was the only *novus homo* from a purely equestrian family to attain the consulship. It was much more difficult for a *novus homo* whose ancestors had never attained the praetorship to reach the consulship, Gelzer (1969) 35, 50–52. However, J. Paterson (1095) 28–29 records examples of non-noble candidates defeating noble candidates in consular elections.
8. Q. Cic. *Comment. Pet.* 9.
9. Q. Cic. *Comment. Pet.* 9 claims that Catiline was raised in poverty.
10. Suet. *Gram et Rhet.* 17.
11. See Marshall (1985b) 294 for a discussion of these qualifications.
12. Catiline is accused of wasting his resources by both Sall. *Cat.* 5.4 and Cic. *Cat.* 1.14. It is likely that Catiline spent his money in running for office rather than wasting it. See App. *B. Civ.* 2.2. Catiline was frequently criticized on the grounds that he was in debt as a result of his efforts to achieve higher office. See Sall. *Cat.* 5.7; Q. Cicero, *Comment. Pet.* 9. Tatum (2018) 198 suggests that this charge is one of the canards frequently launched at political opponents.
13. Gelzer (1969) 36.
14. Verg. *Aen.* 5.1.121.
15. It is not clear from the manuscripts what his first name (*praenomen*) was. A *Praenomen* was indicated by an initial because there were so few of them that there was no need to write the *praenomen* out, (2) a *nomen* which was often the name of the gens or clan and (3) a *cognomen* which was written out in full and generally but not necessarily always was the name of the particular family to which the individual belonged or into which he was adopted. Some Romans had a fourth name or even fifth name which could be a nickname or could reflect the family name before adoption. Because the males in many families had the same *praenomen*, *nomen* and *cognomen* as their fathers

and grandfathers, it is often difficult to distinguish to whom a given reference is. See Salway (1994) 124–131.
16. Broughton (1952) 2. 617; Diod. Sic. 12:24.
17. Liv. 4: 17.
18. Broughton (1952) 2. 617.
19. Broughton, 2.617. He attacked and captured the Volscian town of Artena in 404. Liv. 4:61. However, in 402 he and a fellow tribune were responsible for a Roman defeat by the Veiians. When he was attacked from two sides he did not send for assistance from his fellow tribune Verginius – who was his personal enemy – and Verginius did not send the obviously-needed aid. For their conduct they were prosecuted by the tribunes of the *plebs* and ended up being heavily fined. Liv. 5: 8–9, 11–12.
20. He was also a legate/ambassador in 395. Broughton (1952) 2. 617.
21. Broughton (1952) 2. 617.
22. Plin. *HN*. 7: 104–5. Trans. Bostock and Riley.

Verum in his sunt quidem virtutis opera magna, sed maiora fortunae. M. Sergio, ut equidem arbitror, nemo quemquam hominum iure praetulerit, licet pronepos Catilina gratiam nomini deroget. secundo stipendio dextram manum perdidit; stipendis duobus ter et viciens vulneratus est, ob id neutra manu, neutro pede satis utilis, uno tantum salvus, plurimis postea stipendiis debilis miles. his ab Hannibale captus — neque enim cum quolibet hoste res fuit —, his vinculorum eius profugus, in viginti mensibus nullo non die in catenis aut compedibus custoditus.	*sinistra manu sola quater pugnavit, uno die duobus equis insidente eo suffossis. dextram sibi ferream fecit eaque religata proeliatus Cremonam obsidione exemit, Placentiam tutatus est, duodena castra hostium in Gallia cepit, quae omnia ex oratione eius apparent habita cum in praetura sacris arceretur a collegis ut debilis...!*

23. Broughton (1952) 2. 617. See Corbeill (2010) 443 for Roman views of deformity.
24. Broughton (1952) 1: 323, 328; Liv. 31:50 and 32:1.
25. Broughton (1952) 1. 313. Liv. 30:25 notes that he was almost killed by the Carthaginians.
26. Liv. 29.6 and 9.
27. Liv. 34. 40.
28. He may be the individual identified as M. Sergius who was sent in 164 along with C. Sulpicius Gallus, a *consulare,* to arbitrate a dispute between Sparta and Megalopolis. Broughton (1952) 1, 439–440.
29. The coin shows helmeted bust of Roma right; EX•S•C ROMA XVI around; monogram behind / Horseman galloping left with sword and severed head held aloft; Q below the horse's leg; M•SERGI below; SILVS in exergue. Sydenham (1952) 534; Crawford (1974) 286/1. 3.89g, 20mm, 8h and 302. The *quaestor* may have issued another coin showing Roma, the twins and the wolf. Crawford, 68, 601.
30. Broughton (1952) II, 13; Gelzer, *RE* 'Sergius', No. 42.
31. CIL (2) 709 = ILS 8888.

32. It is unknown how Catiline acquired the *cognomen* Catilina, since his father's *cognomen* was Silus. Cichorius (1922) 172–3 suggests that L. Sergius Silus was not Catiline's father, but that Catiline came from an unknown branch of the Sergius *gens*.
33. Another member of the *gens* Sergius, Gn. Sergius Silo – a contemporary of Catiline – was prosecuted successfully by Q. Caecilius Metellus Celer for attempting to seduce a *mater familiae* (a married woman) (Val. Max. 6.1.8), while another member of the *gens*, Q. Sergius, was convicted of murder (Cic. *Clu.* 21) and a third, L. Sergius, presumably a cousin of Catiline, was allegedly Catiline's bodyguard during the conspiracy. This individual survived the exposure of the conspiracy and according to Cicero ended up as part of Clodius' gang of ruffians. Cic. *Dom.* 5.13.
34. Q. Cic. *Comment. Pet.* 9 which alleges that Catiline debauched his sister and murdered his brother-in-law, Q. Caecilius. This identification of Q. Caecilius as Catiline's brother-in-law does not appear in any other source. Q. Caecilius is the name of a brother-in-law of Clodius so it would not be surprising if this identification is a later deliberate or mistaken addition. Richardson (1971) 437–438. Plut. *Cic.* 10 changed Q. Cicero's story to say that Catiline seduced his daughter and murdered his brother.
35. Bonner (1977) 9.
36. Sall. *Cat.* 35 quotes Catiline's letter to Catulus stating *quod non dignos homines honore honestatos videbam*. (I have seen unworthy men accorded places of honour) referring to the fact that Cicero, a *novus homo*, who was unworthy of the consulship, had attained the same where Catiline despite his ancestry had not.
37. North (2010) 264. Accord: Badian (1964) 151–152. See Liv 6.42 for the struggle between the patricians and the plebeians which resulted in the *lex de consule altero ex plebe* providing that no more than one consul could be a patrician.
38. These two laws represented the only distinction between patricians and plebeians.
39. Habicht (1990) 24–25.
40. Sall. *Cat.* 18; Macdonald (1977) 3.
41. Ramsey (2007) 229 and some others misdate Catiline's birth as having occurred in 108 because they failed to realize that patricians could run for office two years earlier than plebeians.
42. Bonner (1977) 41.
43. Bonner (1977) 34–35.
44. David (2007) 421–422.
45. Bonner (1977) 66.
46. David (2007) 431.
47. Connolly (2007) 69.
48. David (1977) 421. Significantly, Alexander (1990) in his monumental work which lists all known Roman criminal trials in the late Republic does not identify Catiline as an advocate for either the prosecution or defence in any of the cases listed.
49. See Sall. *Cat.* 5; Cic. *Cat.* 1.26 and *Cat* 2. 9.
50. Dolansky (2008) 47–70. Dolansky notes that there was no fixed age for assumption of the *toga virilis*, but that 16 or 17 were the common ages. (2008) 48.
51. Dolansky (2008) 48.
52. Steel (2013) 49, 64.
53. A *consilium* in both military and civilian life was a gathering of advisors to assist the leader in making an important decision. Wiseman (1985) 14–16.
54. CIL I (2) 709 = ILS 8888.
55. Gelzer (1969) 101–102.

56. Liv. *Per.* 52. 8 and 10.
57. CIL I (2) 709 = ILS 8888.
58. CIL I (2) 709 = ILS 8888. Kaplan (1968) 19 points out that the Sergii had given their name to one of Rome's thirty-five tribes and accordingly questions why Catiline was enrolled in the Tromentian tribe as opposed to the Sergian tribe.
59. Syme (1964) 102 states that the whole subject of Catiline's relationship with Pompey needs further study as did Badian (1956) 99. Badian (1956) 94–95 (citing Munzer, 'Gabinus', no. 11 *Real Encyclopedie*) contends that the Pompeian A. Gabinus (cos. 58) was a good friend of Catiline and suggests that he served as the connection between Catiline and Pompey's innermost circle. None of Pompey's subsequent biographers have taken up Syme's and Badian's challenge. Greenhalgh (1981) does not even mention the fact that Pompey and Catiline served together under Pompeius Strabo; Seager (2002) notes the fact that Pompey and Catiline served together in 89, but does not discuss the further relationship, if any, between the two. Some other historians have speculated about the existence of a connection between the two, but have not made persuasive cases for such a connection. Meier (1962) 103–125 suggests that there was an alliance between Pompey and Catiline in 63 although the bulk of his article deals with the activities of Metellus Nepos in attacking Cicero in December, 63 and early 62. Levick (2015) 91–94 hypothesizes that in 63 Pompey and Catiline were corresponding with each other and coordinating their plans.
60. Cic. *Phil.* 12. 27; *Div.* 1. 72. Gelzer (1969) 93 seems to date this meeting as occurring not after the Battle of Mt. Falernus, but later on when Vettius Scato led the Italian army which attempted to relieve Asculum. However, Gelzer does not cite any source for his claim that Vettius Scato led the relieving army.
61. App. *B. Civ.* 1.47; Rickard (2017) www.historyofwar.org/articles/battles_mount_falernus.html.
62. Plut. *Cic.* 3; Cic. *Div.* 1.72.
63. Cic. *Phil.* 12.27 refers to the meeting between Scato and Strabo in 90 as evidence that enemies can meet peaceably during a truce and Cic. *Div.* 1. 72 and 2.65 records an omen that Cicero had observed during the Nola campaign under Sulla in 89. Cic. *Lig.* 21 indicates that Cicero served in Sulla's army with an old friend – Tuberus.
64. Liv. *Per.* 111.
65. Levick (2015) 1.
66. Tatum (2018) 189.
67. Q. Cic. *Comment. Pet.* 51. Ward (1970a) 123–134 goes to great lengths to contend that Cicero and Pompey had so many connections in common that they must have known each other as young men. It is, of course, possible that at some time they may have encountered each other; however, it seems clear that there was no meaningful relationship between the two stemming back to their youth. See Ransom (1978) 4–5.
68. Habicht (1990) 28.
69. Keaveney (1986) 74 and sources cited therein at fn. 32.
70. Plut. *Pomp.* 3.
71. Plut. *Pomp.* 1. Some have incorrectly interpreted Cicero's description *In Toga Candida* (Asc. 79) of a *hominem dis ac nobilitati perinvisum* (a man hated by the gods and the nobility) as referring to Strabo. However, since the Gn. Pompeius referred to in this speech was charged with *maiestas* (literally, of damaging the majesty of the Roman people or treason) under the Lex Varia passed in 90 (Gruen (1974) 263), it is unlikely that Cicero was referring to Gn. Pompeius Strabo who was never charged

with *maiestas*. Moreover, since Cicero was claiming to be Pompey's friend at this time, it seems unlikely that he would have gratuitously insulted Pompey's father however unpopular Strabo had been.

Chapter 2
1. Plut. *Sull.*, 1.
2. Sall. *Cat.* 5 commences 'L. Catilina, born of a noble clan…'
3. Syme (1939) 18.
4. Keaveney (1986) 7. Contra Plut. *Sull.* 1.
5. Keaveney (1986) 8.
6. Keaveney (1986) 7–8; Plut. *Sull.* 1; Q. Cic. *Comment. Pet.* 9.
7. Keaveney (1986) 11–12; Sall. *Cat.* 14 and 16.
8. Cic. *Cae.* 12–14.; Plut. *Sull.* 2; Keaveney (1986) 8–11.
9. Keaveney (1986) 11.
10. Plut. *Sull.* 3–4.
11. Plut. *Mar.* 28; Keaveney (1986) 30. My account of Sulla's career in this chapter follows Keaveney (1986) 28–77.
12. Sall. *Cat.* 60; Cic. *Cae.* 2.
13. Badian (1964) 229 suggests that Catiline stayed in Italy when the Marians/Cinnans were in power and joined Sulla only when Sulla returned from Asia.
14. Keaveney (1984) 143 follows Badian's view that Catiline remained in Italy when the Marians/Cinnans were in power. Neither Badian nor Keaveney can cite any ancient source for their claim that Catiline remained in Italy until Sulla returned from the Mithradatic war. Similarly, I cannot cite any source for the view that Catiline served with Sulla in Asia.
15. Keaveney (1984) 125, citing Plut. *Sull.* 7 as his source.
16. App. *B. Civ.* 2.2.
17. Cic. *Cat.* 1. 6; Sall. *Cat.* 15 who alleges that Catiline murdered his son in order to marry Aurelia Orestilla who did not want to deal with a stepson. Sall. *Cat.* 15.2 picks up this charge from the *First Catilinarian*. Murder of a child to please a potential spouse seems to have been a favourite charge of Cicero since he also used it against Oppianius in *Clu.* 28–29.
18. Syme (1964) 85–86 and (2016) 154. This suggestion is based on Sall. *Hist.* 1:45 which simply states that Gratidianus was the uncle of the unnamed murderer's children and on Scholia Bernensia on Lucan 2: 173 which identifies the decedent as identifies the body '*hunc Marium Gratidianum, uxoris suae fratem*' (this Marius Gratidianus was the brother of his wife). This identification does not necessarily identify the murderer as Catiline. It is possible that the Scholia combines two traditions – the one that Catiline murdered his brother-in-law (Q. Cic. *Comment. Pet.* 9) and the other that Catiline executed M. Marius Gratidianus (Asc. 75, 78 and 80) into one. See Marshall (1985b) 292.
19. Gruen (1968) 243, 250 and 254 suggests that Catiline had Marian connections and sympathies. However, he cites no authorities as a basis for these statements although one suspects they are based on the theory that Catiline's first wife was a Gratidiani.
20. Roman women were given the feminine version of the family *praenomen* and, subject to some exceptions, received little public or historical recognition.
21. Plut. *Mar.* 43–44.
22. Keaveney (1986) 32–34.

23. Alexander (1990) 60. Catulus the elder may have had an *inimicitia* with Gratidianus as well as with Marius.
24. Riggsby (2010) 195–204
25. Alexander (2002) 7; Steel (2016) 205–225.
26. Gruen (1974) 260.
27. Steel (2016) 223; Morrell (2017) 44–49.
28. Plut. *Cic.* 7.
29. Schol. Bob. 176 states: *Cum Q. Catulus (et) patre et filio:ambo Cinnana dominatio proscripti sent odiose* (at the same time. Q. Catulus, both father and son, had been odiously proscribed by the lawless Cinnan regime). Badian (1964) 217 suggests that the younger Catulus remained in Italy since his brother-in-law, Hortensius, remained in Rome without attack by the Cinnan regime. This speculation ignores the above statement from the *Scholia* as well as the fact that Catulus the younger's presence in Athens in 86 is attested to by an inscription. Keaveney (1986) 127; Meritt (1954) 254–255. Hortensius could not save his father-in-law, the elder Catulus, and there is no reason to believe that he could have saved the younger Catulus had the latter foolishly remained in Rome.
30. See Harders (2009) 44–46 for the importance of *amicitia* in Roman life.
31. Some of the fighting against the Italians who supported the Marians continued through 79. Keaveney (1986) 197–198.
32. Q. Cic. *Comment Pet.* 10 For Cicero's frequent references to the killing of Gratidianus *In Toga Candida*, see Asc. 84, 87, 89–90; Plut. *Sull.* 32.
33. Plut. *Sull.* 38.
34. Keaveney (1986) 166, fn. 13.
35. Sen. *De Ira*, 3.18.
36. Sall. Hist. 1. 36 says that Gratidianus' arms and legs were broken and his eyes were gouged out.
37. Plut. *Sull.* 32.
38. Galassi (2014) 57–61 and Marshall (1985b) 124–133.
39. Cic. *Off.* 3:80.
40. Crawford (1994) 185.
41. 2:173.
42. Val. Max. 9.2.2
43. Liv. *Per.* 88. Recent scholarship has produced no consensus. Tatum (2018) 204.
44. Q. Cic. *Comment Pet.* 10.
45. While Roman politicians made the wildest accusations possible against their opponents, there was normally some minor basis in fact for the claim. One would not accuse an opponent of killing his wife unless the opponent had been married and the opponent's wife had died.
46. Syme (1964) 85.
47. Cic. *Off.* 2:80–81.
48. Rawson (1991) 21–2. Significantly, Cicero served on the staffs of Pompeius Strabo and Sulla during the Social War; he did not serve on Marius' staff although one would have thought that if the Tullii's relationship with the Gratidiani was good, the Tullii would have used M. Gratidianus' influence with his uncle to have secured Cicero's appointment to Marius' *consilium*.
49. Given Cicero's views of Gratidianus' policies as well as the hostility between the Tullii and Gratidiani, Cicero's attacks on Catiline's execution of Gratidianus seem particularly hypocritical.
50. Keaveney (1986) 79–145.

51. Plut. *Sull.* 31.
52. Keaveney (1986) 159.
53. Plut. *Sull.* 31.
54. Plut. *Sull.* 32 identifies the victim as Catiline's brother; Q. Cicero's *Comment Pet.* 9 says that Catiline murdered Q. Caecilius, his brother-in-law during the proscriptions. Obviously Plutarch's account is another version of the charge made by Q. Cicero which has led me to combine the details from both accounts in the text.
55. Q. Cic. *Comment. Pet.* 9. This claim was picked up by Dio Cass. 37.10.3. This list differs slightly from the list used by Cicero *In Toga Candida*, Asc. 84 and the inconsistency between the lists damages their credibility.
56. Tatum (2018) 202–203 records his inability to identify these individuals and 200–201 indicates that there are no other sources supporting Q. Cicero's claim that Catiline headed a Gallic murder squad although he suggests that this story may reflect the fact that Catiline during the Sullan civil war may have been placed in charge of auxiliary forces recruited from Cisalpine Gaul on the Italian side of the Alps. (Cisalpine Gaul was not really Gaul at all; it was the part of northern Italy).
57. Bringmann (2002) 212.
58. Cic. *Att.* 1.1 and 2.
59. Asc. 84, 87, 89–90; Cic. *Cat.* 1.18.
60. Gruen (1968) 42, like many historians, claims without citing authority that Catiline was '..one of the more successful executioners and profiteers in the Sullan proscriptions.' See Dyck (2008) 2. However, there is no reliable sources which support this claim that Catiline was active in the proscriptions and emerged rich therefrom. Dyck's citation of Sall. *Cat.* 5.2 *huic adulescentia bella intestina...gratia fuere* (civil wars were pleasing to him since his youth) does not support Dyck's claim that Catiline had grown rich from the proscriptions. Indeed, there were no allegations of Catiline's involvement in the proscriptions before the Ciceronian claims *In Toga Candida* and in the *Commentariolum Petitionis*.
61. Plut. *Crass.* 2.
62. Keaveney (1986) 201–12.
63. Keaveney (1986) 118–50; Badian (1964) groups the individuals somewhat differently and takes a more cynical view of their motivations.
64. Keaveney (1986) 146–150.
65. Keaveney (1986) 148–150. Con. As noted earlier, Gruen believed that the Sullan constitution remained intact despite minor modifications and would have endured but for Caesar's decision to cross the Rubicon and destroy the Republic. Morstein-Marx and Rosenstein (2010) 628.
66. Plut. *Sull.* 34; *Pomp.* 15.
67. Syme (1964) 186–7.
68. There is no record showing the date of Catiline's quaestorship.
69. Taylor (1949) notes that this type of assignment occurred frequently.
70. Sall. *Hist.* 1.46.
71. Syme (1964) 66.
72. Keaveney and Strachan (1981) 363–366.
73. Sall. *Hist.* 1.1. Moreover, Keaveney and Strachan (1981) 364 have demonstrated that Ofella was the sole commander responsible for this siege.
74. Admittedly, Pompey, who was Catiline's age, commanded an army in the Sullan civil war but he had raised these troops from his family's *clientes* in Picenum; in addition, Pompey was an exception to almost every rule. Plut. *Pomp.* 6.

75. Taylor (1949) 31. Con. Keaveney and Strachan (1981) 364 who contend that a *legatus* did not have to be a member of the senate. In addition, they contend that Catiline might have been elected *quaestor* earlier or that he might have been enrolled in the senate by Sulla in 81 when Sulla named 200 new senators. There is no evidence to support either of these theories.
76. Cichorius (1922) 130.
77. Badian (1956) 87–99.
78. Sall. *Cat.* 19.
79. Gruen (1974) 71.
80. Gruen (1974) 11 and 50–51.
81. Plut. *Sert.* 12 et seq.
82. Plut. *Sert.* 13.
83. Asc. 87.
84. Marshall (1985a) 298; Lewis (2006) 294–295.
85. Gruen (1974) 129–130.
86. Ward (1977) 61 refers to Metellus as a 'testy aristocrat' who quarrelled with Crassus when they were trying to oppose the Cinnan/Marian regime. However, others had quarrelled with Crassus too. The Romans were a rather quarrelsome bunch.
87. Epstein (1987) 28–29, 36–37.
88. Ward (1977) 14.

Chapter 3

1. In this section of the book, I am following the example of Tatum (1999) 2 who started off his biography of Clodius with a 'synthetic representation of the nature of Roman politics' not because he was trying to write an original description of it, but because 'it serves to indicate the understanding of Roman politics and society' which would subtend his account of Clodius' career.
2. Millar (2002) 1 and the works cited in fn. 1 to Millar's book.
3. Tatum (2018) 7.
4. Mouritsen (2001) 32.
5. The *comitia tributa* (popular assembly) whose consent was necessary to enact either a *senatus consultum* (decree of the senate) or a tribunicial proposal into law was organized by tribes and voted by tribes; however, within a given tribe, each man had one vote; accordingly, the popular assembly was not dominated by the upper classes as was the *comitia centuria*. Taylor (1966) 59. However, because any one of the ten tribunes could veto a *consultum* or other proposal to enact legislation, it was easy for any one of influence to prevent the adoption of proposed legislation by suborning a tribune. Taylor (1966) 75.
6. Mouritsen (2001) 32, 91.
7. Taylor (1966) 64–67.
8. Millar (2002) 17–18; Mouritsen (2001) 94–5.
9. Taylor (1966) 84–88.
10. Taylor (1966) 86.
11. Q. Cic. *Comment. Pet.* 33.
12. Bringmann (2002) 39; Brunt (1988) 24; Taylor (1966) 86–90.
13. Tatum (2108) 18 who points out that candidates could not ignore the lower orders because their support might prove decisive in a given election as seems to have occurred in the consular election in 64.

14. Fundamental to an understanding of the Roman political system is the recognition that the populace elected all office holders; while the successful candidates were normally members of the nobility, so were the unsuccessful candidates. Popular support was earned, not commanded. Yakobson (2010) 398.
15. Paterson (1985) 32.
16. Brunt (1988) 43; Mouritsen (2001) 97–8. Certainly Cicero seems to have done so. Habicht (1990) 28.
17. Brunt (1988) 16.
18. Mouritsen (2001) 97–100 notes that there were a number of these voters.
19. Cic. *Cat.* 1. 26, and also *Cat.* 2. 9.
20. Cic. *Cae.* 12.
21. Another advantage to a military career was that it often gave the candidate the support of those who served with him either as a peer or as a superior. See Cic. *Mur.* 3, 20–21 and 37–38 arguing that Murena had won the consular election in 63 due in part to the support of his fellow soldiers.
22. Cicero obtained much support from younger members of the nobility who were attracted by his oratorical skills.
23. Suet. *Iul.* 10.
24. Habicht (1990) 22; Tatum (2018) 87.
25. Q. Cic. *Comment. Pet.* 18.
26. Q. Cic. *Comment. Pet.* 25 and 29.
27. Tatum (2018) 37–39.
28. Q. Cic. *Comment Pet.* 37; Cic. *Mur.* 77.
29. Cic. *Mur.* 49. It is significant that Q. Cic. *Comment. Pet.* 28 accuses Antonius of being a lazy campaigner but makes no such criticism of Catiline.
30. Q. Cic. *Comment. Pet.* 50: Cic. *Cae.*
31. Tatum (2018) 187–191.
32. Tatum (2018) 39.
33. Q. Cic. *Comment. Pet.* 52–53, 56–57.
34. Q. Cic. *Comment, Pet.* 49.
35. Family connections included those freedman who owed their former owner a duty of *obsequium* (support and assistance). Cic. *Fa.* 13.23.
36. Hollander (2016) 17; Brunt (1988) 37–40 points out that the importance of family connections has been overemphasized because almost every member of the nobility had some kind of family tie to almost every other member of the nobility. Accord: Gruen (1974) 57–61. Family connections included those freedman who owed their former owner a duty of *obsequium* (support and assistance). Cic. *Fa.* 13.23. A key reason that former freedman and their dependents did not supply great electoral support was that they were enrolled in the four urban tribes as opposed to the tribes in which their former masters had been enrolled and that they did not have enough money to have great voting power. Paterson (1985) 27. However, if they remained loyal to their former masters, they could be of significant help in campaigning by accompanying their former masters on their daily rounds of the city.
37. Cic. *Cae.* 11.
38. Tatum (2018) 223–224.
39. Q. Cic. *Comment. Pet.* 17; Cic. *Mur.* 72–73.
40. Tatum (2018) 284.
41. Q. Cic. *Comment. Pet.* 19.

42. Q. Cic. *Comment. Pet.* 10. Curius became a member of the conspiracy which he betrayed; Vettius became an informer for the government at the time of the conspiracy; Annius, if he was Annius Chilo, became a member of the conspiracy. Who these others were is not really known. Tatum (2018) 208–209.
43. Cic. *Att.* 1.1.3.
44. Q. Cic. *Comment. Pet.* 18 and 45–49.
45. Q. Cic. *Comment. Pet.* 24.
46. Cic. *Att.* 2.2.
47. Cic. *Att.* 1.2. These were not illegal but considered unethical, although they were frequent in Roman politics. Marshall (1985) 284–5.
48. Tatum (2018) 178–180.
49. Q. Cic. *Comment. Pet.* 4, 22–24, and 38. Significantly, Q. Cicero does not mention possession of *clientelae* as being a significant factor in the electoral process.
50. Gelzer (1969) passim.
51. Deniaux (2010) 416–7; Paterson (1985) 27–28. Tatum (2018) 26; Steel (2013) 41.
52. Tatum (2018) 227–228.
53. Vishnia (2012) 139–140; Mouritsen (2001) 111–115.
54. Vishnia (2012) 139–140.
55. Hollander (2016) 22 points out that during the late Republic money assumed a much greater role in political life than it had previously. See Rosillo-Lopez (2016) 28, 33 who describes the monetization of Roman politics in the late Republic. Vishnia 138–145.
56. Paterson (1985) 33.
57. Q. Cic. *Comment. Pet.* 53. *Sed haec tibi sunt retinenda: ut senatus te existimet ex eo quod ita vixeris defensorem auctoritatis suae fore, equites R. et viri boni ac locupletes ex vita acta te studiosum oti ac rerum tranquillarum, multitudo ex eo quod dumtaxat oratione in contionibus ac iudicio popularis fuisti te a suis commodis non alienum futurum.*
58. See Hardy (1924b) 3–5. For a comprehensive review of the various analyses of the Roman political system, see Jehne (2006) 3–28.
59. Cic. *Sest.* 96. *Duo genera semper in hac civitate fuerunt eorum qui versari in re publica atque in ea se excellentius gerere studuerunt; quibus ex generibus alteri se populares, alteri optimates et haberi et esse voluerunt. qui ea quae faciebant quaeque dicebant multitudini iucunda volebant esse, populares, qui autem ita se gerebant ut sua consilia optimo cuique probarent, optimates habebantur*
60. North (2007) 266.
61. The legality of the *senatus consultum* will be discussed in some detail in Chapter VIII. Suffice it to say that this decree gave some protection to extra legal action by the consuls to repress their political opponents if the latter seemed to be disturbing the peace of the Republic. Sall. *Cat.* 29.
62. Arena (2012) 5. Taylor (1949) 22.
63. Odahl (2010) 9.
64. Odahl (2010) 8–11; Taylor (1949) 22.
65. Paterson (1985) 38.
66. Tatum (1999) 4–5. Indeed, the *optimates* would on occasion sponsor *popularis* measures to deal with a matter which was disturbing the peace of the Republic. Tatum (1999) 13.
67. Tatum (1999) 3.
68. Tatum (1999) 5.

69. Syme (1939) and Scullard (1959) are the leading exponents of this approach.
70. This prosopographical approach owed much to Namier (1957) which analysed British politics in 1760 from the standpoint of family relationships and neighbourhood connections.
71. Hardin (2009) 33–42.
72. See Gruen (1974) 57–61 for the dissolution of certain family allegiances in the decade of the 60s due to this phenomenon.
73. Brunt (1988) 470–488.
74. Sall. *Cat.* 18.
75. (1964) 102.
76. (1988) 63.
77. (1973) 357.
78. See Ward (1977) 14–19 describing the seven leading *optimates* and some of family connections between them.
79. Rosillo-Lopez (2017) 156. Accord: Levick (2105) 13; Ward (1977) 9, fn. 15.
80. Syme (1939) 11–12.
81. Sall. *Cat.* 38. *Nam postquam Cn. Pompeio et M. Crasso consulibus tribunicia potestas restituta est, homines adulescentes summam potestatem nacti, quibus aetas animusque ferox erat, coepere senatum criminando plebem exagitare, dein largiundo atque pollicitando magis incendere, ita ipsi clari potentesque fieri. Contra eos summa ope nitebatur pleraque nobilitas senatus specie pro sua magnitudine. Namque, uti paucis verum absolvam, post illa tempora quicumque rem publicam agitavere honestis nominibus, alii sicuti populi iura defenderent, pars quo senatus auctoritas maxuma foret, bonum publicum simulantes pro sua quisque potentia certabant..*
82. Brunt (1988) 487–8.
83. Wiseman (1985) 4.
84. Sall. *Cat.* 5.
85. Sall. *Agitabatur magis magisque in dies animus ferox inopia rei familiaris et conscientia scelerum, quae utraque iis artibus auxerat, quas supra memoravi incitabant praeterea corrupti civitatis mores, quos pessuma ac divorsa inter se mala, luxuria atque avaritia, vexabant.* In the earlier portion of this passage Sallust utilized Cicero's phraseology from Cic. *Cat* 1.26: *Habes, ubi ostentes tuam illam praeclaram patientiam famis, frigoris, inopiae rerum omnium, quibus te brevi tempore confectum esse senties* 'You have an opportunity to demonstrate your famous ability to endure hunger, cold and the lack of every necessity' and *Cat.* 2. 9: *frigore et fame et siti et vigiliis perferundis fortis ab istis praedicabatur* (it can demonstrate your ability endure cold, hunger, thirst and lack of sleep.)
86. Cic. *Cat.* 2. 7–8.
87. Cic. *Att.* 1.1.
88. See Marshall (1976) 1–3. Crassus' reputation has suffered from Cicero's attacks on him following Cicero's return from exile. Cicero somewhat unfairly blamed Crassus for the latter's support of Clodius' bill which sent Cicero into exile. Marshall (1976) 34–41.
89. Plut. *Crass.* 6 and 11.
90. Plut. *Crass.*, 2. Ultimately, both Pompey and Caesar became wealthier than Crassus. Ward (1977) 69.
91. Plut. *Crass.* 6; Odahl (2010) 22.
92. Plut. *Crass.* 3.

93. Plut. *Crass.* 7.
94. See Gelzer (1969) 114: 'The richest man in the world thus became the most powerful, because by lending money, he could put most politicians under an obligation.'
95. Plut. *Crass.* 7. See Marshall (1976) 16–17.
96. Plut. *Crass.* 7; Ward (1977) 99; Marshall (1974) 810–13. Con. Gruen (1974) 40–41 who argues that there was a real *inimicitia* between the two men,
97. Ward (1977) 99. Con. Waters (1970) 20 and Marshall (1974) 809–813.
98. Marshall (1974) 804–813.
99. Ward (1977) 243–245. Ward notes that Crassus had attempted to restrain Clodius' attack on Cicero.
100. Plut. *Crass.* 7. Gruen (1974) 138 questions the existence of Crassus-Catiline alliance on the grounds that Crassus would not have supported a friend of Catulus. Politics, however, make strange bedfellows. Moreover, both Crassus and Catulus were *Sullani*; while they were sometimes opposed politically, there is no evidence of any *inimicitia* between them. When Crassus and Catulus were censors in 65, they disagreed over Crassus' efforts to support Roman citizenship for the Transpadani and subsequently agreed that they should both resign office. In any event this dispute took place years later. Plut. *Crass.* 13.
101. Sall. *Cat.* 17; Asc. 83. Asconius cites Cicero as writing that both Crassus and Caesar were his bitterest foes in the 64 consular campaign. Seager (1964) 347–8 disputes Asconius' claim about the alliance between Catiline and Crassus, alleging that Asconius' position is based on Cicero's *Expositio Consiliorum Suorum* which Seager claims is untrustworthy. However, there is no evidence that this work was the sole source of Asconius' view that Crassus and Caesar supported Catiline in 64. In placing Caesar on the same level of importance as Crassus, Asconius, like many other ancient and modern historians, takes an anachronistic view of Caesar's significance and places him on equal terms with Crassus. For example Hardy (1924a) entitles three of his first four chapters 'Crassus, Caesar...' or 'Caesar and Crassus'. The truth of the matter is that Caesar, like Catiline, started off as a dependent of Crassus but became an independent figure in his own right in 63 when he achieved election as *pontifex maximus* and played a prominent role in the debate over the fate of the conspirators. Suet. *Iul.* 13; Gruen (1974) 75. However, Caesar, even when allied to Crassus, tried to pursue and independent course, particularly with respect to Pompey whose favour he sought to win. Gruen (1974) 79–81. For example, Caesar supported the Manilian law to give Pompey the command of the war with Mithridates and Caesar attempted in 62 to transfer the honour of rebuilding the temple of Jupiter from Catulus to Pompey. Dio. Cass. 37: 44.1. For a contrary view, see Altman (2015) 235–46.
102. Asc. 91; Plut. *Crass.* 1; Oros. 6: 3.1; Sall. *Cat.* 15; Plut. *Cat. Min*, 19; Cic. *Brut.* 236 (which suggests that there may have been more than two Vestal Virgins involved.) See Cic. *Cat.* 3. 9 and Oros. 6: 3.1. for the date. Some historians believe that Fabia was only a half-sister of Terentia or a cousin of Terentia. See Lintott (2008) 157 and Levick (2015) 26. The identity of the two other defendants is not known; it is probable, however, that they were members of Crassus' *factio*. See Lewis (2001) 141. There is no classical source which specifically ties the prosecutions together. It is of course, possible that the accusations against Crassus, Catiline and others were not related although such a coincidence seems improbable.
103. Plut. *Crass.* 1. If one accepts Gruen's suggestion (1974) 41 that Plotius was the Pompeian Plautius whose agrarian bill provided land for Pompey's veterans in 70,

the explanation for the prosecutions becomes obvious. Epstein (1986) 290 suggests without citing any authority that Clodius was the prosecutor in Catiline's case. Apparently, however, Epstein was following Broughton (1952) II. 114 who infers from a tale in Plut. *Cato. Min.* 19 to the effect that Clodius was inciting public anger against Fabia because of her acquittal until Cato intervened and forced Clodius to leave the city. Cato, upon being thanked by Cicero for his actions, somewhat insultingly replied that Cicero should be thankful to Rome because it was for Rome that he had taken this the action. See Tatum (1999) 44, fn. 65 who says that the theory that Clodius was Catiline's prosecutor has been discredited. Cadoux (2005) 177–179 suggests, however, that the events depicted in Plutarch's story occurred after the acquittal of the Vestal Virgins – allegedly an unpopular verdict – and reflected an effort by Clodius to take advantage of the situation by attacking the acquitted Vestal Virgins. Lewis (2001) 147–149 suggests that Plutarch's story refers to an event which occurred in 62/ 61.

104. Cadoux (2005) 164.
105. Cic. *Brut.* 236; Cadoux (2005) 167.
106. Plut. *Crass.* 1.
107. Licinia survived the scandal and was in 63 reported to have lent her cousin, L. Licinius Murena, her seat at gladiatorial games, thereby endorsing his consular candidacy. Cic. *Mur.* 73.
108. Plut. *Crass.* 1.
109. Asc. 91.
110. Oros. 6:3.1.
111. Cadoux (2005) 167.
112. Cic. Brut. 133.
113. Lewis (2001) 141–9. Accord: Keaveney (1992) 193–194.
114. Cic. *Pis.* 95; Cic. *Att.* 1. 16. However, Marshall (1985b) 310 contends that the same procedure followed with respect to Licinia and Crassus was followed in Fabia and Catiline's case – i e. that both Fabia and Catiline were tried together and acquitted together. He suggests that the acquittals reflect Catulus' advocacy for Catiline. Cadoux agrees with Marshall that Catiline was acquitted after trial and contends that Cicero omitted the Vestal Virgin acquittal in his discussion of Catiline's acquittals because he did not want to remind his audience of his sister-in-law's involvement in this affair. Cadoux (2005) 162–179. (Marshall does not discuss this point.) Cadoux's explanation for Cicero's reference to only two acquittals is unconvincing since Cicero had no problem *In Toga Candida* in 64 to referring to Catiline's involvement with a Vestal Virgin. Asc. 91. and would have had no difficulty in referring to a third trial (even if it involved Fabia) had it in fact occurred.
115. Sall. *Cat.* 15.
116. Taylor (1949) 76–97. Most of the major pontifical offices were dominated by members of the nobility. Taylor (1949) 90; Riggsby (2010) 212 who points out that in the year 57 eight of the fifteen pontifical offices were held by ex-consuls and the others were held by younger members of the nobility.
117. Poly. 6.56.
118. Plut. *Cat. Min.* 19.
119. Plut. *Crass.* 10.1 states that many young nobles joined Crassus to help put down the servile insurrection.
120. See Syme (1939) 10.
121. Taylor (1949) 31.

122. Blosel (2016) 68–81 suggests that provincial assignments had become less desirable in the late Republic because of the increased opportunities to invest money while staying in Rome at the centre of things. For someone such as Catiline, who did not have large sums to invest, a provincial assignment would have been desirable.
123. Gelzer (1969) 24; Gruen (1968) 31–33; Blosel (2016) 31.
124. Asc. 85, 89.
125. Sallust made himself rich from serving as *pro praetor* of Africa. Dio Cass. 43.9.

Chapter 4

1. Livy, *Per.* 70 relates one incident where an honest governor was condemned and exiled for trying to protect the provincials from the *publicani*. The reality was that Rome's system for governing the provinces and collecting taxes was defective in almost every respect. Tac. *Annals*, 1. 2: wrote in referring to the provinces' reaction to the establishment of Principate: *neque provinciae illum rerum statum abnuebant, suspecto senatus populusque imperio ob certamina potentium et avaritiam magsratuum invalido legum auxilio. Quae vi ambitu postremo pecuiai turbabantur* (Neither were the provinces disturbed by the [new] state of affairs, looking on with suspicion on the rule of the senate and the people on account of the rivalry of the powerful and the greed of the magistrates with the power of the law being weak and being overcome by violence, ambition and finally money.) See MacDonald (1977) 415–32.
2. Asc. 85; Seager (2002) 67. See Gruen (1974) 309 for the political nature of criminal prosecutions.
3. Gelzer (1968) 331.
4. Gelzer (1968) 148, 151. The one exception to the immunity rule was a prosecution for electoral bribery which could be brought against a successful candidate.
5. Macdonald (1977) 427–8; Odahl (1971) 35.
6. Sall. *Cat.* 15 states that it was believed for certain that the son was murdered by Catiline because Aurelia Orestilla was unwilling to enter into a household that contained an adult stepson. Cic. *Cat.* 1. 14 and App. *B Civ.* 2. 2 make the same claim. One of the remarkable things about the ancient world was the paucity of wealthy or prominent people who died a natural death despite the prevailing horrible sanitary conditions.
7. Sall. *Cat.* 15. The date of this marriage was probably in the mid-60s since a relative of Orestilla vetoed a measure directed against Catiline in the consular election in 64 and Cicero alleged that Catiline had murdered his first wife to marry a second. Asc. 83. See Marshall (1985b) 311 and (1977b) 151–154.
8. See Evans (1987) 68–72 for the prominence of Aurelia Orestilla's family.
9. Sal. *Cat.* 34.
10. Asc. 91–92. Plut. *Cic.* 10 picks up the accusation of incest but does not allege a marriage.
11. Asc. 91–92.
12. See Marshall (1977b) 152–4. Aurelia Orestilla survived Catiline's fall, possibly due to the protection of Q. Catulus. See Sall. *Cat.* 35. Cic. *Fam.* 8:7 writing in 50 to M. Caelius Rufus notes that Orestilla's daughter was engaged to marry Q. Cornificius, an eminent Caesarian, the son of Q. Cornificius, who had been one of the five men into whose custody the conspirators were given on 3 December. See Rawson (1967) 188–201.
13. Sall. *Cato Min.* 39.
14. Syme (1939) 20–21.

15. Syme (1964) 102 notes that Sulla was the brother-in-law of Pompey at this time while Seager (1988) 63 notes that Torquatus had served with Pompey in the East and was married to a woman from Picenum which was the Pompeian stronghold. Thus the two opposing patrician candidates both had Pompeian connections but the anti-Pompeian *optimates* seemed to have closed their eyes to Torquatus' Pompeian connection. This fact indicates some limitation on the Syme/Namier theory that political factions were determined by blood, marriage, military service and neighbourhood. Given the relatively small size of the Roman nobility, almost everyone had some connection to almost everyone else. Thus, the existence of a particular connection did not necessarily explain political allegiances or choices. As Phillips (1973) 357 notes, examples such as these 'should be adequate warning against rigid application of the labels Pompeian and anti-Pompeian. While these terms possessed a certain validity, it must be realized that Pompey was only one of a number of factors in the politics of the period.'
16. Cic. *Sull.* 91.
17. Sall. *Cat.* 18. The younger Torquatus may have assisted his father in the prosecution of Sulla in 66. Alexander (1999) 65–69. However, the younger Torquatus was not the main prosecutor in the 66 case as implied by Cic. *Sull.* 49–50 in an effort to suggest the younger Torquatus was being vindictive by prosecuting Sulla for a second time.
18. Sall. *Cat.* 18.
19. The question of whether Catiline applied to run in the first election or the second has been the subject of much scholarly debate. The analysis of Hardy (1924) 6 and Summer (1965) 441–448 seem more consistent with the evidence-especially since Sall. Cat. 18 makes it clear that Catiline sought to run in the second election. Con. Ryan (1995) 45–48.
20. Gelzer (1969) 45–46 who notes that these meetings would occur at the consul's home. See also Wiseman (1985) 14–16.
21. Sall. *Cat.* 18; Asc. 89
22. Seager (1964) 338–339. It is quite possible that Catiline had actually started campaigning against Torquatus prior to having his candidacy accepted. Cic. *Sull.* 68; Ramsey (1982) 129–131.
23. Woodman (2012) 55.
24. Asc. 89.
25. Marshall (1976–7) 127–135 states correctly that the mere fact that a candidate had been accused of a crime did not preclude him from running in an election.
26. Hardy (1924b) 7 states that candidacy was not barred until after the *nominis delatio* and the establishment of the *iuducium* (time and place of trial). Catiline's prosecution did not reach this state until after July 65. See Cic. *Att.* 2. 2. Accordingly the impending prosecution did not cause Volcatius to refuse his candidacy. See Summer (1965) 227–228. Con. Gruen (1974) 271 who claims that the impending prosecution blocked Catiline from running in 65 as well as in 66.
27. Most scholars have accepted this conclusion. Alexander (2002) 228, n. 30.
28. Asc. 89. A consul had the legal authority to reject a given individual's candidacy. See Earl (1965) 325–32.
29. Asc. 87.
30. Dio Cass. 36.44 claims that Catiline was angered by the decision; however, this statement is made as a way of explaining Catiline's joining the fictitious 'First Catilinarian Conspiracy' and is not consistent with Torquatus' relationship with Catiline.

31. Marshall (1976–7) 133–135; Tatum (2018) 13–14.
32. Asc. 92; Cic. Cic. *Cat.* 1:15; *Mur.* 81; Cic. *Sull.* 66–8. According to Asc. 83 Cicero in his secret history of his consulship made the unlikely accusation that Crassus was behind the First Catilinarian conspiracy. Marshall (1985) 287–8 suggests that Asconius failed to recognize that Cicero's later hostility to Crassus led Cicero to falsely accuse Crassus of deeds which Cicero had made no mention of until years after the events allegedly occurred.
33. Asc. 92.
34. Cic. *Cat.* 1.15.
35. Cic. *Mur.* 81.
36. Cic. *Sull.* 66–8. Ironically, in *Sull.* 11 Cicero denied any real knowledge of the First Catilinarian Conspiracy: 'I played no part in that crisis and these discussions; I believe because I was not yet at the heart of political life and had not yet attained the goal of office which I had set for myself and my work at the bar continued to divert me from all thought about this matter.' *Patris tui, fortissimi viri atque optimi consulis, scis me consiliis non interfuisse; scis me, cum mihi summus tecum usus esset, tamen illorum expertem temporum et sermonum fuisse, credo quod nondum penitus in re publica versabar, quod nondum ad propositum rnihi finem honoris perveneram, quod me ambitio et forensis labor ab omni illa cogitatione abstrahebat.* This from someone who was *praetor* in that year and who himself invented the story of the First Catilinarian Conspiracy. See Lintott (2008) 34 who points out that this is one of many lies contained in Cicero's speeches.
37. Sall. *Cat.* 18–19 continues this fairy tale by saying that afterwards Piso, at the instigation of Crassus but with the support of the *optimates*, was sent off to the province of Nearer Spain to govern the same as though *pro praetor* and create a bulwark for Crassus and others in the event that Pompey followed the example of Sulla and seized power when he returned from the Mithridatic war. Dio Cas. 36. 44 says that part of the senate's motivation in sending Piso to Spain was to get him out of the city where he had supporters who could cause a riot. Sallust's account fails to recognize the fact that Piso's family had a long tradition of service in Spain – something which may have been the motivating factor in sending him to Spain. Phillips (1973) 356. During his journey to the province Piso was murdered by some Spanish cavalry men who were part of his army. Some alleged that these men had resented Piso's haughty and cruel conduct; others, more skeptical, believed that the cavalrymen were *clientes* of Pompey (as a result of Pompey's involvement in the Sertorian war) and acted on his behalf. Sallust does not take a position as to which theory was correct. Asc. 92 repeats Sallust's story about Piso. For Piso's identification with Catiline see Cic. *Mur.* 81 and *Sull.* 67; Dio Cass. 37: 44 and Asc. 66, 92. For an argument that Crassus was not behind the dispatch of Piso to Spain, see Lowe (2004) 115–25. In all events, the dispatch of Piso to Spain with the approval of the *optimates* was obviously not connected to the fictitious First Catilinarian Conspiracy. Seager (1964) 341–2. When Piso was killed is not known although it would seem to have happened early in 65 on his journey to Spain. Sallust has Catiline refer to Piso in Sallust's invented Catiline's speech on 1 June 64 as though Piso was still alive at that point although Sallust's own chronology suggest the opposite.
38. Piso was a well-known opponent of Pompey. Val. Max. 6. 24. Since Piso was probably dead at the time of Cicero's speech, it was easy to cast blame on him for any event that the orator chose.

39. Sall. *Cat.* 18. Asc. 92 seems to be referring to the version of the plot which provided for a second assassination attempt in February.
40. Cic. *Sull.* 11. Cic. *Sull.* 68 claims that Torquatus also charged that Sulla had led armed gangs in an effort to make Catiline consul in place of Torquatus. This charge may suggest that Catiline had actually commenced a campaign against Torquatus in 66 before his candidacy was disallowed. Ramsey (1982) 127–131. However, it seems unlikely that Catiline would have commenced campaigning before his candidacy was formally accepted. It is possible that Torquatus had alleged that Autronius, had the plot succeeded, intended to help Catiline attain the consulship in 65 and that Cicero has simply distorted Torquatus' statement beyond recognition in an effort to demonstrate an inconsistency in Torquatus' charges about Sulla's actions in 63. See Seager (1964) 340.
41. Suet. *Iul,* 9.
42. Dio Cass. 36:44.
43. Liv. *Epit.* 101.
44. Cic. *Sull.* 81.
45. Cic. *Sull.* 81.
46. Woodman (2021) 56, n. 5 which gives an expansive list of the sceptics.
47. For modern advocates of some version of the First Catilinarian Conspiracy see. Stevens (1963) 397–435, Odahl. (2010) x-xi, 20–21; Altman (2015) 241–3 and Woodman (2021) 55–63.
48. Asc. 92.
49. Syme (1964) 88–9.
50. Dio Cass. 36.44. See Marshall, (1977a) 318–20.
51. Dio Cass. 36.44.
52. Syme (1964) 87–8.
53. Dio Cass. 36.44.
54. Ramsey (1980a) 331 suggests that Manilius was also charged with *maiestas* in a case which would be tried the next year.
55. Ramsey (1980a) 331. See Asc. 59 for the normal practice of giving the defendant ten days to respond to the charge. Ward (1977) 137–138 contends that the reason that Manilius wanted to delay the trial so that Cicero, his praetorship over, could defend him while Cicero wanted to get the trial over in 65 so that he would not have to defend Manilius and incur the wrath of the *optimate*s who were already suspicious of Cicero's Pompeian views.
56. Dio Cass. 36.44.
57. Dio Cass. 36.44; Plut. *Cic.* 9. Ramsey (1980a) 332–6 suggests that Cicero's lost *Pro Manilio* was a speech delivered not at Manilius' trial but at this *contio*.
58. Plut. *Cic.* 9; Dio Cass. 36.44.
59. Dio Cass. 36.44.
60. Dio Cass. 36.44. This disruption seems to have ended the prosecution for extortion. It appears that Cicero did not defend Manilius when the latter's trial came up the next year. At the direction of the senate both consuls supervised the trial to preclude disruptions; Manilius fled Rome and was convicted *in absentia*. Asc. 60. Phillips (1970) contends that there was only one charge involving Manilius – extortion – and that the trial was postponed until 65.
61. Asc. 66.

62. Asc. 66. Of course, the fact that Cicero referred to Catiline and Piso as the disrupters does not mean that his charge was accurate.
63. Cic. *Cat.* 1.15 and 18.
64. Gruen (1969) 20–4.
65. Phillips (1973) 353–7.
66. Habicht (1990) 28.
67. Ward (1977) 140–141.
68. Seager (1964) 345.
69. Q. Cic. *Comment. Pet.* 53.
70. Seager (1964) 344–45, Phillips (1973) 355–6 and Ward (1977) Con. Gruen (1969) 23–4.
71. Cic. *Att.* 1. 1 and 2 which were written right before and right after 17 July 65 respectively indicate that Catiline had not yet been tried.
72. Cic. *Att.* 1.1.
73. Ward (1977) 30.
74. Asc. 87.
75. Gruen (1974) 271 has suggested this possibility by seizing on a fanciful story in Plut. *Cato Min.* 19 that Clodius tried to take advantage of the acquittal of the Vestal Virgins in 73 to cause political trouble even though nothing in Plutarch's story suggests that Clodius' action was directed against Catiline.
76. Asc. 87.
77. Cic. *Att.* 1.2.
78. Plut. *Cic.* 29.
79. Asc. 87. Metellus Pius' actions may have been motivated by an *inimicitia* with Catiline; on the other hand, they may have motivated by his and his father's connection with Africa.
80. Cic. *Sull.* 81. Torquatus may have been repaying the favour he owed Catiline because of the latter's ready acceptance of disqualification from the second consular election in 66.
81. Cic. *Sull.* 81. Catiline might well have had the support of the other consul, L. Aurelius Cotta, who was related to Aurelia Orestilla.
82. Cic. *Tog. Cand.* Asc. 85–87 and 92. Asconius and Q. Cic. *Comment Pet.* 10 make the stock charge that the acquittal was the result of bribery. Cic. *Har. Res.* 42 and *Cat.* 1.18 insinuate the same.
83. Asc. 89. Gruen (1974) 28–30 contends that the Lex Aurelia in 70 provided for a jury to be composed from these three groups. It seems that the *tribuni aerarii* were well off citizens whose wealth was not great enough to qualify them for the equestrian order. Marshall (1985b) states that the division of the jury into three classes did not occur until 59 and that Asconius' views as to how the jury voted reflected his own views of the significance of senatorial criticism of Catiline. There is no contemporary evidence of the jury's vote.
84. Asc. 87 who says that the rumour that Clodius was colluding with Catiline was due to (1) the fact that Catiline was acquitted and (2) the prosecution had been cooperative in jury selection. Phillips (1970) 291–294 and Gruen (1974) 271 contend that Clodius did not collude with Catiline to ensure a verdict favourable to Catiline.
85. Riggsby (2010).

86. See Federal Rule of Evidence 404(1): 'Evidence of a person's character or character trait is not admissible to prove that on a particular occasion the person acted in accordance with the character of trait.'

Chapter 5
1. Brunt (1988) 46 says that it is important not to underestimate the political significance of Cicero's oratorical skills.
2. Habicht (1990) 25. Cicero was a trial lawyer rather than a legal scholar or jurist; however, he had studied under the Roman jurist Q. Mucius Scaevola and was not simply a mouthpiece as Riggsby (2010) 59 suggests.
3. He did accept payments from his *clientes* through the form of uncollected loans or bequests in wills, thereby avoiding the basic prohibition against receiving payment for legal services. Polo (2016) 175–176. Cic. *Att* 1.12 alleges that Antonius was spreading rumours that Cicero had agreed to give Antonius the province of Macedonia in exchange for a share of the spoils from Antonius' anticipated depredations. Cic. *Att.* 1. 12. denies this improbable story. For skeptical views, see Bailey (1965) 297; Habicht (1990) 29 and Polo (2016) 172–3. In all events, Cicero's somewhat modest fortune (augmented by his wife's dowry) increased some twenty-fold in the years following his consulship. Polo (2016) 174–5. Being the leader of the Roman bar was not without its financial rewards.
4. Syme (1964) 15–16.
5. Peterson (1985) 31–32.
6. Plut. *Cic.* 24. For a trenchant criticism of Cicero's vanity by his friend Brutus, see Cic. *Brut.* 1:17.
7. Plut. *Cic.* 25–27.
8. Cicero's defence of an obviously guilty Murena reflected his belief that the end (installation of a second consul at the start of January, 62) justified the means. Certainly, his consideration of a *coitio* with Catiline, whom he considered guilty of extortion, is another example of his belief in the same principle. Even Stockton, Cicero's admirer, admitted that Cicero '… sometimes did trim his sails to the prevailing wind (though by no means always).' Stockton (1970) 166. Dio 36.43 was far less charitable: 'Cicero …was aspiring to leadership in the state and was endeavouring to make it clear to both the people and the *optimates* that he was sure to make whichever side he should join predominate. He was accustomed to play a double role and would espouse now the cause of one party, and again that of the other, so that he might be courted by both.' (translation Jeffrey Henderson). See Paterson (1985) 36 who writes about Cicero in his early years: '…when he does lend his support to a political issue, it represented a fine piece of calculated self-interest, rather than a stand on a matter of principle.'
9. Van Der Blom (2010) 55–56.
10. See Cic. *Fam.* 3. 7: In writing to Appius Claudius, head of the *gens* Claudia, Cicero pleaded for acceptance by the aristocracy: '…after I had won and filled positions of the highest authority in such fashion as to let me feel no need of additional rank or fame, I hoped to become the equal (never the superior) of you and your peers.' In another letter Cicero sickeningly says that he has embraced Appius in his mind and smothered his letters to Appius with kisses. Cic. *Fam.* 3.11.2.
11. There is no evidence that Cicero ever helped any other *novus homo* to attain the consulship. Cicero's demagogic opposition to the Rullian land bill, *De lege Agraria*,

during his consulship, epitomizes his doctrinaire conservatism. Odahl (2010) 32–34: Habicht (1990) 29–31.
12. App. *B. Civ.*2:15
13. Dio Cass. 38:18; Sen. *Suas.* 6.22 App. *B. Civ.* 2:15.
14. Sen. *Suas.* 6.17
15. It is significant that Cicero in *Nat. D.* 3.9 had C. Aurelius Cotta say, *Mihi enim unum sat erat, it nobis maioris nostros tradisse.* (For my part, a single argument would have sufficed, namely that is has been handed down to us by our ancestors.) trans. Van der Blom.
16. Cic., *Att.* 1.1.
17. Vishnia (2012) 118–119.
18. Cic. *Att.* 1.2 It was not until later that Cicero charged that Clodius had taken a bribe from Catiline to throw the case. *De Has. Resp.* 42. Asc. 87 reports this claim but does not endorse it.
19. One Roman historian, Fenestella, claimed that Cicero did defend Catiline, but Asc. 85–86 has conclusively demonstrated that Fenestella's claim was not accurate.
20. Marshall (1976) 73 assumes that Cicero did not offer to defend Catiline. However, there is no proof either way.
21. Asc. 93–4.
22. Cic. *Att.* 1:1.
23. Cic. *Att.* 1.1. For the lethargy of Galba and Cassius, see Q. Cic. *Comment. Pet.* 7.
24. Gruen (1974) 136, n. 6.
25. Asc. 82.
26. Asc. 82.
27. Gruen (1974) 260.
28. Asc. 82.
29. Tatum (2018) 100.
30. Tatum (2018) 100.
31. Ac. 85.
32. Plut. *Cic.* 11; Sall. *Cat.* 21; Asc. 83. See Syme (1939) 19 for the power of the Antonii.
33. Asc. 82–83.
34. Asc. 86.
35. It is likely that Orestinus was a relative of Catiline's wife, Aurelia Orestilla, and thus was acting in Catiline's interest. See Crawford (1994) 188 citing various scholars who make this suggestion.
36. Asc. 83. Con. Brunt (1957) 193–5 who argues that Asconius' statements are based on Cicero's secret history of his consulship which Brunt considers unreliable as being biased against Crassus and Caesar. However, the language of Cicero's speech- *cuiusdam hominis noblilis et valde in hoc largitionis quasetu noti* (a certain noble well known for profiting by supplying funds for bribery) seems a clear reference to Crassus. Gruen (1974) 138 contends that Caesar would not have supported the Catiline-Antonius ticket in 64 because a decade before Caesar had prosecuted Antonius for extortion when he had been *pro praetor* in Greece. This argument is unconvincing. Politics has always made strange bedfellows. Stone (1998b) contends that the house in question was that of P. Cornelius Sulla (the defeated candidate from 66) who was responsible for financing Catiline's (and Antonius') campaign in order to elect consuls who would support efforts to void the penalties imposed on him by his conviction in 66 for *ambitus*. Voiding the penalties would permit Sulla to run for consul again.

37. Asc. 85–86.
38. Asc. 83 says this is a reference to Crassus or Caesar; given Caesar's financial situation at this time, the source of the money must have been Crassus who was financing both Caesar and Catiline although Marshall (1984) 286–7 points out that Crassus nay have been using Caesar's house as a meeting place. Asconius' suggestion that the reference could have been to Caesar reflects Asconius' anachronistic view of Caesar's political significance in 64. Marshall (1984).
39. Asc. 83.
40. Marshall (1984) 286–7.
41. Ward (1977) 125.
42. Of course, Roman political speeches always involved personal invective. See Syme (1939) 149–150; Odahl (2010) x; Kaplan (1968) 2–3.
43. Tatum (2018) 211 suggest that Cicero may have circulated forged versions of the affidavits submitted by witnesses in Catiline's extortion trial in an effort to blacken Catiline.
44. Asc. 83 mistakenly identifies that unnamed person as Gallius. Asconius' identification is mistaken for the reasons pointed out in by Ramsey (1980b) 417–21.
45. Syme (1964) 125–6 suggests Cicero embroidered further on this story in *Pro Sulla* (delivered in the first part of July, 62) and, in an effort to defend Sulla, attributes to Catiline the role actually played by Sulla in the events of 66. Cicero may also have made an attack *In Toga Candida* on Q. Curius, the later Catilinarian conspirator. Asc. 93. See Marshall (1978) 207–9.
46. Asc. 93.
47. Asc. 93–4. Schol. Bob 80: 14 states that Clodius may have made the same type of attack on Cicero. This claim is doubtful in view of the fact that Clodius and Cicero seemed to have been on good terms during this period.
48. Quin. *Inst.* 9.3.94.
49. Asc. 94.
50. Habicht (1990) 25. Cicero certainly considered (correctly or incorrectly) Hortensius among his enemies because of the latter's chagrin at Cicero' surpassing him as the leader of the Roman bar. Habicht (1990) 74 (and sources cited therein.) Any 'alliance' between Cicero and Catulus/Hortensius had to have occurred after the suppression of the conspiracy.
51. Asc. 95.
52. Cic. *Sull.* 81.
53. Epstein (1987) 55–56.
54. Asc. 83. Some scholars have questioned the view that Crassus and Caesar supported Catiline' candidacy in 64. See Blunt (1957) 7 and Marshall (1974) 84–809. Con. Ward (1977) 145–151.
55. Q. Cic. *Comment. Pet.* 3 and 24; Odahl (2010) 27.
56. See Q. Cic. *Comment. Pet.* 6 for Cicero's support from younger members of the nobility.
57. Asc. 94.
58. Q. Cic. *Comment. Pet.* 3. *Deinde fac ut amicorum et multitudo et genera appareant; habes enim ea quae qui novi habuerunt? - omnis publicanos, totum fere equestrem ordinem, multa propria municipia, multos abs te defensos homines cuiusque ordinis, aliquot conlegia, praeterea studio dicendi conciliatos plurimos adulescentulos, cottidianam amicorum adsiduitatem et frequentiam* See Gruen (1974) 137–8. Ward (1972) 247 suggests that Cicero's election was due to the support of Pompey. However, there is no evidence of

such support and Cicero's letter to Pompey after the suppression of the conspiracy does not suggest that Pompey had helped him to win the consulship. Cic. *Fam.* 5. 7. 3. Q. Cic. *Comment Pet.* 51 does advise his brother to claim that Pompey viewed him with favour.
59. Q. Cic. *Comment. Pet.* 6, 51. Cicero's support of the *Lex Manilia* which gave Pompey command of the war against Mithridates may have been motivated by a desire to win the support of Pompey's friends and allies as opposed to the support of Pompey himself who was overseas with the army and not active in Roman politics at this time. Rawson (1978) 57–58.
60. Asc. 94. Marshall (1985) 318 suggests that Antonius may have received help from the then consul, L. Caesar, who had connections with the Antonii.
61. Gruen (1974) ix-x. Con. Habicht (1990) 24 who claims that a *repulsa* (defeat) was nearly always fatal. Cic. *Agr.* 2.3 boasts of the fact that he won the consulship on his first try which suggests that many others took several attempts to reach the goal.
62. Suet. *Iulus* 13. Of course, there is one other possible explanation. The *amicitia* between Catulus and Catiline may have been purely personal and did not carry over into politics. However, this theory is unlikely because the Romans did not tend to separate personal friendship from political alliances.
63. Sall. *Cat.* 23–24 which is followed by App. *B. Civ.* 2. 2 and Plut. *Cic.*11
64. B. Levick (2015) 39–40.
65. Cic. *Agr.* 2.6. does suggest that at one point Cicero had claimed to be a *popularis*.
66. See Syme (1939) 24 and. Odahl (2010) 29–30. For a partial endorsement of the theory that the older *optimates* carried the day for Cicero, albeit out of a desire to frustrate Crassus, see Marshall (1976) 74.
67. Q. Cic. *Comment. Pet.* 14, and 51.
68. Cic. *Att* 1.2.
69. Q. Cic. *Comment Pet.* 14.
70. Cic. *Att.* 1.1; Seager, (1976) 46; Stockton (1971) 62.
71. Cic. *Agr.* 2. 1. See Seager (1976) 46.
72. So Phillips (1973) 357 speculates. See Cic. *Ver.* 2.1.139 which names Ahenobarbus as a prosecution witness for the Verrine trial.
73. Cic. Att. 1.1; See Gruen (1974) 139, 267.
74. Asc. 91 dates these convictions as occurring several months before the consular election in 64. Dio Cass. 37:10 dates them as occurring in 64.
75. Asc. 91.
76. Cic. *Fam.* 5.12–15 which contains a series of letters between Cicero and Lucceius. The first letter asks Lucceius to include a laudatory account of Cicero's handling of the Catilinarian conspiracy in his history of Rome or, even better, to write a monograph on that subject. Gruen (1974) 277 contends that Lucceius was a Pompeian.
77. Seager (1964) 347.
78. Asc. 92. Since Asconius refers to the writings of Lucceius against Catiline, it would seem that Lucceius later wrote down and published his speech to the jury.
79. Cic. *Sull.* 81. There is no explanation for Torquatus' absence given his support of Catiline the year before in Catiline's trial for extortion.
80. Dio Cass. 37: 10.
81. Asc. 91–2.
82. Marshall (1985) 307.
83. Marshall (1976–7) 127.

84. Cic. *Lig.* 12.
85. Dio Cass. 37.10. Instigating such actions would be consistent with Caesar's strategy in arranging for T. Labienus to prosecute Rabirius for his extra judicial killing in 100 of Apuleius Saturinus under the protection of the *senatus consultum ultimum*. Caesar was trying to re-establish the rule of law which had been destroyed by the optimates and Sulla.
86. Taylor (1949) 62–3.
87. If he did, his efforts in this regard did not enable him to compete with Cicero's longstanding alliances with leaders of the Italian municipalities. See Q. Cic. *Comment. Pet.* 32, 50.
88. Taylor (1960) 115.
89. Mouritsen (2001) 90–6 and 119–23.
90. Dio Cass. 37.30; Plut. *Cic.* 14.
91. Sall. *Cat.* 16; How small farmers could raise enough cash to engage in riotous and luxurious living is something that neither Cicero or Sallust ever explained.
92. Brunt (1971) 310–11; (1988) 271. See Sall. *Hist.* 1.55.23 for the speech of Lepidus which hints at this point. Accord: Keaveney (1982) 184–185. Con. Gruen (1974) 424.
93. Hutchinson (1966) 21.
94. Brunt (1971) 309 suggests that this explanation may be accurate with respect to some veterans.
95. Plut. *Cic.* 14; Dio Cass. 37:30 states that Manlius was among this group.
96. Cic. *Mur.* 49; Odahl (2010) 15.
97. Hutchinson (1966) 21–23. This view is based on Plut. *Ti. Gracch.* 8 who reports that Tiberius Gracchus became convinced of the need for agrarian reform after observing the dearth of small farms during his trip through Etruria and on App. *B Civ.* 1.7 who records the growth of large farms owned by wealthy individuals who bought out smaller farmers.
98. (2013) 342–50.
99. (1983) 287–331.
100. (2010) 603. Accord: Patterson (2010) 619 who notes that the coastal areas of Etruria were cultivated primarily by servile workforces.
101. Odahl (2010) 26–44.
102. Ward (1977) 170–171.
103. Cic. *Vat.* 12; *Flac.* 67.
104. Cicero, *Att.*1:12.
105. Hudson (2000) 135.
106. J.T. Ramsey (2007) 95; Giovannini (1995) 25–7 who notes that the rates of loans in the provinces could hit 48 per cent.
107. Giovanni (1995) 29.
108. Odahl (2010) 46.
109. Cic. *Cat.* 2.18.
110. Sall. *Cat.* 21. Accord: Dio Cass. 37.30.
111. MacDonald (1977) 87; Woodman (2007) 16, n. 43.
112. Giovannini (1995) 30–32.
113. International Money Fund, '100 Percent Debt Cancellation? A Response from the IMF and the World Bank' (2007) III-IV.
114. Giovannini (1995) 30.
115. Val. Max. 4.8.3.
116. Giovannini (1995) 132.

117. Sal. *Cat.* 33.
118. Cic. *Off.* 2.84
119. Di Cass, 37. 25
120. Cic. *Cat.* 2.18–19. See Gruen (1974) 423–7; Frederiksen (1966) 128–133.
121. P.A. Brunt (1988) 271.
122. H. Mouritsen (2001) 94. Giovanni (1995) 31 fails to recognize that this group had little voting power but their support would be significant in any insurgent effort to seize Rome by force.
123. Yavetz (1958) 500–577; (1963) 495.
124. Cic. Cat. 2.18–23.
125. Antonius was deeply in debt and obviously supported proposals for debt reform. Plut. *Cic.* 12. Cicero had bought Antonius's support by exchanging Cicero's assignment as pro-consul to the rich province of Macedonia for Antonius's assignment to the poor province of Cisalpine Gaul. See Plut. Cic. 12; Sall. *Cat.* 26. There is a good deal of controversy about the exact date of Cicero's deal with Antonius, but it could not have occurred until the assignment of provinces had been announced in 63 and probably did not occur until after the consular election in 63 since Cic. *Mur.* 49 says Catiline made public statements during the campaign that he had Antonius's support. Dio Cas. 37.30 implies that the deal is made after the election since he places Antonius in the initial meeting of the conspirators. Con. Sall. *Cat.* 26 who implies that the deal had been made before the elections.
126. Sall. *Cat.* 14; Cic. *Cael.* 10; *Mur.* 49.
127. Cic. *Cat.* 2: 18–21. Cicero, of course, opposed any legislation to cancel debts in whole or in part. Cic. *Off.* 2: 78.
128. Dio Cass. 37.30 indicates that agrarian reform was one of the objectives of the conspiracy (and logically one of the platforms of Catiline's consular campaign). On the other hand, Dio may have automatically attributed to Catiline a key plank to the *popularis* platform.
129. Ward (1977).
130. Ward (1977) 172 n.9 lists the various authorities who believe that Crassus and Caesar supported Catiline as well as those who believe the opposite.
131. Tatum (2018) 42.
132. Sall. *Cat.* 24–25 claims that many of these were matrons who had once satisfied their avaricious desires through prostitution but, driven by age from this source of livelihood, had not only spent the fortunes they had accumulated in their salad days but had incurred large debts that they were unable to pay. See Rawson (2010) 327 and 332 and Syme (1939) 12 and (1964) 25–27 for the influence of noble women. Rawson indicates that the political power of women was due to three factors: (a) existence of independent wealth (327); (b) superior social status with the ability to influence non-nobles (330); and (c) influence on male relatives (327). Sexual favours may have been involved. (330) Sallust's claim that Catiline thought these women would help him incite slaves to rebellion, set fire to the city, and either bring their husbands over to his side or kill them is a piece of hyperbole that makes no sense at all. For a similar hyperbolic claim, see App. *B. Civ.* 2:6. See Waters (1970) 199–200 for a criticism of Sallust's claims.
133. Sall. *Cat.* 25. *Sed in iis erat Sempronia, quae multa saepe virilis audaciae facinora conmiserat. 2 Haec mulier genere atque forma, praeterea viro atque liberis satis fortunata fuit; litteris Graecis et Latinis docta, psallere et saltare elegantius quam necesse est probae, multa alia, quae instrumenta luxuriae sunt. 3 Sed ei cariora semper omnia quam decus*

atque pudicitia fuit; pecuniae an famae minus parceret, haud facile discerneres; lubido sic accensa, ut saepius peteret viros quam peteretur. 4 Sed ea saepe antehac fidem prodiderat, creditum abiuraverat, caedis conscia fuerat; luxuria atque inopia praeceps abierat. Verum ingenium eius haud absurdum: posse versus facere, iocum movere, sermone uti vel modesto vel molli vel procaci; prorsus multae facetiae multusque lepos inerat. This portrait may reflect the Caesarian Sallust's disdain for Sempronia's son /stepson, D. Junius Brutus, one of the most hated of Caesar's assassins. Syme (1964) 134; (2016) 177. It may also reflect Sallust's misogynistic views of women whom he sees as embodying the *luxuria* to which he attributes Rome's fall. Syme (2016) 173 (and others) suggest that Sempronia was an artistic invention intended as a female counterpart to Catiline and as a contrast to his allegedly effeminate supporters since her only ostensible involvement in the conspiracy was hosting the initial meeting between the Gauls and the conspirators. See the scholars listed in Boyd (1987) 182, fn. 2 as advancing this view. This approach underestimates the importance of Sempronia and other noble women by failing to recognize that women in a male-dominated society exercised their power behind the scenes and their actions were not readily visible.

134. Sall. *Cat.* 24.
135. Ramsey (2007) 134.
136. Plut. *Cat. Min.* 21.
137. Cic. *Mur.* 20. See Plut. *Luc.* 38 for Lucullus' status as an *optimate* although not very active in politics towards the end of his life. Cic. *Att.* 12:6. Gruen (1974) 52 dates Lucullus' retirement from politics to 59, three years before his death in 56.
138. Cic. *Mur.* 37–38. Cicero seems to be the only source for the impact of Lucullus' soldiers on the election; he certainly exaggerated their influence.
139. Tatum (1999) 55–61.
140. Cic. Mur. 7.
141. Cicero did not list this speech among the ten speeches from 62 which he considered his consular speeches – presumably because he made it in a private capacity. Cic. *Att.* 2.1.
142. As with all of Cicero's speeches, there is a question to what extent the written version corresponds to the version delivered orally.
143. Cic. *Mur.* 47–49.
144. Syme (1939) 526.
145. Dio Cass. 37.29.
146. Dio Cass. 37.29.
147. Cic. *Vat.* 37; MacDonald (1977) 175.
148. Certainly, one of the charges against P. Sulla in 62 was that he had assisted Catiline by financing such gladiatorial games. Cic. *Sull.* 54–55.
149. Cic. *Mur.* 47.
150. Ward (1977) 175. Con. Hardy (1917) 178–179 who explain the absence of veto on the grounds that Crassus and Caesar were not supporting Catiline at this point and Salmon (1935) 311 who improbably suggests that by not having the bill vetoed Crassus hoped to drive a despairing Catiline to attempt a *coup d'etat*.
151. Ward (1977) 174.
152. Cic. *Mur.* 47.
153. Taylor (1949) 56.
154. Despite all of these factors, Jehne (2016) 202–3 points out that the results of Roman elections frequently defied prediction which meant that the electorate was not totally dominated by either *optimates* or *populares*.

155. Cic. *Mur.* 47; *Plan.* 41.
156. Cic. *Mur.* 49; Plut. *Cic.*14. In an effort to blacken Catiline's reputation, Cicero may have exaggerated the number of unpopular Sullan colonists who supported Catiline. Berry (2006) 138: Harris (1971) 289–294. On the other hand, Plut. *Cic.* 14 reports that a large number of the Sullan colonists came to Rome to support Catiline in the election.
157. Cic. *Mur.* 49–51.
158. Cic. *Mur.* 7.
159. Cic. *Mur.* 51.
160. Cic. *Mur.* 51–52. See Plut. *Cato Min.* 21 for Cato's threat to prosecute the successful candidates other than his own brother-in-law, Silanus.
161. Ramsey (2019) 212 and fn. 3.
162. Ramsey (2019) 213–214, Table I, 217–221 which certainly demonstrates that many consular elections occurred at other than the 'normal' date of mid to late July.
163. Cic. *Mur.* 50. *cum miserorum fidelem defensorem negasset inveniri posse nisi eum qui ipse miser esset; integrorum et fortunatorum promissis saucios et miseros credere non oportere; qua re qui consumpta replere, erepta recipere vellent, spectarent quid ipse deberet, quid possideret, quid auderet; minime timidum et valde calamitosum esse oportere eum qui esset futurus dux et signifer calamitosorum.*
164. Cic. *Mur.* 50–51. Plut. *Cic.* 14.5
165. Cic. *Mur.* 51.
166. Cic. *Mur.* 51. Suet. *Aug.* 5 and 94.5 states that Augustus was born on September 23 and that the senate discussed the Catilinarian conspiracy on that date. The discussion on that date could not have involved the conspiracy, since no knowledge of the conspiracy surfaced before mid to late October. Ramsey (2019) 230–232 theorizes that the discussion on September 23 is the one in which Cicero reported Catiline's remarks and postponed the election. Ramsey's theory is based on the assumption that there were two postponements of the election- one from July to September (to enable enactment of the *lex Tullia)* and the other for a couple of days in September so that the senate could have considered Catiline's remarks. However, the classical sources only report one postponement. The absence of evidence of two postponements seems to invalidate Ramsey's theory that Catiline's remarks were the subject of the 23 September discussion. Since there may have been several discussions about the Catiline in the senate, one cannot determine which discussion Suetonius is referring to as having occurred on 23 September.
167. Plut. *Cic.* 14.
168. Cic. *Mur.* 14. Cicero's account of this incident seems exaggerated and his view reflects Monday morning quarterbacking.
169. Lintott (2008) 142, n. 39 contends that the reason for the postponement was the need to draft and consider the *lex Tullia* – a process which would have taken several weeks. Ramsey (2019) 226–227 adopts Lintott's theory. However, Lintott's claim is specifically contradicted by Cicero's statement that it was Catiline's remarks that led to the postponement of the election – not the need to draft the bill which presumably had been enacted into law some time before.
170. Dio Cass. 37.29 states that Cicero started wearing a cuirass on election day; however, it is more likely that it happened during the campaign particularly since Dio indicates that one of the purposes of the masquerade was to arouse prejudice against his

opponents which would make more sense if this action occurred pre-election than it if occurred only on election day.
171. Dio Cass. 37.29.
172. Suet Iul. 14; Plut. *Caes.* 8; Cic. *Cat.*3.5
173. See Benson (1986) 234–41 for a discussion of the various arguments advanced by historians with respect to the date on which the election was originally scheduled to be held and the date on which it was actually held.
174. Cic. *Mur.* 51–52.
175. Plut. *Cic.* 15.
176. (1949) 71. Taylor (1966) 105 noted that in 55 the First Triumvirate delayed the election for months so that Caesar's soldiers could come to Rome after the conclusion of the summer campaigning season and vote for the Triumvirate's candidates. See Gruen (1974) 160–161 for his view that postponing elections was a common political manoeuvre and that the postponement of elections in 67, 63, 62, 59, 56, 55, 54, and 53 had been politically motivated. Gruen's observations are certainly consistent with Ramsey's detailed study referred to in fn. 161.
177. Cic. *Mur.* 49.
178. Herlihy (1967) 108 indicates that many Etrurian farmers had vineyards and that grapes had to be harvested starting in mid-September.
179. Ramsey (2019) 214 agrees that the elections did not take place until September, 63 for two reasons: (1) Sulpicius' challenge to Murena's election was heard in late November, 63 and normally challenges to the result of an election were heard a month or two after the election itself and (2) and Cicero's speech, *De Proscriptorum Filiis* delivered no earlier than August dealt with upholding Sulla's disqualification of the sons of the Marians and therefore had to be a pre-election speech. Ramsey (2019) 226–227.
180. It seems that Manlius, at least, did remain for the election. Sall. *Cat.* 27.
181. Cic. *Mur.* 37 and 69. Miller (1998) 99 indicates that soldiers who had served in the Roman army with a given candidate were often impressive witnesses to the candidate's military experience and virtue and thus persuasive advocates of his cause on the election field. However, they had little direct impact on the election since most of them were enrolled in the last century and thus had no real voting power.
182. Tatum (1999) 57.
183. Cic. *Mur.* 52; Plut. *Cic.* 14.
184. Cic. *Sull.* 51–52. This claim of Autronius' involvement seems to have resulted from Cicero's need in *Pro Sulla* to contrast Autronius, the bad convicted politician, who continued in his evil ways, to Sulla, the good convicted politician, who abandoned his evil ways to stand by the Republic in its time of need. Cic. *Cat.* 1:11 claimed that Catiline planned to kill not just Cicero on the election field but the other consular candidates as well. This seems to be another one of Cicero's fabrications.
185. Cic. *Mur.* 52.
186. Cic. *Sull.* 51.
187. It is also possible that Cicero saw Catiline as a useful bogeyman to frighten the senators and the *equites* into a *concordia ordinum*. Galassi (2104) 128 improbably suggests that Terentia may have been behind Cicero's vendetta against Catiline because of Catiline's alleged involvement in 73 B.C. with her sister, the vestal virgin Fabia. This suggestion is based on the suppositions that Fabia was Terentia's sister, that Terentia was enraged by Catiline's alleged actions and that Terentia has such influence over Cicero that she could cause him to hate Catiline. There is no evidence for the last two of these suppositions. Moreover, while Asconius 92 states that Fabia

was Terentia's sister, some historians contend that she was only a half-sister or perhaps only an adopted sister. If these views are correct, then there is even less basis for Galassi's theory.
188. Cicero identified Clodius and Anthony with Catiline. Tatum (1999) 143–145. Of course, demonization of one's opponents was usual in Roman politics, but Cicero seems to have believed in his own charges. Trial lawyers often lose their sense of perspective in cases which they are vigorously pursuing and believe the evidence in favour of their side is stronger than it is.

Chapter 6

1. Taylor (1949) 31. Habicht (1990) 24 notes that Cicero attained each office in the year in which he was first eligible.
2. Cic. *Cat.* 1:14 claims that Catiline was bankrupt. Catiline in his letter to Catulus, written after Cicero's *First Catilinarian*, claimed that he could pay his own debts and with the aid of Aurelia Orestilla and her daughter could pay the debts contracted in the names of others. Sall. *Cat* 35. Sall. *Cat.* 5 and 14 comments on Catiline's general lack of financial resources and prodigal expenditures. Sall. *Cat.* 24 states that Catiline was able to obtain loans to buy arms for the insurgents in Etruria- an action which had to take place after his electoral defeat in 63. For someone who allegedly was profligate and always in debt, Catiline seems to have remained amazingly creditworthy.
3. Sall. *Cat.*16. Sallust overstates the situation. There were at least two armies outside of Rome waiting for their generals to be awarded triumphs; the government used these forces with great effect to crush the Catilinarians.
4. Ramsey (2019) 226, who suggests that the postponement of the elections from July to September would have led Catiline to conclude that his supporters from Etruria would be unlikely to attend and that the enactment of the *lex Tullia* was a presage to a prosecution if he was successful in the election.
5. Sall. *Cat.* 17. Sampson (2019) 73–78 claims that most of the conspirators were unsuccessful *Sullani* and that Catiline's conspiracy was an attempt by unsuccessful *Sullani* to seize power and wealth. The fact that most of the conspirators were *Sullani* or descendants of *Sullani* is hardly surprising, since almost everyone in politics in this period were *Sullani*; the Marians had been killed off and their descendants barred from political office. The only prominent Marian was Caesar, who had narrowly survived Sulla and had adopted the Marian mantle to launch his career. Ward (1977) 120–121.
6. Sall. *Cat.* 47; Cic. *Sull.* 70 and *Cat.* 3.9.
7. Sall. *Cat.* 43. *semper querebatur de ignavia sociorum: illos dubitando et dies prolatando magnas opportunitates corrumpere; facto, non consulto in tali periculo opus esse seque, si pauci adiuvarent, languentibus aliis impetum in curiam facturum. Natura ferox, vehemens, manu promptus erat, maxumum bonum in celeritate putababit.*
8. Cic. *Cat.* 3.16. When in charge of the *maiestas* court as *praetor*, he had failed to appear for the hearing which he had set in the case of the ex-tribune Cornelius, which suggests that he had been bribed to let Cornelius off. See Asc. 60. and 82 where Cassius is described as an idiot.
9. Sall. *Cat.* 23.
10. Cic. *Sull.* 71. Of course, Cic. *Sull.* 18–9 makes much of the fact that he refused to defend his 'boyhood friend' Autronius despite the latter's imploring. Since there is no evidence that Autronius came from Arpinum, it is doubtful that Cicero's reference to him as a 'boyhood friend' is accurate.

11. See Forsythe (1991) 407–412 for his origins and Linderski (1963) 511–2 for his conviction. Sal *Cat.* 28 calls him a senator, which is probably a reference to his former rank which he lost upon conviction.
12. This is not the P. Cornelius Sulla who was the defeated candidate in 65.
13. Badian (1959) 97–8 suggest that this individual may have been a relative of the Pompeian A. Gabinus (cos. 58) but admits that 'any such conclusion is anything but certain'.
14. Sall. *Cat.* 17.
15. Cic. *Dom.* 5.13.
16. Sall. *Cat.* 17.
17. Sall. *Cat.* 17.
18. Stories of Crassus' alleged involvement were publicized later on by Cicero.
19. Suet. *Iul.* 13.
20. Suet. *Iul.* 13 and 17.
21. Miller (1975) 45–57.
22. Fomin (206) 219, 225.
23. Syme (1964) 196–201.
24. Fomin (2016) 218.
25. Thuc. 2.1 (Rex Warner translation, Penguin Books, 1954).
26. Miller (1975) 48 notes that Sallust followed the Thucydidean approach of writing speeches not for artistic effect but to reflect the historian's view as to what the speaker had probably said. Sallust probably had a reasonably accurate idea of the substance of what Catiline said at some point and used that information as the basis for this fictional speech. The fact that the speech contains some anachronistic references to Piso (since Piso had been sent to Spain in 65 and was killed shortly thereafter. (Sall. *Cat.* 19)) as well as to the consular campaign of 64 suggests that Sallust may have drawn on information about an earlier speech that Catiline had made when he was running for the consulship. Schaffer (1973) 88–89 improbably views Sallust's fictional speech as a genuine speech made by Catiline in the 64 campaign. It is likely that Sallust's re-creation tracks the substance of Catiline's speech more accurately than the writer's re-creations of Caesar's and Cato's speeches in the Senate debate over the fate of the conspirators, since these speeches focused on philosophy which would have been no more appealing to the members of the Roman senate than they would be to members of the U.S. Senate.
27. Sall. *Cat.* 20.
28. Sall. *Cat.* 21.
29. Sall. *Cat.* 21.
30. Dio Cass. 37.30.
31. See Sall. *Cat.* 22; Plut. *Cic.* 10 and Dio Cass. 37.30 for versions of the story that Catiline had the conspirators drink from a bowl containing the blood of a murdered slave before swearing the oath of allegiance. Sallust refused to vouch for the story and stated that many believed that this story was invented later on by Ciceronian supporters who sought to mitigate the popular hostility against Cicero for his later actions against the conspirators by exaggerating the wickedness of the conspirators.
32. Sall. *Cat.* 27; Cic. *Cat.* 2. 6; App. *B Civ.* 2.2. See Levick (2015) 47–8 for a list of areas in which discontent was prominent.
33. Oro. 6.6.7.
34. Sall. *Cat.* 37.9.

35. Plut. *Cic.* 10.
36. Dio Cassius, 37.2
37. Sall. *Cat.* 21.
38. Sall. *Cat.* 21.
39. Sall. *Cat.*37. *sed omnino cuncta plebes novarum rerum studio Catilinae incepta probabat. Id adeo more suo videbatur facere. Nam semper in civitate, quibus opes nullae sunt, bonis invident, malos extollunt, vetera odere, nova exoptant, odio suarum rerum mutari omnia student, turba atque seditionibus sine cura aluntur, quoniam egestas facile habetur sine damno.*
40. Sall. *Cat.* 37. Brunt (1971) 13–14 indicates that in the preceding century the population of the city had grown from 400,000 to 900,000/910,000.
41. Sall. *Cat.* 27. Sallust, of course, attributes this frantic activity over Catiline's guilty conscience caused by his murder of his son. Sal. *Cat.* 15.
42. Sall. *Cat.* 17. Of course, it is possible that the meeting was a *contio domestica* (pre-election rally). However, it seems logical that Catiline would have had at least one meeting with the conspirators so that each individual would draw confidence from the presence of the others. Certainly, the men called to the meeting would have been those of the *factio* which supported Catiline in the campaign. Sall. *Cat.* 17; Gelzer (169) 124.
43. Plut. *Cic.* 10–11, App. *B Civ.* 2.2. However, Appian correctly dates the beginning of the conspiracy after the consular elections in 64.
44. Dio Cass. 37.30.1.
45. Stone (1993) 230, fn. 1. See Syme (2002) 75–7 for a trenchant criticism of Sallust's dating.
46. Stone (1993) 230–41.
47. Woodman (2021) 63–67.
48. Sall. *Cat.* 26.
49. Sall. *Cat.* 56.
50. Even Woodman (2021) 63 admits that ancient historians frequently made transposition of events as Sallust obviously did.
51. Sall. *Cat.* 5.
52. Woodman (2021) 67. Using *a priori* reasoning, Woodman then seizes on every piece of 'evidence' to support his conclusion. Thus, he accepts the myth of the First Catilinarian conspiracy. Second, he relies on the speeches which Sallust invented for Catiline to show that Catiline's seeking the consulship was not inconsistent with planning to establish a dictatorship. This evidence would have been more persuasive, but for the fact that the speeches were invented by Sallust who designed them to be consistent with his picture of Catiline as the eternal conspirator. Third, Woodman credits a series of Cicero's incredible claims in the First Catilinarian that (1) that Catiline had plotted against Cicero when the latter was consul designate (2) that Catiline tried to kill Cicero on the election grounds in 63 (even though Cicero did not even see Catiline on the election grounds) and (3) that on a number of occasions Catiline had tried to kill Cicero both as consul designate and consul as evidencing Catiline's omnipresent criminal intent. This account of frequent but unsuccessful and unpublicized attacks on Cicero's life sounds like the fairy tale that it is. Fourth, Woodman claims that Catiline may have been impressed by Sulla or by Q. Lucretius Ofella whom he may have met at the siege of Praeneste in 82 and wanted to follow Ofella's efforts to seize power. There is no evidence that Catiline was present at

such siege or had any contact with Ofella. Finally, Woodman relies of a charge by Cicero that Caesar when Caesar was *aedile* hoped to seize sole power in the Republic which he allegedly did in 59 when he became consul proved that Catiline's election as consul would not have precluded an attempt by Caesar to establish a dictatorship despite Catiline's consulship. Ironically, despite his comparison of Catiline to Hitler, Woodman considers Catiline to be an incompetent fool who fails to declare his candidacy in 66 within the required time limits, who appears armed on December,66 although he was trying to conceal his presence in the forum and who in February 65 gives the signal for the attack on the consuls too soon.

53. Sall. *Cat.* 56. 6 and App. *B. Civ.* 2. 1.2.
54. Sall. *Cat.* 28 and 37.
55. Sall. *Cat.* 39. In a sense, all were waiting for Pompey. Seager (2002) 71 suggests that one reason for Cicero's attacks on Catiline was his desire to ensure that there were no dissident agents in the Republic who would cause dissension in the state and give Pompey an excuse for using his army to restore law and order. Certainly, Pompey was less than happy that the *optimates* led by Cato took advantage of Cicero's success to defeat a proposal made by the Pompeian tribune, Q. Metellus Nepos, to recall Pompey to crush the conspiracy. Plut. *Cato Min.* 27–29. See also Cic. *Fam.* 5.7 for Pompey's coolness to Cicero and his lack of praise for Cicero's defeat of the conspirators. However, Cicero was an ardent Pompeian throughout his career and there is no evidence that he ever sought to thwart any plan by Pompey.
56. For some hints as to Catiline's possible plans to deal with Pompey see Cic. *Cat.* 3.9 for Lentulus' efforts to have Gallic cavalry sent to Italy. The only need for this cavalry would have been to oppose Pompey on his return. See Cic. *Red. Pop.* 17 for the conspirators' attempts to subvert the fleet for possible use against Pompey and Plut. *Cic.* 18 for the insurgents' plans to seize Pompey's family to use as a bargaining chip with Pompey.
57. Levick (2015) 91–4.
58. Suet. *Iul.* 17.
59. Plut. *Cic.* 15; *Crass.* 13. Plutarch cites as his source Cicero's now lost history of his consulship, *Expositio Consiliorum Suorum*. Dio Cass. 37.31 says that the letters were addressed to various *optimates*.
60. Since Plutarch indicates that all three were powerful and distinguished Romans, it is likely that the third man is M. Claudius Marcellus, although he certainly was not in the same league as Crassus and Metellus Pius.
61. Plut. *Cic.* 15.
62. This theory suggests that Crassus may have forged the letters himself. See Hardy (1917) 104. The first theory was far more likely because Crassus had a real interest in escaping charges of involvement in the conspiracy.
63. Ward (1977) 182.
64. Plut. *Cic.* 15
65. Arrius may have been acting in concert with Cicero since the latter describes Arrius as an intimate friend in *Vat.* 30. Marshall and Baker (1975) 220–231 claim that Arrius was a long-time ally of Crassus and suggest that Arrius was acting as an agent of Crassus in this matter. See Cic. *Brut.* 242–3 which describes Arrius as sitting as a second chair to Crassus in cases where the latter was the lead attorney. Accord: Ward (1977) 79–90.
66. Dio Cass. 37.30. Con. Sall. *Cat.* 29 and Plut. *Cic.* 15 who confuse the *tumultus* decree with the *senatus consultum ultimum* which was passed later on. Since the *senatus*

consultum ultimum was passed on October 21, the incident involving Crassus and the letters must have occurred earlier. The reason that many scholars date incident involving the letters as occurring on the evening of October 20 is that they do not distinguish between the passage of a decree of *tumultus* and the passage of the *senatus consultum ultimum*.
67. Asc. 93.
68. Florus 2.12 claimed that she was a common prostitute.
69. Sall. *Cat.* 23 and Diod. Sic. 40:5. Sallust makes the improbable claim that Fulvia told all and sundry about the conspiracy.
70. Sall. *Cat.* 26.
71. Suet. *Iul.* 17.
72. Sall. *Cat.* 26 claims that this contact occurred at the beginning of Cicero's consulship. This claim is part and parcel of Sallust' fairy tale account of the conspiracy as beginning on June 1 64. Fulvia seems to disappear from history after the suppression of the conspiracy. Syme (2016) 183 identifies her as being the Flavia/Fulvia (the texts vary) described by Val. Max. 9.8.1 as attending along with Mucia a party at a brothel where they acted as prostitutes. Valerius Maximus states that both women were daughters or husbands of famous men but does not otherwise identify them. Syme's effort to identify Curius' Fulvia with Valerius Maximus' Fulvia/Flavia seems to be based on the similarity of the *praenomen*s and nothing else. Florus, 2:12 claims that she was a common whore.
73. Cic. *Cat.* 1.7. See Hardy (1924a) 57–8. Cicero's charge of planning to murder the *optimate*s seemed to be part of his stock in trade when denouncing conspiracies. He made the same charge *In Toga Candida* (Asc. 92 in connection with the First Catilinarian Conspiracy. When Fulvia and Curius came into contact with Cicero is not known (assuming one rejects Sallust's anachronistic claim at *Cat.* 26 that the couple had started their course of betrayal at the beginning of Cicero's consulship.) It seems likely, however, that the first contact occurred immediately before 21 October since Cicero obviously had obtained significant information about the conspiracy immediately before that date.
74. Cic. *Cat.* 1.4. Although Cicero said on 8 November (the date of the *First Catilinarian*) that the *senatus consultum ultimum* had lain unused for some twenty days, Asc. 5 points out that Cicero was rounding off and it had actually been only eighteen days since the passage of the *senatus consultum ultimum*.
75. Cic. *Cat.* 1.5; 2. 4, 12 and 14 states that there were many citizens of Rome who were not convinced that Catiline posed a threat to the Republic.
76. Cic. *Cat.* 1., 6, 22 and 29; 2. 3 and 27 and 4.1, 9, 20 and 23 all reveal Cicero's justified fear that taking extra legal action against the conspirators could endanger Cicero himself.
77. Dio Cass. 37:31. See Cic. *Cat.* 1.1 for reference to these bands. Con. Sall. *Cat.* 30 who states that the bands were not established until the news of the rising in Etruria reached Rome.
78. Cic. *Cat.*1.7.
79. Plut. *Cic.* 16.
80. Dio Cass. 37.31. It is highly improbable that Catiline had any plans for wholesale murder. What benefit would such action been to him?
81. Cic. *Cat.* 1.8. Cicero undoubtedly was warned by Curius of any planned attempt on his life. However, since no attempt took place, one cannot be sure that any was planned. It is possible that Cicero fabricated this entire story.

82. Harvey (1975) 33 et seq.
83. The report of servile insurrection near Capua in Campania may have been a rumour; at least Cic. *Sull.* 55 claimed that all of Campania was devoid of Catilinarian supporters. Apulia could be a different case since Catiline sent one conspirator there to rouse the countryside. Sall. *Cat.* 27; however, as noted elsewhere, Catiline steadfastly refused to admit slaves to the insurgency so the report about a slave rebellion in Apulia was probably a rumour also.
84. Sall. *Cat.* 32; Dio Cass. 37.31. The date of this event is uncertain but must have occurred by 1 November since it would not have taken more than three or four days for the news of the rising in Etruria to reach Rome.
85. Sall. *Cat.* 30.
86. Plut. *Cic.* 16.
87. Sall. *Cat.* 30. Capua was the headquarters for the schools which trained gladiators and a logical place to send gladiator bands from Rome. Edmundson (2016) 43.
88. Sall. *Cat.* 31.
89. Sall. *Cat.* 37.
90. Sall. *Cat.* 33. *Deos hominesque testamur, imperator, nos arma neque contra patriam cepisse neque quo periculum aliis faceremus, sed uti corpora nostra ab iniuria tuta forent, qui miseri, egentes, violentia atque crudelitate faeneratorum plerique patriae, sed omnes fama atque fortunis expertes sumus. Neque cuiquam nostrum licuit more maiorum lege uti, neque amisso patrimonio liberum corpus habere: tanta saevitia faeneratorum atque praetoris fuit. Saepe maiores vostrum, miseriti plebis Romanae, decretis suis inopiae eius opitulati sunt; ac novissume memoria nostra propter magnitudinem aeris alieni volentibus omnibus bonis argentum aere solutum est. Saepe ipsa plebs, aut dominandi studio permota aut superbia magistratuum armata, a patribus secessit. At nos non imperium neque divitias petimus, quarum rerum causa bella atque certamina omnia inter mortalis sunt, sed libertatem, quam nemo bonus nisi cum anima simul amittit. Te atque senatum obtestamur: consulatis miseris civibus, legis praesidium, quod iniquitas praetoris eripuit, restituatis neve nobis eam necessitudinem inponatis, ut quaeramus, quonam modo maxume ulti sanguinem nostrum pereamus*
91. Sall. *Cat.* 32.
92. Despite Sallust's statement that that this 'document' recreated the oral message which Manlius told his envoys to convey to Marcius Rex, a series of historians have mistakenly assumed (1) that Manlius' message took the form of a written letter and (2) that Sallust's recreation of the message is a copy of an actual letter sent by Manlius as opposed to a recreation of it. See Levick (2015) 60, Waters (1970) 201 and Earl (1961) 94–5.
93. Sall. *Cat.* 34.
94. Seager (1973) 241 fails to recognize this message for what it was – a public relations stunt – and relies on it to support his theory that the story of a unitary conspiracy involving Catiline and Manlius was a Ciceronian invention and that the two were not closely allied.
95. Sall. *Cat.* 31; Dio Cass. 37.31. This seems to have been the first prosecution under this law. The Schol. Bob. 149 St. states that Cethegus was charged under the same law.
96. Cic. *Fam.* 14. 13.
97. Dio Cass. 37.31.

98. Cic. *Cat.* 1.19. The surviving manuscripts differ as to whether the host's name was Marcellus or Metellus. Dio Cass. 37. 32 incorrectly identifies the individual as Metellus Celer who presumably had left the city to deal with the insurgents. W. E. Gwatkin Jr. (1934) 275–281 speculates that this individual may have been the Pompeian tribune, Metellus Nepos.
99. Cic. *Cat.* 1.19.
100. App. *B Civ.* 2. 3.
101. Sall. *Cat.* 27, Cic. *Cat.* 1. 9; *Sull.* 52; Plut. *Cic.* 16.
102. Sall. *Cat.* 27; Cic. *Cat.* 1. 8; Dio Cass. 37.32. For the date which is not disputed, see Cic. *Sull.* 52.
103. Sall. *Cat.* 27; Cic. *Cat.* 1.9. Sallust said that initially the conspirators were shocked and terrified by this proposal. This claim seems questionable; if one is engaged in a conspiracy to overthrow the government, one would expect to shed some blood.
104. Sall. *Cat.* 27–28; Cic. *Cat.* 1.9 and *Sull.* 18 and 5; Dio Cass. 37.32–3. Plut. *Cic.* 16 names Cethegus and one Marcus as the would-be assassins.
105. Sall. *Cat.* 26; Cic. *Cat.* 1. 9 and *Sull.* 52.
106. Sall. *Cat.* 28; Cic. *Cat.* 1. 10; Plut. *Cic.* 16 and Dio Cass. 37.32. This date seems undisputed.
107. Cic. *Cat.* 1.1; Plut. *Cic.* 16.
108. Cic. *Cat.*1.11.
109. See Cic. *Sull.* 34 for his practice of meeting with Torquatus and the other *optimate* leaders during this period. Of course, it would be standard for a consul to meet with the *consulares* (ex-consuls) – at least those who shared his political view – on a regular basis.
110. This date is subject to some dispute; however, a fair reading of Cic. *Cat.* 1.1, '*Quid proxima, quid superior nocte egeris, ubi fueri*'(What you did last night, what you did the night before and where you were) and *Cat.*1. 8, '*Dico te priore nocte venisse inter falcarios…*'(I say you came the prior night to the street of the scythe-makers) indicates that Cicero was referring to both the meeting on 6 November and the meeting on 7 November. See Van Dyck (2008) 243–244. For some articles containing convoluted arguments against this generally accepted dating see; Holmes (1918) 15–25; Potter (1925–26) 164–176; Crane (1966) 264–7 and Berry (2006) 142. Scholars are often unwilling to apply the Occam's Razor analysis to disputes such as this.
111. Plut. *Cic.* 16.
112. Sall. *Cat.* 31.
113. Sall. *Cat.* 31 indicates that the speech was extemporaneous and was written down later. While the beginning of the speech was probably extemporaneous (since Cicero could not have anticipated that Catiline would attend the meeting of the senate) much of the rest of it was probably prepared by Cicero on November 7. While some of the polished oratory contained in the written version may have reflected Cicero's later revision, the speech even as originally delivered was probably the most brilliant of Cicero's career and had to reflect some preparation.
114. Cic. *Cat.* 1.1.
115. Cicero would change this story to suit the needs of the day. In *Cat.*4.13 he blames the plot on Lentulus and names Cassius and Cethegus as the would-be murderers; in *Sull.* 18 he blames the plot on Autronius (because he was trying to contrast Sulla's conduct with that of Autronius) and names Cornelius as the would-be assassin. The changes in the names of the would-be assassins support the view that Cicero made up this story.

116. Cic. *Cat.* 1.16.
117. Cic. *Cat.* 1.13.
118. Dio. Sic. 40.5a.
119. Dio. Sic. 40.5a. Cicero revised *Cat.* 1.20 in 60 to cover up the fact that he actually made such a motion and omitted any reference to Catulus in the revised version of the speech. Rosillo-Lopez (2017) 165–166 suggests that Cicero's tactic here were designed to force the senators to adopt his position by claiming that the failure of anyone to disagree with him openly constituted an endorsement of his position, thereby forcing an unanimity of opinion by capitalizing on the unwillingness of a minority to speak out when its members know that its views are contrary to the majority. Dio Cass. 37.33 incorrectly states that the senate voted to send Catiline into exile.
120. Cic. Cat. 1.27–32. Although this statement may be seen as an accurate prediction of what actually happened after Catiline left the city, it is likely that it was added by Cicero in his later revision of the speech to justify his inaction at the time. Cic. Cat. 1.27 and 32 falsely accused Catiline of recruiting slaves- a step which Catiline had always rejected. Sall. *Cat.* 44. Con. Dio Cass. 37. 33 and App. *B. Civ.* 2. 2.
121. Van der Blom (2010) 122 notes that Cicero's speeches were partly intended to pass on to posterity his own assessment of both past historical figures as well as his own contemporaries.
122. See Phillips (1998) 109, fn. 12 for a list of articles dealing with the *First Catilinarian* and for trenchant criticism of the logical inconsistencies in Cicero's position. However, at least one logical inconsistency pointed out by Phillips at 121, Cicero's suggestion that he was acting out of *clementia* (Cic. *Cat.*1. 4) – is probably a later addition in the revised version of the speech intended to defend Cicero's execution of the conspirators by emphasizing that *clementia* was a basic part of his character.
123. Cic. *Cat.* 2.17: '*murus interest, non timeo*;' (I do not fear you if the city wall lies between us.) Plut. *Cic.* 16. See Van Dyck (2008) 10–11 for a discussion of possible substantive changes in the *Catilinarians* in Cicero's revisions three years later.
124. Sall. *Cat.* 31.
125. Plut. *Cic.* 16.
126. Cic. *Cat.* 1.10
127. Dio. Sic. 4.5a.
128. Cic. *Cat.* 1 21.
129. Sall. *Cat.* 32.
130. App. *B. Civ.* 2. 3.
131. Plut. *Cic.* 18.
132. Plut. *Cic.* 16 and 18; Cic. *Cat.* 2. 4 says that Tongilius was Catiline's catamite and the other two were heavily in debt.
133. Despite Cicero's favourable references in the First Catilinarian and other speeches to the example of L. Opimius, the consul who was responsible for the murder of G. Gracchus, Cicero had no real desire to follow the *exemplum* he cited. Van der Blom (2010) 208–213.
134. Cic. *Cat.* 2. 6, 14; and 16; Sall. *Cat.* 34.
135. Milo went to Massilia as an exile. Asc. 54. See Van Dyck (2008) 145.
136. Sall. *Cat.* 34. The purpose of these letters was to delay governmental action against Catiline and his followers since until Catiline arrived in the camp of Manlius because the road that he took- the Via Aurelia- ran through Faesulae and until he went to Manlius' camp, it was possible that he could go into exile in Massilia. Seager (1973)

247–8 in his rejection of the theory that Manlius and Catiline were working together from the start suggests that Catiline had not made up his mind to join Manlius until he got to Arretium.
137. Sal. *Cat.* 1. 34–35. *L. Catilina Q. Catulo. Egregia tua fides re cognita, grata mihi magnis in meis periculis, fiduciam commendationi meae tribuit. Quam ob rem defensionem in novo consilio non statui parare; satisfactionem ex nulla conscientia de culpa proponere decrevi, quam, medius fidius veram licet cognoscas. Iniuriis contumeliisque concitatus, quod fructu laboris industriaeque meae privatus statum dignitatis non optinebam, publicam miserorum causam pro mea consuetudine suscepi, non quia aes alienum meis nominibus ex possessionibus solvere non possem (et alienis nominibus liberalitas Orestillae suis filiaeque copiis persolveret); sed quod non dignos homines honore honestatos videbam meque falsa suspicione alienatum esse sentiebam. Hoc nomine satis honestas pro meo casu spes reliquae dignitatis conservandae sum secutus. Plura cum scribere vellem, nuntiatum est vim mihi parari. Nunc Orestillam commendo tuaeque fidei trado. Eam ab iniuria defendas, per liberos tuos rogatus. Haveto.* Sallust states that this is an accurate text of Catiline's letter and Syme (1964) 72 points out that this letter 'is remote from the style and language of Sallust.' As noted in Chapter IV, it appears that Catulus honoured Catiline's request and Aurelia maintained a respectable position in society.
138. The reference in both the letters circulated by Catiline's supporters and in this letter to '*inimici*' indicate that Catiline was blaming his situation on his personal enemies – i.e. Cicero. Cadoux (2005) 167 believes this statement that Catulus' loyalty to Catiline is known to Catiline by experience refers to the Vestal Virgin incident.
139. Cic. *Cat.* 2 14.
140. Cicero was trying to take advantage of the popular hostility to the *Sullani* who had benefited from the proscriptions. Paterson (1985) 26.
141. Cic. *Cat.* 2. 18–23.
142. Sall. *Cat.* 37 set forth a somewhat similar list although in more poetic terms. Although he focused on the *plebs* consistent with his aristocratic disdain for the commons; his list includes the following groups (a) debtors, (b) men, mindful of the riches gained by Sulla's soldiers, hoped to benefit similarly in another civil war, (c) idlers who preferred to live up the public purse than work (the Roman equivalent of welfare queens), (d) those whose civil rights and property had been taken away by Sulla and, finally, (e) those opposed to the *optimate* domination of the Republic.
143. Plut. *Cic.* 18. However, having dinner parties was a Roman custom and the conspirators may have used dinner parties as a way of meeting without causing suspicion. See Rosillo-Lopez (2017) 72–73.
144. Sall. *Cat.* 36.
145. Cic. *Cat.* 2. 13.
146. Sall. *Cat.* 56.
147. Sall. *Cat.* 56. In adopting this approach, Catiline was following the traditional method of raising a levy; that is to create a core force first and then add newcomers to it. Brunt (1971) 688; Plut. *Cic.* 16.
148. Plut. *Cic.* 16. Bradley (1978) 336 records that slaves in Southern Italy who whose duties included sheepherding often carried sharpened sticks and suggests that some of these men were escaped slaves who were dismissed after Catiline took charge of Manlius' army.
149. Ramsey (2019) 247, n. 82.

150. Sall. *Cat.* 36. Plut. *Cato Min.* 22 mistakenly claims that Cicero convicted Catiline, causing the latter to flee the city. Cicero as consul was not a judicial officer and had no authority to convict anyone.
151. Sall. *Cat.* 36.3; Ramsey (2019) 149, n. 82.
152. Sall. *Cat.* 36. For the reward offer, see Sall. *Cat.* 30. See also Dio Cass. 37.33.
153. Sall. *Cat.* 39; Dio Cass. 37. 36; Val. Max. 5: 8. Syme (2016) 184 suggests that the man put to death may have been the son of an A. Fulvius who was part of Strabo's *consilium*. There seems to be no basis for Syme's speculation except for the fact that the name A. Fulvius appears on the inscription listing the members of the *consilium*. Va. Max. 5.8.5.
154. Asc. 50.
155. Tatum (1999) 57. Plut. *Cic.* 19 states that Clodius was of great assistance to Cicero in dealing with the conspiracy.
156. Cic. *Sull.* 17.
157. The story that Aulanus was intriguing in Gallic territories does not make sense since Pisaurum was not near Transalpine Gaul.
158. Cic. *Ses.* 8– 9. See Sall. *Cat.* 30 for the quartering of the gladiator bands in Capua.
159. Sall. *Cat.* 42. Sallust calls the legate C. Murena rather than L. Murena which seems a clear mistake. (Sallust's mistake is followed by Van Dyck (2008) 217.) There is considerable dispute about whether L. Murena was governor of both Gauls or just Cisalpine Gaul. See Allen (1953) 176–177 and Badian (1966) 913–918.
160. Stewart (1995) 78.
161 Bradley (1978) 331-2.
162. Cato was extremely supportive of Cicero in his struggle with Catiline. Plut. *Cat. Min.* 22.
163. Cic. *Mur.* 3–7. Plut. *Cato Min.* 21.
164. Cic. *Mur.* 84 indicates that at the time Cicero delivered is speech at the trial, Antonius had left with forces to oppose Catiline.
165. Cic. *Mur.* 48.
166. Cic. *Mur.* 48.
167. Plut. *Cic.* 35.
168. Cic. *Mur.* 19–31 hypocritically praises the martial virtues of Murena over the civilian virtues of Sulpicius even though Cicero looked down upon (but also envied) those whose reputations were won on the battlefield. See Badian (1956) 89, 93.
169. Cic. *Mur.* 78–86; *Flac.* 98.
170. Another example of Cicero's expert handling of humour and sarcasm against opposing counsel may be found in his treatment of the younger Torquatus in *Pro Sulla*.
171. Plut. *Cato Min.* 21. Dio Cass. 37.22 states that Cato was the one *optimate* who sympathized with the lot of the urban poor.
172. Val. Max. 4.8.3.
173. Plut. *Cato Min.* 26. This action was consistent with an *optimate* tradition of making minor concessions to avoid any serious disruption of their control over the Republic.

Chapter 7
1. Sall. *Cat.* 32 names both, but at *Cat.* 29 seems to focus on Lentulus. Plut. *Cic.* 18 names Lentulus as the head. App. *B. Civ.* 2.2 names the two as co-heads. It seems that Lentulus took the lead with Cethegus as his second in command.
2. Cic, *Cat.* 3.16 and *Brut.* 235 for a description of Lentulus.

3. Plut. *Cic.* 17.
4. Plut. *Cic.* 17.
5. Sall. *Cat.* 43.
6. Cic. *Sull.* 70. There is no other support for this story which seems to have been one of Cicero's many inventions.
7. Dio. Sic. 40.5.
8. Sall. *Cat.* 43.
9. So goes Sallust's preposterous story in *Cat.* 43.
10. Dio. Sic. 40. 5. This story is obviously incredible and probably reflects a rumour at the time. As in any pre-printing society, rumour was a main source of public information and was often recorded as fact. See Rosillo-Lopez (2017) for the significance of rumours and gossip in Roman political life. One of the problems facing ancient historians writing after the fall of the Republic was distinguishing rumours from facts when both had been recorded in their sources.
11. Sall. *Cat.* 43. Cic. *Cat.* 3.8 claims the whole city was to be set on fire while Plut. *Cic.* 17 states that there were to be a 100 separate fires. Cic. *Cat.* 4. 13 says that Cethegus was to be responsible for Cicero's assassination, Gabinus was to murder the leading *optimates* and Cassius was to burn the whole city. Of course, the conspirators had no intention of burning to the ground the city that they hoped to rule.
12. Sall. *Cat.* 43. Syme (1964) 132–133 and (2016) 126–136 discredits this story and argues that Bestia had no involvement in the conspiracy which is why he was never prosecuted.
13. Cic. *Cat.* 3.8 and Sall. *Cat.* 43 repeated the cover story. Since Cic. *Cat.* 2. 27 promised to permit all of Catiline's followers to leave the city unscathed, it is questionable if Cicero was taken in by the cover story since he knew that there was no need for the Catilinarians to break out of the city. The text of Sallust which has come down to us says that the rising was to occur when Catiline arrived in Faesulae. Sall. *Cat.* 39. As. Stockton (1971) 121 points out, this is clearly an error in the text itself; to implement the plan, Catiline had to be near Rome- not 150 miles away in Faesulae; presumably, the original text referred to a location nearer Rome such as Falerianum or Aefulanum.
14. Plut. *Cic.* 18 even accepts the extreme claim that the conspirators planned to stop up the aqueducts and kill any who attempted to open them so that no water would be available for the fire fighters and the city could be burned to the ground. In reality, however, setting any fires in Rome was a dangerous tactic because most buildings were constructed of combustible material and warehouses had inflammable goods stored in them. Schaffer (1973) 108–110
15. Sall. *Cat.* 39.
16. Sall. *Cat.* 39; Cic. *Cat.* 3.10.
17. Plut. *Cic.* 18.
18. Sall. *Cat.* 40.
19. Sall. *Cat.* 40. This paragraph is a rough paraphrase of Sall. *Cat.* 40.
20. The conspirators apparently stated that P. Autronius and P. Sulla (the defeated candidates in 65) were involved in the conspiracy. Cic. *Sull.* 36.
21. Sall. *Cat.* 40. This paragraph is a rough paraphrase of Sallust's text.
22. The Allobroges has been conquered by Q. Fabius Maximus Allobrogius who became the patron of the tribe and whose patronage was assumed by Q. Fabius Sanga, his descendant. Ramsey (2007) 171.
23. This paragraph is a rough paraphrase of Sall. *Cat.* 41.
24. Cic. *Dom* 134.

25. Sall. *Cat.* 41.
26. Cicero's *Third Catilinarian* was delivered to the people on the evening of 3 December with the exposure of the conspirators in the senate having taken place earlier that day, the Gauls having been seized on the night of 2/3 December and the Gauls' final meeting with the conspirators having occurred the prior night which would have been the night of 1/2 December.
27. Sall. *Cat.* 44.
28. Cic. *Cat.* 3.9.
29. Cic. *Cat.* 3.10; Sall. *Cat.* 43
30. Supposedly the books containing the Sibylline prophecies were kept as a closely guarded secret. Parke (1988) chapter 7. However, this particular prophecy seems to have been commonly known. Cic. *Cat.* 3.9.
31. Cic. *Cat.* 3. 9; Sall. *Cat.* 47.
32. See Forsythe (1992) 407–412.
33. Sall. *Cat.* 44
34. Cic. *Cat.* 3.4; Sall. *Cat.* 45.
35. Cic. *Cat.* 3.8; Sall. *Cat.* 45.
36. Sall. *Cat.* 44.
37. Cic. *Cat.* 3. 6. Sall. *Cat.* 44 dates the delivery of the letter as 1 December when Lentulus and the others met with the Gauls.
38. Cic. *Cat.* 3 8 and 12; Sall. *Cat.* 44.
39. Sall. *Cat.* 45; Cic. *Cat.* 3. 6.
40. Sall. *Cat.* 46 who writes *ingens cura atque laetitia simul occupavere.* (at the same time great care and great joy seized the consul).
41. Sall. *Cat.* 46.
42. March (1989) 230.
43. Sall. *Cat.* 46. Cic. *Cat.* 3.4 gives the same account except he does not mention Caeparius at this point; however, later on (at 3.14) he alleges that Caeparius had been sent to Apulia to incite the slave shepherds there.
44. Cic. *Cat.* 3. 6. Cicero was being sarcastic in suggesting that Lentulus' late appearance at Cicero's house that morning was due to Lentulus staying up late at night to write this cryptic letter. MacDonald (1977) 106–7.
45. Sall. *Cat.* 46.
46. See March (1988–89) 232.
47. Cic. *Cat.* 3. 6–8.
48. Sall. *Cat.* 46.
49. Cic. *Sull.* 42.
50. Alexander (2002) 17–18.
51. Cic. *Cat.* 3.8. Cicero, contrary to Sall. *Cat.* 46, claims that he led in Volturcius without the Gauls. I think Sallust's version that they were brought into together makes more sense but that Cicero then sent out the Gauls and proceeded to question Volturcius alone before having the Gauls brought back in. Sall. *Cat.* 46 says that Volturcius started to lie and disassemble before being given immunity; Cicero says nothing about this. I suspect that Sallust has embellished the story at this point.
52. Cic. *Cat.* 3.8. Assuming Rome had 900,000 inhabitants, the conspirators had a lot of massacring to do.
53. Sall. *Cat.* 47. Volturcius' statements about the conspirators' plans strain credulity since it is unlikely that Lentulus would not have entrusted a new recruit with the important

mission of communicating with Catiline. Sallust alleges that Volturcius named Ser. Sulla and P. Autronius as conspirators. These men had been named by the Gauls as conspirators or possible conspirators. Cic. *Sull.* 36–39. It seems that Sallust's account has garbled the story and attributed to Volturcius a statement actually made by the Gauls.

54. Cic. *Cat.* 3.10. See Plut. *Cic.* 19.
55. Individuals who were not senators were not permitted to attend- let alone appear at- meeting of the senate unless specially invited in. Alexander (2002) 194.
56. Cic. *Cat.* 3. 9–10, Sall. *Cat.* 47.
57. Plut. *Cic.* 19.
58. Cic. *Cat.* 3. 10.
59. Cicero does not indicate what the remaining evidence was.
60. Cic. *Cat.* 3. 11.
61. Sall. *Cat.* 44. Cic. *Cat.* 3. 12 gives a slightly different version of the letter. I am inclined to accept Sallust's version because he indicates that he got a copy of the letter from the official files while Cicero was probably relying on his memory when he revised the Third Catilinarian several years later. See Gejrot (2005) 20–25. Con. Syme (1964) 72 who argues that Cicero's recollection was more credible than Sallust's research and Ramsey (2007) who believes that Sallust's version reflects Sallust's polishing of Lentulus' actual language. In all events, the two versions of the letter are almost identical from a substantive standpoint.
62. Cic. *Cat*. 4. 13.
63. Levick (2015) 71–72 and. Seager (1973) 244–5 contends that the statements in the letter dealing with the identity of the writer and letter and Lentulus' tone of a superior issuing instructions to a subordinate indicates that the conspirators in Rome and the forces with Catiline and Manlius were not parts of unitary conspiracy. I think this is reading too much into the grammar of the letters.
64. Sall. *Cat.* 56 states that Catiline rebuffed the slaves who sought to join him because he was advancing the cause of free men, not leading a slave rebellion as Spartacus had done. Gruen concludes (1974) 428–29 that any rumours that Catiline was enlisting slaves were clearly false.
65. Cic. *Cat.* 3. 14–15.
66. Sall. *Cat.* 47. Con. Plut. *Cic.* 19 who says that the conspirators were handed over to the *praetors*.
67. Mommsen (1904) 4: 487. Levick (2015) 77–78 suggests that Crassus did not attend this meeting, but Caesar did. It is hard to see how Cicero could have turned Gabinus over to Crassus following the meeting unless Crassus had attended the meeting.
68. Ward (1977) 189. Crassus and Caesar voted for the motion to arrest the conspirators and voted for the thanksgiving. Cic. *Cat.* 4. 10. See Sall. *Cat.* 60.
69. Since it was night when Cicero finished this speech (Cic. *Cat*.3.29) he must have left the senate house as dusk was descending and started his oration to the people immediately.
70. Cic. *Cat.* 2.25. See J. Paterson (1985) 22.
71. This statement may have been added in Cicero's revision of the speech since it seems to be directed at the criticism he received in later years for his execution of the conspirators.
72. Sall. *Cat.* 48. This particular incident is certainly a validation of Rosillo-Lopez's (2017) claim that public opinion existed in the Roman Republic.

73. Cic. Ses. 11.
74. Drummond (1995) 18–19. See also I. Harrison (2008) 95–118.

Chapter 8

1. Plut. *Cic.* 19–20. Dio Cass. 37.34.4 improbably places his account of this episode as occurring on the morning of 5 December.
2. Cic. *Cat.* 1. 3–4.
3. Plut. *Cic.* 19.
4. Sall. *Cat.* 55.
5. Mommsen (1899) 960–963. Caesar was to propose confinement for life in various municipalities (Cic. *Cat.* 4.7–8).
6. Cic. *Cat.* 4.20, 22, and 24.
7. Plut. *Cic.* 19.
8. It was both those characteristics which precluded the conspirators in 44 from enlisting Cicero in the conspiracy to assassinate Caesar. Plut. *Cic.* 42.
9. Tatum (2018) 7.
10. Bringmann (2013) 151–153.
11. Mitchell (1971) 47–61.
12. Hardy (1924b) 92; Habicht (1990) 31, 36–37.
13. Dio Cass. 37. 26–28; Suet. *Iul.* 12. See Millar (2002) 106–108. This action was designed to send a thinly veiled message to the *optimates* not to rely on the *senatus consultum ultimum* in the future.
14. Robinson (2007) 34; Drummond (1995) 63–64.
15. Riggsby (2010) 198.
16. Drummond (1995) 108–11. Mitchell (1971) 47–61 argues that Cicero believed as a lawyer that the *senatus consultum ultimum* authorized the consuls to take only those actions which the senate intended them to take so that Cicero was acting within the law in referring this matter to the senate. This theory ignores the basic reality that Cicero had no interest in the law as such; it was simply a means to be used in achieving political ends. His motivation in referring the matter to the senate was political, not legal. The naïveté of Mitchell's analysis is best demonstrated by his assertion that Sallust reported the actual text of Caesar's and Cato's speeches on 5 December. Mitchell (1971) 56–7.
17. See Drummond (1995) 80–113 for recognition that the debate on 5 December did not focus on legal arguments regarding the conspirators right to a trial, the impact of the declaration that they were *hostes* or the applicability of the *senatus consultum ultimum*; rather the key question in the debate was what action was in the best interest of the Republic.
18. It is likely that the others were members of Cicero's *consilium*. Wiseman (1985) 15.
19. Plut. *Cic.* 20; Cic. *Sull,* 34 and *Fam.* 5.13.
20. Plut. *Cic.* 20.
21. Plut. *Cic.* 20.
22. Sall. *Cat.* 48.
23. Sall. *Cat.* 48.
24. It does seem unlikely that one the greatest property owners in Rome would favour a group whose tactics involved starting fires which once lit could easily spread and destroy a large part of the city; on the other hand, Crassus had his own fire company and had made a great deal of money by buying buildings on fire on the cheap and

then having his fire company put out the fire before it caused considerable amount of damage, leaving him with the ownership of a valuable property purchased literally at fire sale prices. Plut. *Cras.* 2.4.
25. Sall. *Cat.* 48; Dio Cass. 37.35.
26. Plut. *Crass.* 7.
27. Sall. *Cat.* 48. Ramsey (2010) suggests that Sallust may be relying on a speech that Crassus made. However, the context clearly indicated that Crassus was speaking directly to Sallust. If the remarks had been made in a speech, Sallust would simply have recorded that fact and not have emphasized his personal knowledge of Crassus' statement.
28. Dio Cass. 39.10.3.
29. Dio Cass. 39.10.3 claims that Cicero delivered the text of this work to his son with the injunction that it not be published until after Cicero's death. There are differing titles ascribed to this work because it was never formally published.
30. Asc. 93.
31. Plut. *Caes.* 8. Suet. *Iul.* 17.
32. Plut. Crass. 13:3–4.
33. Cic. *Off.* 3. 73 stated with respect to Crassus. 'I do not hate the other [Crassus] now that he is dead.' Plut. *Crass.* 13.4 records the enmity between the two men. See Marshall (1976) 173–5.
34. Sall. *Cat.* 49. Plut. *Cic.* 20 indicates that some believed Caesar was involved in the conspiracy, but Cicero was unable to find evidence against him while others felt that Cicero had the evidence but did not use it in fear that accusing Caesar of complicity would result not in Caesar's conviction but in the acquittal of the conspirators. Plutarch's account reflects an anachronistic approach which assigns greater importance to Caesar in this period than is warranted.
35. Dio Cass. 36.36a; Plut. *Pomp.* 25. See Cic. *Leg. Man.* 51 for the high regard with which Catulus was held.
36. Drummond (1995) 20 suggests this story should be regarded with scepticism.
37. Syme (1964) 104–5.
38. Epstein (1987) 69–74.
39. Sall. *Cat.* 50; Cic. *Cat.* 4.17; Dio Cass. 37.35.
40. Dio Cass. 37.35. Although Dio does not so state, it seems logical that the only citizens the *praetors* would have enlisted for temporary military service would have been veterans.
41. App. *B Civ.* 2.5.
42. Dio Cass. 37.35 Cic. *Att.* 12. 21. See Cic. *Att.* 2. 1 for the date.
43. Cic. *Phil.* 12. 16.
44. Cic. *Att.* 2.1. Atticus eschewed involvement in public affairs. Nep. *Att.* 6.
45. Ramsey (2010) 181. Plut. *Cat. Min.* 23 wrote that the proceedings were taken down by scribes who knew shorthand. This story is not credible for three reasons. One, Cicero would have had no reason to change the procedure of 3 December, which involved having eminent senators take down the proceedings, guaranteeing by their eminence the accuracy of the transcription. Two, normally non-senators were not allowed to listen to the deliberations it seems unlikely that mere scribes would have been permitted to attend this most important meeting of the senate. Three, it seems that true shorthand was not used until the early days of the Empire. Alexander (2002) 18.

46. Sall. *Cat.* 50.
47. Drummond (1995) 97–98.
48. Plut. *Cato Min.* 23.
49. Aul. Gell. 14. 7. See M. Jehne (2016) 192. I
50. Ramsey (2010) 191.
51. Furius was identified by Cic. *Cat* 3.14 as a Sullan colonist from Faesulae and may very well be the individual who commanded one of Catiline's wings in the battle of Pistoria. See Sall. *Cat.* 59.3.
52. Sall. *Cat.* 50; Plut. *Cato Min.* 22. Cic. *Cat.* 4.7 mentions only Silanus' proposal that the five captured conspirators should be put to death. It is likely that Cicero had consulted with all the *consulares* before the meeting and obtained their consensus that the conspirators should be put to death.
53. Ramsey (2010) 191.
54. Cic. *Att.* 12. 21. This list is more accurate than the list that Cicero gave in *Phil.* 2 12 which includes Crassus and Hortensius but omits Poplicola and Torquatus. It is possible, however, that the listing of Hortensius in *Phil.* 2.12 corrects a mistake an omission in Cicero's letter to Atticus and that Hortensius was present for the great debate.
55. Cic. *Cat.* 4. 10–11 notes the absåence of Crassus and points out that Crassus had voted only two days before to take the conspirators into custody and had voted Cicero a thanksgiving and that on the day before Crassus had voted to provide rewards to the informants. Con. Drummond (1995) 14–15 who suggests unconvincingly that the senator who was absent is one of the two anti-Ciceronian tribunes-elect (Nepos or Bestia).
56. Sall. *Cat.* 50.
57. Suet. *Iul.* 10 and 13.
58. Plut. *Cic.* 20.
59. Suet. *Iul.* 60.
60. Suet. *Iul.* 13.
61. Sall. *Cat.* 51; Cic. *Cat.* 4. 7–8; Plut. *Caes.* 7, *Cato Min.* 22 and *Cic.* 21; Suet. *Iul*, 14.1. Accord: Dio Cass. 37.36 except that Dio adds that the proposal included a provision that if any Italian city which permitted a conspirator to escape would be considered at war with Rome. It is likely that Sallust's version of Caesar's speech is much more philosophical and intellectual in nature than the real version.
62. Cic. *Cat.* 4. 7.
63. Gruen (1974) 281.
64. Plut. *Cic.* 21 and *Caes.* 7 and App. *B Civ.* 2. 6 both claim that Caesar's proposal was to keep the conspirators in prison until Catiline's defeat at which point they would be tried. Even if Caesar's ostensible proposal had been for lifetime imprisonment, it would not have been practical to keep the conspirators under guard for the rest of their lives; accordingly, if they were not put to death, they would have ended up being tried for their crimes.
65. Suet. *Iul.* 14; Dio Cass. 37.36; App. *B Civ.* 2.6; Plut. *Cato Min.* 22; *Caes.* 8, *Cic.* 20–21.
66. Cic. *Att.* 12. 21 in which Cicero complains about Brutus' treatment of the debate in an account that Brutus has written.
67. On the other hand, Dio Cass. 37.35 claims that Cicero by exciting and terrifying the members of the senate persuaded them to endorse the death penalty for the conspirators.

68. Drummond (1995) 45.
69. Lintott (2008) 17.
70. Stockton (1971) 135.
71. Sall. *Cat.* 53. Indeed, Sallust writes what is in effect a eulogy for each of these men in *Cat.* 54.
72. Drummond (1995) 51 suggests that the debate is a Roman version of Thucydides 3.36–49 dealing with the fate of the citizens of Mytilene.
73. Cic. *Pis.* 11, 15–16 and 23; *Mil.* 17; *Dom.* 72, 75; *Ses.* 28, 95.
74. Cic. *Cat.* 4.20. Van Dyck (2008) 235 contends that this passage could not have been added after Cicero's exile in 58 because the addition of Cicero's consular speeches was published in 60. However, there was nothing to prevent Cicero from making additional changes after the publication of the consular speeches in 60 particularly since at some points the speeches were published separately. Van Dyck (2008) 10. On the other hand, Cicero may have been quite prescient in foreseeing future attacks on his conduct.
75. Cic. *Cat.* 4. 23. See Van Dyck (2008) 238.
76. Sall. *Cat.* 50. Con. Dio Cass. 37.36 who says that all who spoke before Cato endorsed Caesar's proposal and App. *B. Civ.* 2.5 who says that T. Nero spoke before Caesar – a clear mistake in chronology.
77. Suet. *Iul.* 14.
78. Sall. *Cat.* 50.
79. Plut. *Cato Min.* 22.
80. Plut. *Caes.* 8 and *Cic.*21; *Cic. Att.* 12.21.
81. Sall. *Cat.* 52.
82. Sall. *Cat.* 53 and Vellius Paterculus 2.35.3–4 See Plut. *Cato Min.* 24 for a claim that Cato denounced Caesar as a friend of the conspirators and abused Silanus for changing his opinion.
83. Vel. Pate. 2.35.4
84. Plut. *Cato Min.* 24; Plut. *Brut.* 5.
85. Plut. *Cato Min.* 6.
86. Plut. *Cic.* 21. Sall. *Cat.* 52. Drummond (1995) 53–56 suggests that Sallust shows Cato using demagogic tactics in his effort to rally the senators.
87. Plut. *Cic.* 21.
88. Dio Cass, 37.36; Suet. *Iul.* 14.
89. Plut. *Cic.* 21.
90. Plut. *Cic.* 21. Cicero in later years wrote Atticus that it was Cato's motion that was voted on by the senate. Cic. *Att.* 12. 21.
91. Cic. *Att.* 12.21.
92. Sall. *Cat.* 53; Cic. *Att.* 12. 21; Plut. *Cato Min.* 23 and Dio Cass. 37.36 all say that Cato's motion was for execution of the conspirators only and do not indicate that it proposed the confiscation of their property.
93. Ampelius, *liber memorialis.* 31.
94. Plut. *Caes.* 8.
95. Plut. *Caes.* 8.
96. Plut. *Caes.* 8. Sall. *Cat.* 49 dates this incident as occurring on 4 December. It may be that Sallust's dating was designed to avoid ascribing any events other than the senate debate to 5 December and thus detract from his description of Caesar and Cato as each rose to prominence on that day. Suet. *Iul.* 14, consistent with Plutarch, dates the

incident as occurring on 5 December and states that the guards threatened Caesar in an effort to keep him from filibustering Cato's motion.
97. Sall. *Cat.* 55.
98. Plut. *Cic.* 22.
99. Sall. *Cat.* 55.
100. Cic. *Phill.* 2.17–18. See Van Der Blom (2003) 296.
101. Plut. *Cic.* 22; App. *B Civ.* 2. 6.
102. Plut. *Cic.* 22.
103. In 62, Cicero, *Att.* 1.14 proudly informed Atticus that Crassus had made a great speech in the senate stating that 'he owed it to me that he was still a senator, a citizen, nay, a free man; and that he never beheld wife, home, or country without beholding the fruits of my conduct.' Cicero may have been totally oblivious both to the sarcasm involved in Crassus' extravagant endorsement and also to Crassus' motivation which was to embarrass Pompey, the previous speaker, who had made only an oblique acknowledgment of Cicero's accomplishments. See Lintott (2008) 156. Keeline (2018) 296 suggest that Cicero was making fun of Crassus for the latter's bombastic style and possibly making a sly dig at his own bombastic descriptions of his consulship. While Cicero had good sense of humour which he used to great effect in some of his speeches for defendants, he had almost no ability to see any humour in his own actions; accordingly Keeline's hypothesis is unlikely.
104. Dio Cas. 37.36.
105. Pseudo Sallust, *In Ciceronem*, 2. Of course, Roman officials had no offices in which they could conduct official business so Cicero and others had to use their own homes for governmental purposes. Keeline (2018) 154–64 claims that all of these charges were false and that they were made by members of an anti-Ciceronian school in the Principate.
106. Plut. *Caes.* 8. Suet. *Iul.* 14 claims that Caesar did not attend the senate between 5 December and the start of the next year. However, Plutarch clearly dates this incident as occurring in late December 62.
107. App. *Mith.* 14.94. For the relationship between Nepos, Mucia and Pompey see Marshall (1976) 95.
108. Plut. *Cato. Min.* 20–21.
109. Cic. *Fam.* 2. 2.
110. Cic. *Ses.* 11.
111. Cic, *Ses.* 12.
112. Plut. *Cic.* 23.
113. Dio Cass. 37.38.
115. Cic. *Fam* 2.2.
114. Sall, *Cat.* 57.
115. Cic. *Fam.* 5.1 and 5.2; *Pis.* 6.
116. Dio Cass. 37.42.
117. See Cic. *Fam.* 5. 2.8 for the date. Dio Cass. 37.43. Summers (1963) speculates that Nepos may have heard from his brother, Celer, that he was about to engage Catiline's forces and tried to push through the proposal before Catiline's defeat. Plut. *Cic.* 23 improbably claims that Nepos had changed the rationale of the proposal to claim that that Pompey should be recalled to save the Republic from Cicero's tyranny. Asides from the absurdity of this charge, Catiline had not been defeated as of that date so there was no need to change the rationale for the Pompey recall bill.

186   Catiline: Rebel of the Roman Republic

118. Dio Cass. 37.43. Plut. *Cat. Min.* 26–28; Cic. *Ses.* 62.
119. Dio Cass. 37.43. A by- product of this development was the temporary silencing of Caesar. On 1 January 62 upon entering into his office as *praetor*, Caesar charged Catulus who had been in charge of the rebuilding of the temple of Jupiter with embezzling the funds for such a project. In an effort to curry favour with Pompey, Caesar had moved that the assignment be given to Pompey and that Pompey's name- not Catulus'- should be inscribed on the temple. Caesar ended up withdrawing the proposal in the face of strenuous opposition from the *optimates*. After Nepos' defeat, the senate suspended Caesar from his office as *praetor* whereupon Caesar isolated himself in his mansion. Dio Cass. 37.44. Suet. *Iul.* 16. According to Suet. *Iul.* 16 a crowd gathered around Caesar's home and offered to restore him forcibly to the *praetor*'s tribunal; Caesar however refused the offer and ultimately the senate permitted him to assume his office.
120. Plut. *Cic.* 23. Cic. *Pis.,* 3 says that Catulus gave him this title.

Chapter 9
1. Dio Cass. 37.39 states that Antonius and Celer had been besieging Faesulae. It is possible that Antonius may have seized Faesulae, but it seems unlikely that he had to besiege it. Metellus Celer was on the other side of the Apennines and in no position to attack Faesulae.
2. Sall. *Cat.* 56.4 contains a statement that Catiline was waiting for the conspirators to break out of Rome and add to his force. This statement reflects the conspirators' cover story and not the real plan to attack the city from both outside and inside.
3. Sall. *Cat.* 56. Con. Dio. Cass. 37.22 and App. B. Civ. 2.2 who plausibly state that some may have joined Catiline's army.
4. Sall. *Cat.* 57; Dio. Cass. 37.40; Plut. *Cic.* 22.8
5. Dio Cass. 37.40.
6. Sall. *Cat.* 57.
7. Dio Cass. 37.47.
8. Sall. *Cat.* 57. While Sallust suggests that Catiline was planning to use back routes all the way, it is far more probable that he planned follow the Via Cassia to the neighbourhood of Genoa, since that was the fastest way to get to Gaul. If he desired secrecy rather than speed, he might have stayed in the Apennines and marched north through them. However, this course would have been difficult because of the condition of the roads, the winter weather and the lack of supplies.
9. Sumner (1963) 216.
10. Sumner (1963) 16–217. Summer has Catiline descending on the east side of the Apennines, finding his descent blocked by Celer and then recrossing the Apennines to the west side and descending to Pistoria, apparently with Celer in pursuit. This account is inconsistent with Sallust's account and inherently improbable; no one trying to go to Transalpine Gaul would march east over the Apennines when Transalpine Gaul lay in the opposite direction.
11. Cic. *Ses.* 12.
12. Sall. *Cat.* 57–58. For the date, see Dio Cass. 37.39 and Liv. *Per.* 103. Catiline could not have descended from the mountains using the normal road because Celer was blocking such a movement.
13. Sall. *Cat.* 59.
14. Sall. *Cat.* 59.

15. https://it.wikipedia.org/wiki/Campo_Tizzoro
16. Sall. *Cat.* 58 has Catiline making a lengthy speech to his men. The reality is that no general ever made speeches to his army before battle. Even assuming that the general did not have better things to do, there is no way that more than a few dozen men could any speech he gave even if they cared to listen. A more realistic picture of what a general would do before the start of a battle is seen in the movie *Gettysburg* in which Pickett, prior to making his famous charge, rides up and down in front of his infantry, shouting a few words of encouragement to each brigade. See Hansen (1993) 161–180. For a defence of the romantic but unrealistic tradition of speeches to an army, see Pritchard (1994) 95–115.
17. For references to Marius' eagle, see Cic. *Cat.* 1.24 and *Cat.* 2.13. It is ironic that Catiline, a *Sullani* to the core, carried a standard used by Sulla's greatest enemy-Marius.
18. Sall. *Cat.* 59.
19. Sall. *Cat.* 59 has that Petreius begging his men to remember that they were defending their children, their altars, their hearths and their county against a group of poorly armed bandits. Again, this speech is imaginary.
20. This means that Petreius gave no quarter (Waters (1970) 215) and put all the wounded to sword.
21. Sall. *Cat.* 60–61. *Sed ubi omnibus rebus exploratis Petreius tuba signum dat, cohortis paulatim incedere iubet; idem facit hostium exercitus. Postquam eo ventum est, unde a ferentariis proelium conmitti posset, maxumo clamore cum infestis signis concurrunt: pila omittunt, gladiis res geritur. Veterani pristinae virtutis memores comminus acriter instare, illi haud timidi resistunt: maxuma vi certatur. Interea Catilina cum expeditis in prima acie vorsari, laborantibus succurrere, integros pro sauciis arcessere, omnia providere, multum ipse pugnare, saepe hostem ferire: strenui militis et boni imperatoris officia simul exsequebatur. Petreius ubi videt Catilinam, contra ac ratus erat, magna vi tendere, cohortem praetoriam in medios hostis inducit eosque perturbatos atque alios alibi resistentis interficit. Deinde utrimque ex lateribus ceteros aggreditur. Manlius et Faesulanus in primis pugnantes cadunt. Catilina postquam fusas copias seque cum paucis relictum videt, memor generis atque pristinae suae dignitatis in confertissumos hostis incurrit ibique pugnans confoditur. Sed confecto proelio tum vero cerneres, quanta audacia quantaque animi vis fuisset in exercitu Catilinae. Nam fere quem quisque vivus pugnando locum ceperat, eum amissa anima corpore tegebat. Pauci autem, quos medios cohors praetoria disiecerat, paulo divorsius, sed omnes tamen advorsis volneribus conciderant. Catilina vero longe a suis inter hostium cadavera repertus est paululum etiam spirans ferociamque animi, quam habuerat vivus, in voltu retinens. Postremo ex omni copia neque in proelio neque in fuga quisquam civis ingenuus captus est: ita cuncti suae hostiumque vitae iuxta pepercerant. Neque tamen exercitus populi Romani laetam aut incruentam victoriam adeptus erat; nam strenuissumus quisque aut occiderat in proelio aut graviter volneratus discesserat. Multi autem, qui e castris visundi aut spoliandi gratia processerant, volventes hostilia cadavera amicum alii, pars hospitem aut cognatum reperiebant; fuere item, qui inimicos suos cognoscerent. Ita varie per omnem exercitum laetitia, maeror, luctus atque gaudia agitabantur.*
22. Val. Max 2.8.7.
23. Dio Cass. 37.40; Julius Obsequens (Livy) frag. 61a. Dio Cassius states that Antonius had no right to the title of *imperator* because the number slain fell below the number required for this title. Antonius' right to the title was further questionable because he had won a victory not over alien foes but over his own countrymen.

24. Dio Cass. 37.40.
25. Crawford (1974) 705.
26. Cic. *Sull.* 6–7, 71; *Flac.* 9; Psuedo Sall. *in Cic.* 2.3; Cic. *Cael.* 70 indicates, however, Caelius was prosecuted not under the *Lex Plautia de vi* (force) but under the earlier *Lex Lutatia de vi*.
27. Cic. *Sull.* 21.
28. Plut. *Cic.* 26.
29. Dio. Cass. 37.41. Vettius may betrayed the conspirators in Paelignum. Oros. 6.6.
30. Ryan (1995) 151–6 identifies L. Novius Niger as an urban *quaestor* that year and who was logically assigned the task of investigating the conspirators. Niger was elected a tribune of the people several years later.
31. Suet. *Iul.* 17 names Niger as the individual who received Vettius' list.
32. CIL I (2) 709 = ILS 8888; Syme (2016) 114.
33. Sall. *Hist.* 55. 17. (Speech of Lepidus)
34. Dio. Cass. 37.41
35. Oros. 6.6.7.
36. Suet. *Iul.* 17; Dio Cass. 37.41. Niger, as *quaestor*, was inferior to Caesar, as a *praetor*. In *Att.* 2. 24, Cicero refers to '*Vettius ille, ille noster index*' (that Vettius, our informer) which could mean that Vettius had acquired a reputation as an informer from the events in 63–2; it could also mean that Vettius was Cicero's agent during this period and that his attack on Caesar was at Cicero's instigation. McDermott (1949) 351–367 suggests that Vettius was working for Caesar during the period 63–59 and that he denounced him in 62 to give Caesar an opportunity to clear himself of any involvement in the Catilinarian conspiracy. This theory may be too clever by half; in reality people do not normally engage in such convoluted manoeuvres because the possibility of their backfiring is too great. In addition, Caesar was responsible for Vettius receiving a severe punishment. In 59, Vettius – allegedly at Caesar's instigation – circulated a story that C. Scribonius Curio and some young *optimates* were planning to murder Pompey. His story was not believed by the senate and he was thrown into prison. He was released the next day by Caesar and brought into the senate to speak from the rostrum which he used to denounce a number of older *optimates* as participants in this alleged plot (while omitting the younger *optimates* whom he had previously named). Cic. *Att.* 2.24. He was then recommitted to prison where he was murdered. McDermott (1949) 351–367 gives an interesting account of Vettius' murder. Taylor (1950) 45–51 contends that Vettius was acting at the instigation of Caesar in order to stop Curio's attacks on Caesar's henchmen. Ward (1977) 237–244 contends that Vettius was acting at the instigation of Pompey. It is certainly questionable if there was any plot to murder Pompey. Ironically, Cicero bought a Tusculum mansion formerly owned by Q. Lutatius Catulus the elder who had obtained it from a certain Vettius. Treggiari (2007) 51, n. 68. It would be interesting if the seller was '*vettius ille, ille noster index.*'
37. Dio Cass 37.41 dates these events as occurring after January 62.
38. Cic. *Sull.* 51.
39. MacDonald (1977) 307; Cic. Sull. 2.
40. MacDonald (1977) 308–9.
41. Cic. *Fam.* 5:7; Habicht (1990) 39–40.
42. MacDonald (1977) 309.
43. Gell. 12. 2.

44. Cic, *Sull.* 40.
45. Cic. *Sull.* 36–39. Cicero's account improbably credits the Gauls with an extremely sophisticated knowledge of recent Roman political history and political alliances. While the conspirator Cassius said that he did not know for certain whether Sulla was a member of the conspiracy or not, (Cic. Sull. 36) he may have spoken the literal truth, but his statement does not mean that Sulla had not been in contact with the conspirators and was merely biding his time to join the conspiracy if it succeeded. Alexander (2002) 193.
46. Cic. *Sull.* 40.
47. Cic. *Sull.* 42–45.
48. MacDonald (1977) 302–312. However, it seems unlikely that Cicero would have defended Sulla had he believed the latter had been an ardent Catilinarian. Alexander (2002) 204–205.
49. Gabba (1961) 89–96.
50. See Morrell (2010) 142–144 for an account of the circumstances leading to this trial and for a discussion of the considerable disagreement between scholars as to the exact charge brought against Antonius.
51. Dio Cass. 38.10. In 60, Cicero defended Flaccus (one of the *praetors* at the Mulvian Bridge) from an accurate charge of extortion in connection with Flaccus' governance of Asia. Morrell (2010) 145–146.
52. Dio Cass. 38.10; Cic. *Flac.* 5.
53. Cic. *Flac.* 95.
54. Dio Cas. 38.41.
55. Oros. 6.6.
56. Suet. *Aug.* 3.
57. Cic. *Plan.* 98.
58. See Stewart (1995) 62–65 for recognition of the prompt and effective actions the government took to deal with the Catilinarians.
59. Ramsey (2007) 142.
60. Yaketz (1963) 485–499.
61. Shakespeare (*MacBeth*, 1606) V, ii, 13–14.

Chapter 10

1. Primary sources are contemporaneous sources whose access to information about Catiline and his fellow conspirators was obviously greater than that of secondary sources, who wrote decades – and sometimes centuries – after the events in question.
2. Batstone (2010) xxi.
3. See Keeline (2018) 187, n. 97 and 310–311 for critical comments on Cicero's poetry by ancient authors such as Tacitus, Dio Cassius, Pliny, Martial and Juvenal.
4. Keeline (2018) 102–146, 199–200; Contra: Millar (1964) 46 who contends that most Imperial writers were hostile to Cicero.
5. Plut. *Cic.* 49.3–4. Keeline (2018) 102–18.
6. La Bua (2019) 106–112.; Wibier (2016) 101–102.
7. Keeline (2018) 2, 13–101; La Bua (2019) 125–162.
8. Keeline (2018) 3. La Bua (2019) 22–26. See Cic. *Att.* 2.1.3; *Brut.* 123.
9. Keeline (2018) 16, 25; La Bua (2019) 219–298.
10. Keeline (2018) 196–334.
11. Keeline (2018) 338–340.

12. Asc. 83; Dio Cass. 39.10. Dio claims that Cicero wrote this book in order to defend his policies and actions and to denounce Crassus, Caesar and others. Cic. *Att.* 2. 6 states that that the book was a secret history and Cic. *Att.* 14.17 implied that it contains attacks on Caesar. Rawson (1982) 121–4 contends that this book was meant as a serious history and not a political tract because it was being written for the benefit of Cicero's friend, T. Atticus, who was scrupulously honest. Accordingly, she questions whether it contained scandalous attacks on Crassus and Caesar. However, Cicero, more than most men, had an ability to convince himself that his opponents were evil and to reformulate the past to reflect his later views and positions. Accordingly, there is nothing inconsistent with Cicero's effort to write an honest account of his consulship and his inclusion of fabricated charges against Crassus and Caesar. Cicero had a great ability to believe his own lies.
13. Vell. Pat. 2. 16. 3.
14. CIL I (2) 709 = ILS 8888.
15. Asc. 92.
16. References in the text to the conspiracy, or the Catilinarian conspiracy, are all to the 'second' or 'real' conspiracy.
17. See Ramsey (2007) 8.
18. Syme (1939) 149–52; (1964) 84; Kaplan (1968) 2–3; Hutchinson (1966) 31–32. See Gruen (1968) passim for the general politicization of the criminal court system.
19. Cic. *Cat.* 2. 7.
20. Cic. *Cae.* 12–14. If Catiline's evil characteristics were so prominent, how did he almost fool Cicero?
21. Cic. *Off.* 78–85.
22. Keeline (2018) 152.
23. Plut. *Cic.* 24. (translation E. Thayer) As Seneca pointed out, Cicero praised his consulship *non sine causa, sed sine fine* (not without cause but without end). *Brev. vit.* 5.2. There are some who claim that it was improbable that Cicero kept on boasting about his consulship throughout his career. See Shackleton Bailey (1980) 13. However, this claim is inconsistent with Cicero's self-serving letter to Lucceius begging Lucceius to write a eulogistic account of Cicero's consulship. Cic. *Fam.* 5.1.
24. Cic. *Att.* 2.1. In this letter, Cicero listed his consular speeches which included the Catilinarian orations that he had revised. His list did not include the *Pro Murena* delivered during his consulship because Cicero made this speech in a private capacity. D. Berry (2008) has suggested that the *Pro Murena* had been published earlier. Cic. *Att.* 1. 13 writes of revising his speeches after delivery as though this was his normal practice. Phillips (1998) 108 argues that Cicero published the Catilinarians shortly after their delivery and did not revise them on the second publication because he did not deal with the logical flaws in the *First Catilinarian*. Phillips is correct is pointing out that there are logical inconsistencies in the *First Catilinarian* between Cicero's urging Catiline to leave the city and his refusing to order Catiline to leave or between his invocation of the murder of the Gracchi and his disavowal of any intent to order Catiline's execution. However, these inconsistencies reflect the substantive inconsistencies in Cicero's position at that time; they could not be eliminated without rewriting the substance of the entire speech. Thus, the continued existence of these inconsistencies does not prove that Cicero did not revise the *First Catilinarian*. Our version of the *First Catilinarian* is such a polished and brilliant speech that it cannot be a word for word copy of the extemporaneous speech that Cicero delivered.

25. Political concerns seemed to have permeated the revisions of the *Fourth Catilinarian*. See Berry (2006) 152–3; Lintott (2008) 217.
26. Drummond (1995) 11–12.
27. Plin. *Ep.* 1. 20.8. However, Alexander (2002) 20 questions the validity of Pliny's claim.
28. See Lintott (2008) *passim*.
29. Arena (2012) 211 has suggested that Cicero may have been sent into exile because of the falsification of the records of the senate proceeding on December 3. This theory is not supported by the ancient sources.
30. Pobjoy (2010) 51–62.
31. CIL I (2) 709 = ILS 8888.
32. Culham (1989) 100–15.
33. Culham (1989) 104–5. Cic. *Sull.* 34.
34. Suet. *Iul.* 20.
35. Cic. *Fam.* 5. 1.
36. See Cic. *Fam.* 3. 7
37. Lintott (2008) 4.
38. Cic. *Att.* 1.1.
39. Cic. *Att.* 1.2.
40. Quoted on the cover of Freeman (2012).
41. Tatum (2018) 64.
42. Sall. *Cat.* 4.2.
43. Q. Cic. *Comment. Pet.* 9–10.
44. Q. Cic. *Comment. Pet.* 52 translated Freeman (2012).
45. Richardson (1971) 436–437 lists a number of articles dealing with the authorship of the *Commentariolum Petitionis* which claim that the work was not written by Q. Cicero, but rather by some Augustan author. However, Tatum (2018) 68 who is the most recent and thorough scholar to deal with this work believes that it was written by Q. Cicero. Alexander (2009) has claimed unconvincingly that the work is an ironic attack on historical views of Roman electioneering. See Tatum (2018) 71–73 for a criticism of Alexander's theory.
46. Tatum (2018) 68.
47. Periano (2012) 25–28.
48. Periano (2012) 47–53.
49. Q. Cic. *Comment. Pet.* 47.
50. Freeman (2012) x–xl.
51. Syme (1964) 71; for an extreme claim of Sallust's personal knowledge of the actors, see Levick's suggestion (2015) 113 that Sallust knew Pompey, Cicero and perhaps even Catiline.
52. Sall. *Cat.* 53.
53. Sall. *Cat.* 48.
54. Syme (1964) 73. Woodman (2007) xxi, xxxvi (n. 20) declares that Sallust was thoroughly familiar with Cicero's Catilinarian Orations as well as Cicero's other speeches and cites dozens of examples of Sallust's use of words and phrases from Cicero's Orations.
55. Lewis (1988) 31–42.
56. Sall. *Cat.* 47.5.

57. Treggiari (2007) 149–150. Indeed, Sallust tends to downplay the significance of Cicero's role in defeating the conspiracy.
58. Sall. *Cat.* 4.
59. Woodman (1988) 73–74.
60. Sallust fell into disgrace because he committed extortion when he was governor of Africa in 46. Dio Cass. 38:9.
61. Sall. *Cat.* 5. See Batstone (2010) xxi.
62. Syme (1964) 66–69. See in particular Sal. *Cat.* 1–4 and 5.9–13.
63. Sall. *Cat.* 5.
64. Sall. *Cat.* 18.
65. Sall. *Cat.* 17.
66. Woodman (2021) 55–68.
67. Plut. *Cato Min.* 23.
68. Batstone (2010) xxi.
69. Sall. *Cat.* 22.
70. Sall. *Cat.* 14.
71. Batstone (2010) xxi.
72. Sall. *Cat.* 5.
73. See Sall. *Cat.* 37 for one such slanted description.
74. Sall. *Cat.* 31.
75. Sall. *Cat.* 53.
76. Syme (1964) 136.
77. Sacks (1990) 6–7.
78. Sacks (1990) 179.
79. Sacks (1990) 169.
80. Millar (1964) 28.
81. Dix (1994) 282–96.
82. Pelling (2002) 21.
83. Pelling (2002) 20–2.
84. Pelling (2002) 24.
85. Lushkov (2018) 30–46
86. Liv. *AUC* 1.2.
87. Millar (1964) 32–38.
88. Lushkov (2108) 36.
89. Squires (1990) vii.
90. Jer. *Chron.* at 76 A.D. Marshall (1985) 26.
91. Marshall (1985) 43–4. See Asc. 69 where the writer says, 'My sons, your age makes it necessary for me to explain what dividing to take a vote means.' Keeline (2018) 16, n. 13 cites several other writers as supporting his view that Asconius' claim that he was writing the commentaries for his sons is a literary convention and that Asconius would not have produced such an extensively researched set of commentaries unless his work was designed for a larger audience than his sons. Keeline (2018) 38 makes the further point that Asconius would have recognized that a teacher of rhetoric could use his work as an outline for teaching the Ciceronian orations.
92. Marshall (1985b) 39–50, 284.
93. Marshall (1985b) 75.
94. Asc. 85.
95. Marshall (1985b) 62–75.

96. Stadter (2015) 2, 50, 70–81.
97. Often anecdotes reflect incidents involving others which are attributable to a historical figure because they presaged the historical figure's character. For example, in visiting the school room in Georgetown, Ohio that U.S. Grant had attended as a young boy, I noticed that there were several dozen accounts of incidents involving Grant as a young boy which foretold his great genius. These incidents could have involved boys other than Grant but were attributed to Grant to show that his genius was remarkable at an early age.
98. Plut. Cic. 25.
99. Pelling (2002) 142–162.
100. Morrell (2017) 16.
101. Stadter (2015) 83.
102. Stadter (2015) 83–87.
103. Winter (1997) 139.
104. Bowersock (1969) 112.
105. Pelling (2002) 46–7.
106. Pelling (2002) 53–55.
107. Wallace-Hadrill (1983) 78–86.
108. Baldwin (1983) 24–45.
109. Culham (1989) 107.
110. Baldwin (1983) 104–123; Wallace-Hadrill (1983) 21.
111. *HA, Had.*, 11.3.
112. Brennan (2018) 83–84.
113. Brennan (2018) 84.
114. Brennan (2018) 209.
115. Wallace-Hadrill (1983) 10, 18.
116. Power and Tristan (2014) 11, n. 4.
117. C. Lange and J. Madsen (2016) 3.
118. Millar (1964) 24.
119. Millar (1964) 32; See Westall (2016) 51–75 for Dio's use of sources besides Livy for the Civil Wars of 49–30.
120. Fomin (2016) 217–237.
121. Millar (1964) 46–55. For a somewhat more nuanced view of Dio's attitude to Cicero see Mallan (2016) 258–269.
122. Dio Cass. 36:43–44.
123. Millar (1964) 32.
124. Drummond (1995) 13 contends that Dio Cassius' account of the Catilinarian conspiracy reflects pro-Cicero bias.
125. Morrell (2017) 17.
126. Morrell (2017) 17.
127. Millar (1964) 34–38.
128. Levick (2015) 118.

Chapter 11

1. Levick (2015) 120.
2. Virg. *Aen.* 8.668
3. Juv. *Sat.*, 2: 25–8.
4. Juv. *Sat*, 8: 231–241.

> *quid, Catilina, tuis natalibus atque Cethegi*
> *inueniet quisquam sublimius? arma tamen uos*
> *nocturna et flammas domibus templisque paratis,*
> *ut bracatorum pueri Senonumque minores,*
> *ausi quod liceat tunica punire molesta*
> *sed uigilat consul uexillaque uestra coercet.*
>
> Translation by A.S. Kline.

5. Bolton and Gardner (1973) x1.
6. Ben Jonson (1611) III.
7. *The Works of Voltaire, A Contemporary Version*, IX, Part I.
8. *The Works of Voltaire: A Contemporary Version*, XI, Part 1, 226.
9. *The Oxford Ibsen*. Volume I. *Early Plays*.
10. Saylor (1993) 429 indicates that this novel was greatly influenced by his reading of Hutchinson (1966).
11. Harris (2006) 243–244.
12. Cic. *Cae.* 12–14. *Habuit enim ille, sicuti meminisse vos arbitror, permulta maximarum non expressa signa, sed adumbrata [lineamenta] virtutum. Utebatur hominibus improbis multis; et quidem optimis se viris deditum esse simulabat. Erant apud illum illecebrae libidinum multae; erant etiam industriae quidam stimuli ac laboris. Flagrabant vitia libidinis apud illum; vigebant etiam studia rei militaris. Neque ego umquam fuisse tale monstrum in terris ullum puto, tam ex contraris diversisque et inter se pugnantibus naturae studiis cupiditatibusque conflatum. Quis clarioribus viris quodam tempore iucundior, quis turpioribus coniunctior? quis civis meliorum partium aliquando, quis taetrior hostis huic civitati? quis in voluptatibus inquinatior, quis in laboribus patientior? quis in rapacitate avarior, quis in largitione effusior? Illa vero, iudices, in illo homine mirabilia fuerunt, comprehendere multos amicitia, tueri obsequio, cum omnibus communicare, quod habebat, servire temporibus suorum omnium pecunia, gratia, labore corporis, scelere etiam, si opus esset, et audacia, versare suam naturam et regere ad tempus atque huc et illuc torquere ac flectere, cum tristibus severe, cum remissis iucunde, cum senibus graviter, cum iuventute comiter, cum facinerosis audaciter, cum libidinosis luxuriose vivere. Hac ille tam varia multiplicique natura cum omnes omnibus ex terris homines improbos audacesque collegarat, tum etiam multos fortes viros et bonos specie quadam virtutis assimulatae tenebat. Neque umquam ex illo delendi huius imperii tam conscelaratus impetus exstitisset, nisi tot vitiorum tanta immanitas quibusdam facultatis et patientiae radicibus niteretur. Quare ista condicio, iudices, respuatur, nec Catilinae familiaritatis crimen haereat; est enim commune cum multis et cum quibusdam etiam bonis. Me ipsum, me, inquam, quondam paene ille decepit, cum et civis mihi bonus et optimi cuiusque cupidus et firmus amicus ac fidelis videretur; cuius ego facinora oculis prius quam opinione, manibus ante quam suspicione deprehendi. Cuius in magnis catervis amicorum si fuit etiam Caelius, magis est ut ipse moleste ferat errasse se, sicuti non numquam in eodem homine me quoque erroris mei paenitet, quam ut istius amicitiae crimen reformidet.*
13. Mommsen (1904); Odahl (1971) and (2010).
14. Bossier (1905); Beesly (1878); Hutchinson (1966); Kaplan (1968); F. Galassi (2014) The last is more cognizant of the self-serving aspects of Catiline's late adoption of some aspects of the *popularis* program. See also Yavetz (1963) 485–9.
15. Gruen (1974) 47.
16. Waters (1970) 195–215; Seager (1973) 240–8.
17. Plut. *Pomp.* 43.2.

18. See Levick (2015) 91–4.
19. Levick (2015) 92.
20. Levick (2015) 91–92.
21. Dio Cass. 37:42. Some modern historians have made the same point. See Yavetz (1963) 497; Waters (1970) 195; MacDonald (1977) 29–30.
22. Sampson (2019) 58–85 claims that the insurrection was in fact a second civil war, Lepidus' revolt being the first and Caesar's the third.

Bibliography

Alexander, Michael C. *Trials in the Late Roman Republic, 149 BC to 50 BC* (Toronto, University of Toronto Press, 1990).
—— 'The Role of Torquatus the Younger in the *Ambitus* Prosecution of Sulla in 66 B.C.' *Classical Philology* (1999) 94: 65–69.
—— *The Case for the Prosecution in the Ciceronian Era* (Ann Arbor, University of Michigan Press, 2002).
—— 'The *Commentariolum Petitionis* as an Attack on Election Campaigns' *Athenaeum* (2009) 97: 331–57; 369–395.
Allen, W. 'The Acting Governor of Ciasalpine Gaul in 63' *Classical Philology* (1953) 48: 176–155.
Altman, William H. F. 'Cicero and the Fourth Triumvirate: Gruen, Syme and Strasburger' in *Brill's Companion to the Reception of Cicero* (Leiden, Koninklijke Brill n.v. 2015).
Arena, V. *Libertas and the Practice of Politics in the Late Roman Republic* (Cambridge, Cambridge University Press, 2012).
Badian, 'The Early Career of A. Gabinius' *Philologus* (1956) 103: 87–99.
—— *Studies in Greek and Roman History* (Oxford, Basil Blackwell, 1964, reprinted 1968).
—— 'Notes on *Provincia Gallia in the Late Republic.*' *Melanges Piganiol* (1966) 2: 901–918.
—— 'Tiberius Gracchus and Beginning of the Roman Revolution' *AMRW* (1972) 1.1, 668–731.
—— 'The Consuls, 179–49 BC' *Chiron* (1990) 371–413.
Bailey, Shackleton. ed. and trans. *Cicero's Letters to Atticus* (Cambridge, Cambridge University Press, 1965).
—— ed. and trans. Valerius Maximus, *Memorable Doings and Sayings* (Cambridge, Harvard University Press, 2000).
Baldwin, Barry. *Suetonius* (Amsterdam, Adolf M. Hakkert, 1983).
Batstone, William. ed. '*Sallust: Catiline's Conspiracy, the Jugurthine War, Histories*' (Oxford, Oxford University Press, 2010).
Benson. J.M. 'Catiline and the Date of the Consular Elections in 63' *Studies in Latin Literature and Roman History* (1986) 4: 234–241.
Berry, D.H. ed. and trans. *Cicero: Political Speeches* (Oxford, Oxford University Press, 2006, paperback).
—— *Where are Cicero's Catilinarians?* (Speech Delivered at the Cicero Away Day, V in Edinburgh (June 2008).
Beesly, Edward Spencer. *Catiline, Clodius and Tiberius* (London, Chapman and Hall, 1878, reprinted paperback).
Blosel, Wolfgang. 'Provincial Commands and Money in the Late Republic' in *Money and Power in the Roman Republic*, ed. Hans Beck, Martin Jehne and John Serrati (Brussels, Latomus, 2016) 68–81.

Bolton, W.F. and Gardner, Jane F. ed. *Ben Jonson; Catiline* (Lincoln, University of Nebraska Press, 1973).
Bonner, Stanley F. *Education in Ancient Rome: From the Elder Cato to the Younger Pliny.* (Berkeley: Univ. of California Press, 1977).
Bossier, Gaston. *La Conjuration de Catilina* (Paris, Hachette, 1905).
Bowersock, G.W. *Greek Sophists in the Roman Empire* (Oxford, Oxford University Press, 1969).
Boyd, Barbara. 'Effeminata and Sallust's Sempronia' *TAPA* (1987) 117: 183–201.
Bradley, K.R. 'Slaves and the Conspiracy of Catiline' *Classical Philology* (1978) 73: 329–336.
Brennan, T. Corey *Sabina Augusta; An Imperial Journey* (Oxford, Oxford University Press, 2018).
Bringmann, Klaus. *A History of the Roman Republic* (Cambridge, Polity Press, 2002, 2013, paperback, translated W.J. Smyth).
Broughton, T.R.S. *The Magistrates of the Roman Republic* (New York: American Philological Association, 1952).
Brunt, P.A. 'Three Passages from Asconius' *Classical Review* (1957) 7: 193–195.
——— 'Amicitia in the Late Roman Republic' *Proceedings of the Cambridge Philological Society*, New Series, No. 11 (191) (1965) 1–20.
——— *Italian Manpower* (Oxford, Oxford University Press, 1971)
——— 'Nobilitas and Novitas' *Journal of Roman Studies* (1982) 72: 1–17.
——— *The Fall of the Roman Republic and Other Essays*, (Oxford, Oxford University Press, 1988).
Cadoux, T.J. 'Catiline and the Vestal Virgins' *Historia* (2005) 54: 162–179.
Carsten, C. and Madsen, J. 'Between History and Politics' in *Cassius Dio: Greek Intellectual and Roman Politician* ed. C. Carsten and J. Madsen (Leiden, Brill, 2016) 1–10.
Cichorius, C. 'Das Offizierkorps eines romainschen Heeres aud dem Bundesgenossenkriege' in *Romische Studien* (Leipzig-Berlin, B.G. Teubner, 1922).
Corpus Inscriptionum Latinarum (CIL)
Connolly, Joy. *The State of Speech* (Princeton, Princeton University Press, 2007).
Corbeill, Anthony. 'The Republican Body' in *A Companion to the Roman Republic* ed. Rosenstein, N. and Morstein-Marx, R. (Wiley-Blackwell, 2010) 439–456.
Cowell, F.R. *Cicero and the Roman Republic* (Baltimore, Penguin Books, 1967, 4th ed.).
Crane, T. 'Times of the Night in Cicero's First Catilinarian' (1966) *Classical Journal*, 61: 264–267.
Crawford, Jane W. *M. Tullius Cicero The Fragmentary Speeches* (Atlanta, Scholars Press, 1994).
Crawford, Michael H. *Roman Republican Coinage* (Cambridge, Cambridge University Press, 1974).
Culham, Phyllis. 'Archives and Alternatives in Republican Rome' *Classical Philology* (1989) 84: 100–115.
David, J.M. 'Rhetoric and Public Life' in *A Companion to the Roman Republic* ed. N. Rosenstein and R. Morstein-Marx (Wiley-Blackwell, 2010) 421–438.
Dahl, R. *Who Governs* (New Haven, Yale University Press, 2005, paperback).
Deniaux, E. 'Patronage, the Exchange of Favors, and Social Harmony' in *A Companion to the Roman Republic* ed. N. Rosenstein and R. Morstein-Marx (Wiley-Blackwell, 2010) 400–420.
Dix, T. Keith. '"Public Libraries" at Rome: Ideology and Reality' *Libraries and Culture* (1994) 29: 282–296.

Dolansky, Fanny. '*Togam Virilem Sumere:* Coming of Age in the Roman World' in *Roman Dress and the Fabrics of Roman Culture* ed. J. Edmondson and A. Keith (Toronto, University of Toronto Press, 2008) 47–80.
Drummond, Andrew. *Law, Politics and Power: Sallust and the Execution of the Catilinarian Conspirators* (Stuttgart, Steiner, 1995).
Dyson, Stephen L. *Rome: A Living Portrait of an Ancient City* (Baltimore, John Hopkins University Press, 2010).
Earl, Donald C. *The Political Thought of Sallust* (Cambridge, Cambridge University Press, 1961).
—— 'Appian B.C. I:14 and "*Professio*"' *Historia* (1965) 14: 325–332.
—— 'The Early Career of Sallust' *Historia* (1966) 15: 302–311.
Edmundson, Jonathan. 'Investing in Death' in *Money and Power in the Roman Republic*, ed. Beck, Hans; Jehne, Martin; and Serrati, John (Brussels, Latomus, 2016) 37–52.
Epstein, D.F. 'Cicero's Testimony at the *Bona Dea* Trial' Classical Philology (1986) 81: 229–235.
—— *Personal Enmity in Roman Politics, 218 -43 B.C.* (London, Croom Helm, 1987).
Evans, Richard J. 'Catiline's Wife' *Acta Classica* (1987) 30: 68–73.
Fomin, Andriy. 'Speeches in Cassio Dio' in *Cassius Dio: Greek Intellectual and Roman Politician*, ed. Lange, C. and Madsen, J. (Leiden, Brill, 2016) 217–237.
Forsythe, Gary. 'The Municipal Origin of the Catilinarian T. Volturcius' *American Journal of Philology* (1992) 113: 407–312.
Frederiksen, M.W. 'Caesar, Cicero and the Problem of Debt' *Journal of Roman Studies* (1966) 56: 128–141.
Freeman, P. ed. and trans. *Q. Cicero's Commentariolum Petitionis (*Princeton, Princeton University Press, 2012).
Frisch, H. 'The First Catilinarian Conspiracy' *Classical and Medieval Studies* (1947) 9: 10–36.
Gabba, E. 'Cicerone e la falsificazione dei senatoconsulti' *Studi Classice e Orientali* (1961) 10: 89–96.
Gejrot, C. 'The Letter from Lentulus' *Eranos* (2005) 103: 21–25.
Gelzer, Matthias. 'Sergius' *Realencyclopodie*, II A 2 ed. Pauly-Wissowa (1923) 1693–1711.
—— *The Roman Nobility* (Oxford: Basil Blackwell, 1969, trans. Robin Seager).
Giovannini, A. '*Catilina et la problem de dettes*' in *Leaders and Masses in the Roman World: Studies in Honor of Zvi Yavet*, ed. Malin, I. and Rubinsohn, Z.W. (Leiden, Brill, 1995).
Galassi, Francis. *Catiline: The Monster of Rome: An Ancient Case of Political Assassination* (Yardley, Westhome, 2014).
Graves, Robert. ed. and trans. *Suetonius: The Twelve Caesars*, (Baltimore, Penguin Books, 1957).
Greenhalgh, P.A.L. *Pompey: The Republican Prince* (Worthing, Littlehampton Book Services, 1981).
Gruen, Erich S. *Roman Politics and the Criminal Courts, 149–78 B.C.* (Cambridge, Harvard University Press, 1968).
—— 'Notes on the First Catilinarian Conspiracy' *Classical Philology* (1969) 64: 20–24.
—— *The Last Generation of the Roman Republic* (Berkeley, University of California Press, 1974).
—— 'Cicero: *Pro Sulla* 68 and Catiline's Candidacy in 66 BC' *Harvard Studies in Philology* (1982) 86: 121–131.
Gwatkin, Jr. W. E. 'Cicero *in Catilinam* 1, 19–Catiline's Attempt to Place Himself in *Libera Custodia*' TAPA (1934) 65: 271–281.

Habicht, Christian. *Cicero the Politician* (Baltimore, John Hopkins University Press, 1990).
Hansen, M.H. 'The Battle Exhortation in Ancient Historiography' *Historia* (1993) 42: 161–180.
Harders, Ann-Cathrin. 'Let Us Join Our Hearts The Role and Meaning of Constructing Kinship And Friendship in Republican Rome' in *De Amicitia: Friendship and Social Networks in Antiquity and the Middle Ages*, ed. Katarina Mustakallio; Christian Krötzl (Roma: Institutum Romanum Finlandiae, 2010) 33–47.
Hardy, E. G. 'The Catilinarian Conspiracy- a re-study of the evidence' *Journal of Roman Studies* (1917) 7: 153–228.
—— *The Catilinarian Conspiracy in its Context: A Restudy of the Evidence* (Oxford, Blackwell, 1924) (a).
—— *Some Problems in Roman History* (Oxford, Clarendon Press, 1924) (b).
Harris, W.V. *Rome in Etruria and Umbria* (Oxford, Oxford University Press, 1971).
Harrison, Ian. 'Catiline, Clodius and Popular Politics at Rome during the 60's and 50's' *Bulletin of the Institute of Classical Studies* (2008) 51:95–118.
Harvey, P. 'The Sullan Colony of Praeneste' *Athenaeum* (1975) 53: 33 et seq.
Heaton, John W. *Mob Violence in the Late Roman Republic, 133–49 B.C.* (Urbana, University of Illinois Press, 1939).
Herlihy, David. *Medieval and Renaissance Pistoia* (New Haven, Yale University Press, 1967).
Hin, Saskia. *The Demography of Roman Italy: Population Dynamics in an Ancient Conquest Society* (Cambridge, Cambridge University Press, 2013).
Hollander, David. 'Lawyers, Friends and Money' in *Money and Power in the Roman Republic*, ed. Beck, Hans; Jehne, Martin; and Serrati, John (Brussels, Latomus, 2016) 18–25.
Holmes, T.R. 'Three Catilinarian Dates' *Journal of Roman Studies* (1918) 8: 15–25.
Hudson, Michael. 'How Interest Rates Were Set, 2500 BC-1000 AD: *Máš*, *tokos* and *fœnus* as Metaphors for Interest Accruals' *Journal of Economic and Social History* (2000) 132–161.
Hutchinson, Lester. *The Conspiracy of Catiline* (London, Arthur Blond, 1966).
Ibsen, Henrik. *The Oxford Ibsen Volume I. Early Plays*. ed. and trans. by McFarlane, James Walter and Orton, Graham. (London, Oxford University Press, 1970).
Jehne, Martin 'Methods, Models and Historiography' in *A Companion to the Roman Republic* ed. Rosenstein, N. and Morstein-Marx, R. (Wiley-Blackwell, 2010) 3–28.
—— 'The Senatorial Economics of Status in the Late Republic' in *Money and Power in the Roman Republic*, ed. Beck, Hans; Jehne, Martin; and Serrati, John (Brussels, Latomus, 2016) 188–207.
Kaplan, Arthur. *Catiline: The Man and His Role in the Roman Revolution* (New York, Exposition Press, 1968).
Keaveney, Arthur. 'Who were the Sullani?' *Klio* (1984) 114–150.
—— *Sulla: The Last Republican* (Beckenham, Croom Holm, 1982, paperback, 1986).
—— *Lucullus: A Life* (London, Routledge, 1990).
Keaveney, Arthur and Strachan, C.J.S. 'L. Catilina Legatus' *Classical Quarterly* (1981) 31: 361–366.
Keeline, Tom. *The Reception of Cicero in the Early Roman Empire: The Rhetorical Schoolroom and the Creation of a Cultural Legend* (Cambridge, Cambridge University Press, 2018).
Konrad, C.F. 'From the Gracchi to the First Civil War (133–70)' in *A Companion to the Roman Republic* ed. Rosenstein, N. and Morstein-Marx, R. (Wiley-Blackwell, 2010) 167–189.
La Bua, G. *Cicero and Roman Education: The Reception of the Speeches and Ancient Scholarship* (Cambridge, Cambridge University Press, 2019).

Lange, C and Masden, J. *Cassius Dio: Greek Intellectual and Roman Politician* (Leiden, Brill, 2016).
Levick, Barbara. *Catiline* (London, Bloomsbury, 2015).
Lewis, R.G. 'Inscriptions of Amiterinum and Catilina's Last Stand' *ZPE (1988)* 74:31–42.
—— 'Catiline and the Vestal' *Classical Quarterly* (2001) 51: 141–149.
—— *Asconius Commentaries on Speeches of Cicero* (Oxford, Oxford University Press, 2006).
Ligt, Luuk de. 'The Economy: Agrarian Change During the Second Century' in *A Companion to the Roman Republic* ed. Rosenstein, N. and Morstein-Marx, R. (Wiley-Blackwell, 2010) 590–605.
Linderski, J. 'Cicero and Sallust on Vargunteius' *Historia* (1963) 12: 511–512.
Lintott, Andrew. *The Constitution of the Roman Republic* (Oxford, Oxford University Press, 1999).
—— *Cicero as Evidence: A Historian's Companion* (Oxford, Clarendon Press, 2008).
Little, Charles E. 'The Authenticity and Form of Cato's Saying "Carthago Delenda Est"' *Classical Journal* (1934) 29: 429–435.
Lovano, Michael. *The Age of Cinna: Crucible of Late Republican Rome* (Stuttgart, Steiner, 2002).
Lowe, Benedict. 'The *Imperium* of Cn. Calpurnius Piso' *Ancient Society* (2004) 34: 115–125.
Lushkov, A. H. 'Citation, Spoilation and Literary Appropriation in Livy's AUC' in *Rome, Empire of Plunder; the Dynamics of Cultural Appropriation* ed. Loar, M; MacDonald, C. and Peralta, D. (Cambridge, Cambridge University Press, 2018).
MacKay, L.A. 'Sallust's Catiline: Date and Purpose' *Phoenix* (1962) 16: 181–194.
MacDonald, C. ed. and trans. *Cicero X,* ed. (Cambridge, Harvard University Press, 1977, reprinted 1996).
Mallan, Christopher '*Parrhesia* in Cassius Dio' in *Cassius Dio: Greek Intellectual and Roman Politician* ed. C. Carsten and J. Madsen (Leiden, Brill Press, 2016) 258–275.
March, Duane A. 'Cicero and the "Gang of Five"' *Classical World* (1989) 82: 225–234.
Marshall, Bruce A. 'Cicero and Sallust on Crassus and Catiline' *Latomus* (1974) 33: 804–813.
—— *Crassus: A Political Biography* (Amsterdam, Adolph M. Hakkert, 1976).
—— 'Catilina: Court Cases and Consular Candidature' *Scripta Classica Israelica* (1976–77) 3: 127–137.
—— 'A Vote of a Bodyguard for the Consuls of 65' *Classical Philology, (1977a)* 72: 318–320.
—— 'The Date of Catiline's Marriage to Aurelia Orestilla' *RFIC* (1977b) 105: 151–154.
—— 'Q. Curius: *Homo Quaestorius*' *L'Antquite Classique* (1978) 207–209.
—— 'Catilina and the Execution of M. Marius Gratidianus' *Classical Quarterly* (1985a) 35: 124–133.
—— *A Historical Commentary on Asconius* (Columbia, University of Missouri Press, 1985b).
Marshall, Bruce A. and Baker, Robert. 'The Aspirations of Q. Arrius' *Historia* (1975) 24: 220–231.
Mattingly, H.B. 'The Consilium of Gn. Pompeius Strabo in 89 B.C.' *Athenaeum* (1975) 53: 262–266.
McDermott, W.C. '*Vettius ille; ille noster index*' *TAPA* (1949) 79: 351–367.
Meier, Christian. 'Pompeius' Ruckkehr aud dem Mithridatischen Kriege und die Catilinarische Verschwurung' *Athenaeum* (1962) 40: 103–125.
Millar, Fergus. *A Study of Dio Cassius* (Oxford, Clarendon Press, 1964).
—— *The Crowd in Rome in the Late Republic* (Ann Arbor, University of Michigan Press, 2002 paperback).

Miller, N.P. 'Dramatic Speeches in Roman Historians' *Greece & Rome* (1975) 22: 45–57.
Mitchell, Th. N. 'Cicero and the *Senatus Consultum Ultimum*' *Historia* (1971) 20: 47–61.
Mommsen, Theodor. *A History of Rome* (New York, Charles Scribner's & Sons, 1904, trans. Scribners).
—— *Romisches Strafrecht (*Leipzig, 1899).
Moreau, *Clodiana Religio* (Paris, Les Belles Lettres, 1982).
Morrell, Kit. *Pompey, Cato and the Governance of the Roman Empire* (Oxford, Oxford University Press, 2017).
Morstein-Marx, R. and Rosenstein, N. 'The Transformation of the Republic' in *A Companion to the Roman Republic* ed. Rosenstein, N. and Morstein-Marx, R. (Wiley-Blackwell, 2010) 625–637.
Henrik Mouritsen, *Plebs and Politics in the Late Roman Republic* (Cambridge, Cambridge Press, 2001, 2007 paperback).
Namier, Lewis B. *The Structure of Politics at the Accession of George III* (London: MacMillan, 1928, 2d. ed. 1957)
Nisbet, R.G. 'The *Commentariolium Petitionis*: Some Arguments against Authenticity' *Journal of Roman Studies* (1961) 51: 84–87.
North, John A. '*The Constitution of the Roman Republic*' in *A Companion to the Roman Republic* ed. Rosenstein, N. and Morstein-Marx, R (Wiley-Blackwell, 2010) 257–277.
Nutting, H.C. 'The Conspiracy at Rome in 66–55 BC' *University of California Publications in Classical Philology* (1911–1916) 2: 43–55.
Odahl, C.M. *The Catilinarian Conspiracy* (New Haven, College & University Press, 1971).
—— *Cicero and the Catilinarian Conspiracy.* (Ann Arbor: College & University Press, 1972).
Paterson, Jeremy. 'Politics in the Late Republic' in *Roman Political Life, 90 B.C.- A.D. 69* ed. Wiseman, T.P (Exeter, Exeter University Press, 1985) 21–43.
Patterson, John R. 'Rome and Italy' in *A Companion to the Roman Republic* ed. Rosenstein, N. and Morstein-Marx, R. (Wiley-Blackwell, 2010) 606–624.
Irene Peirano, *The Rhetoric of the Roman Fake* (Cambridge, Cambridge University Press, 2012).
Pelling, C.B.R. 'Plutarch and Catiline' *Hermes* (1985) 113: 311–329.
—— *Plutarch and History: Eighteen Studies* (London, Classical Press of Wales, 2002).
Phillips, E.J. '*Ad Atticum* I, 2' *Philologus* (1970) 114: 291–294.
Phillips, J.J. 'The failure of Cicero's "First Catilinarian"' *Studies in Latin Literature and Roman History* (1998) 9: 106–28.
Phillips, E.J. 'Cicero and the Prosecution of C. Manilius' *Latomus* (1970) 29: 595–607.
—— 'Asconius' *magni homines*' *Rhein Mus.* (1973) 353–357.
—— 'Catiline's Conspiracy' *Historia:* (1976) 25: 441–448.
Pobjoy, Mark, 'Epigraphy and Numismatics' in *A Companion to the Roman Republic*. ed. Rosenstein, N. and Morstein-Marx, R. (Wiley-Blackwell, 2010) 51–80.
Polo, F.P. '*Cupiditas Pecuniae*: Wealth and Power in Cicero' in *Money and Power in the Roman Republic*, ed. Beck, Hans; Jehne, Martin; and Serrati, John (Brussels, Latomus, 2016) 165–177.
Potter, H.F. 'The Date of Cicero's First Oration Against Catiline' *Classical Journal* (1925–6) 21: 164–176.
Power, Tristan and Gibson, Roy K. (ed.) *Suetonius, the Biographer. Studies in Roman Lives* (Oxford; New York: Oxford University Press, 2014).
Pritchett, W.K. 'The General's Exhortations in Greek Warfare' in *Essays in Greek History* (Amsterdam, Brill, 1994) 95–115.

Ramsey, John T. 'The Prosecution of C. Manilius in 66 BC and Cicero's *Pro Manilio*' *Phoenix* (1980a) 34: 323–36.
—— 'A Reconstruction of Q. Gallius' Trial for *Ambitus*' *Historia* (1980b) 29: 402–421.
—— 'Cicero, *pro Sulla* 68 and Catiline's Candidacy in 66 B.C.' *Harvard Studies in Classical Philology* (1982) 86: 121–131.
—— *Sallust's Bellum Catilinae.* ed. (Oxford, Oxford University Press, 2007).
'The Date of the Consular Elections in 63 and the Inception of Catiline's Conspiracy' *Harvard Studies in Classical Philology* (2019) 110: 213–269.
Rawson, Beryl. *The Politics of Friendship Pompey and Cicero* (Sydney, Sydney University Press, 1978).
—— 'Finding Roman Women' in *A Companion to the Roman Republic* ed. N. Rosenstein and R. Morstein-Marx (Wiley-Blackwell, 2010) 324–341.
Rawson, Elizabeth. 'Cicero the Historian and Cicero the Antiquarian' *Journal of Roman Studies* (1972) 62: 33–45.
—— 'The Identity Problems of Q. Cornificius' *Classical Quarterly* (1978) 38: 188–201.
—— 'Cicero's *Expositio Consiliorum Suorum*' *Liverpool Classical Monthly* (1982) 7: 121–124.
—— 'Sallust on the Eighties' *Classical Quarterly* (1987) 37: 163–180.
—— 'L. Crassus and Cicero: The Formation of a Statesman' in *Roman Culture and Society* (Oxford, Clarendon Press, 1991) 16–33.
—— 'History, Historiography, and Cicero's *Expositio Consiliorum Suorum*' in *Roman Culture and Society* (Oxford, Clarendon Press, 1991) 408–415.
Rich, J.W. 'The Supposed Roman Manpower Shortage of the Later Second Century BC' *Historia* (1983) 32: 287–331.
Richardson, John S. 'The *Commentariolum Petitionis*' *Historia* (1971) 20: 436–442.
Riggsby, Andrew M. *Roman Law and the Legal World of the Romans* (Cambridge, Cambridge University Press, 2010, paperback).
Rickard, J. (17 July 2017), *Battle of Mount Falernus, 90 BC* http://www.historyofwar.org/articles/battles_mount_falernus.html
Robinson, O.F. *Penal Practice and Penal Policy in Ancient Rome* (New York and Abingdon, Routledge, 2007).
Rosillo-Lopez, Cristina. 'Cash is King' in *Money and Power in the Roman Republic,* ed. Beck, Hans; Jehne, Martin; and Serrati, John (Brussels, Latomus, 2016) 26–36.
—— *Public Opinion and Politics in the Late Roman Republic* (Cambridge, Cambridge University Press, 2017).
Ryan, Francis Xavier. 'The Consular Candidacy of Catiline in 66' *Museum Helveticum* (1995a) 52: 45–48.
—— 'Novius Niger' *Classica et Medievala* (1995b) 46: 151–156.
Salmon, E.T. *Samnium and the Samnites* (Cambridge, Cambridge University Press, 1967).
Sacks, Kenneth. *Diodorus Siculus and the First Century* (Princeton, Princeton University Press, 1990).
Salway, Benet. 'What's in a name? A survey of Roman onomastic practice from c. 700 B.C. to 700 A.D.' *Journal of Roman Studies* (1994) 84: 124–145.
Salmon, E.T. 'Catiline, Crassus and Caesar' *American Journal of Philology* (1935) 56: 311.
Sampson, Gareth. *Rome, Blood & Power* (Barnsley, Pen and Sword, 2019).
Saylor, S. *Catilina's Riddle: A Mystery of Ancient Rome* (New York, St. Martin's Press, 1993).
Schaffer, C.A. *Catiline and Clodius: A Social Scientific Approach to Two Practitioners of Violence in the Late Roman Republic* (Phd. Thesis 1973).
Scullard, H.H. *From the Gracchi to Nero,* (London, Routledge 3d. ed. 1970).

Seager, Robin L. 'The First Catilinarian Conspiracy' *Historia* (1964) 13: 338–347.
—— 'Iusta Catilinae' *Historia* (1973) 22: 240–248.
—— 'L. Domitus Ahenobarbus and Cicero's election to the consulship' *Liverpool Classical Monthly* (1976) 1: 46.
—— *Pompey the Great* (Oxford, Blackwell Publishing Company, 2002, paperback).
Squires, Simon. ed. *Asconius: Commentaries on Five Speeches of Cicero* (Wauconda, Bolchazy-Carducci Publishers, 1990).
Stadter, Philip A. *Plutarch and his Roman Readers* (Oxford, Oxford University Press, 2015).
Stevens, C. Burden 'Fictitous Speeches, Envy and Habituation to Authority; Writing the Collapse of the Roman Republic' in *Cassius Dio: Greek Intellectual and Roman Politician*, ed. C. Lange and J. Madsen (Leiden, Brill, 2016) 193–216.
Stewart, Roberta. 'Catiline and the Crisis of 63–60 B.C.: The Italian Perspective' *Latomus* (1995) 54: 62–78.
Stevens, C. Burden, 'Fictitious Speeches, Envy and Habituation to Authority; Writing the Collapse of the Roman Republic' in Lange, C. and Madsen, J ed. *Cassius Dio: Greek Intellectual and Roman Politician*, ed. (Leiden, Brill, 2016) 193–216.
Stevens, C.E. 'The Plotting of BC 66/65' *Latomus* (1963) 26: 397–435.
Stockton, D.L. *Cicero: A Political Biography* (Oxford, Oxford University Press, 1971).
Stone, A.M. 'A House of Notoriety: An Episode in the Campaign for the Consulate in 64 B.C.' *Classical Quarterly* (1998a) 48: 487–491.
—— 'Was Sallust a Liar? A Problem in Modern History' *Ancient History in a Modern University* (1998b) I: 230–243.
Sumner, G.V. 'The Last Journey of L. Sergius Catilina' *Classical Philology* (1963) 58: 215–219.
—— 'The Consular Elections of 66 B.C.' *Phoenix* (1965) 19: 226–231.
Sydenham, E.A. *The Roman Republican Coinage* (London, Spink & Son, 1952).
Syme, Ronald. *The Roman Revolution* (Oxford, Clarendon Press, 1939, paperback in 2002).
—— *Sallust* (Berkeley, University of California Press, 1964, paperback in 2002).
—— *Approaching the Roman Revolution* (Oxford, Oxford University Press, 2016).
Tatum, W.J. *The Patrician Tribune: Publius Clodius Pulcher* (Chapel Hill, University of North Carolina Press, 1991).
—— ed. *Quintus Cicero, A Brief Handbook on Canvassing for Office: COMMENTARIOLUM PETITIONIS*. (Oxford, Oxford University Press 2018).
Taylor, Lily Ross. *Party Politics in the Age of Caesar* (Berkeley, University of California Press, 1949, paperback).
—— 'The Date and Meaning of the Vettius Affair' *Historia* (1950) 1: 45–51.
—— *The Voting Districts of the Roman Republic* (Rome, American Academy in Rome, 1960), (Ann Arbor, University of Michigan Press, paperback, 2013).
—— *Roman Voting Assemblies* (Ann Arbor, University of Michigan Press, 1966, paperback 1990).
Treggiari, Susan. *Terentia, Tullia and Publia: the women of Cicero's Family* (Abingdon, Routledge Press, 2007).
Van Dyck, Andrew. ed. *The Catilinarians* (Cambridge, Cambridge University Press, 2008).
Van Der Blom, Henriette. *Cicero's Role Models: The Political Strategy of a Newcomer* (Oxford, Oxford University Press, 2010).
Vishnia, F. *Roman Elections in the Age of Cicero* (London and New York, Routledge, 2002).
Voltaire, *The Works of Voltaire, A Contemporary Version* (New York, E. R. DuMont, 1901) IX, Part I, 202 trans. William F. Fleming.

Wallace-Hadrill, Andrew *Suetonius: The Scholar and His Caesars* (London, Duckworth, 1983).
Ward, A.M. 'The Early Relationships between Cicero and Pompey until 80 B.C.' *Phoenix* (1970a) 24: 123–4.
—— 'Politics in the Trials of Manlius and Cornelius' *TAPA* (1970b) 101: 545–556).
—— 'Cicero's Fight against Crassus and Caesar in 65 and 63 BC' *Historia* (1972) 21: 244–258.
—— *Marcus Crassus and the Later Roman Republic* (Columbia, University of Missouri Press, 1977).
Waters, K.H. 'Cicero, Sallust and Catiline' *Historia* (1970) 19: 195–215.
—— 'Competition and Cooperation' in *Roman Political Life-90 B.C.-A.D. 69* ed. T.P. Wiseman (Exeter, Exeter University Press, 1985) 3–20.
Werner, S. 'On the History of the *Commenta Berensia* and the *Adnotationes super Lucanum*' *Harvard Studies in Philology* (1994) 96: 343–368.
Westall, Richard. 'The Sources of Cassius Dio for the Roman Civil Wars of 49–30 B.C.' in *Cassius Dio: Greek Intellectual and Roman Politician*, ed. C. Lange and J. Madsen (Leiden, Brill, 2016) 51–75.
Wibier, M. 'Cicero's Reception in the Jurist Tradition of the Early Empire' in P. Du Plessis ed. *Cicero's Law: rethinking Roman law of the Late Republic* (Edinburgh, Edinburgh University Press, 2016) 100–122.
Winter, Bruce C. *Peter and Paul Among the Sophists (*Grand Rapids, Wm B. Eerdmans, 2002).
Woodman, A.J. *Rhetoric in Classical Historiography: Four Studies* (Abingon, Routledge, 1988, digital 2010)
—— ed. '*Sallust: Catiline's War, the Jugurthine War, Histories*' (New York, Penguin Books, 2007)
—— 'Sallust and Catiline: Conspiracy Theories' *Historia* (2021) 70:55–68.
Yakobson, Alexander. 'Popular Power in the Roman Republic' in *A Companion to the Roman Republic* ed. N. Rosenstein and R. Morstein-Marx (Wiley-Blackwell, 2010) 383–400.
Yavetz, Z. 'The Living Conditions of the Urban Plebs in Republican Rome' *Latomus* (1958) 17: 500–517.
—— 'The Failure of Catiline's Conspiracy' *Historia* (1963) 11: 485–499.

Index

Index of Historical Figures

Ahenobardus (L. Domitius Ahenobardus), 20, 45, 57
Anthony (M. Antonius), 58, 103
Antonius (C. Antonius Hybrida), 51, 90
    64 Consular Election, 42, 43
    Directed to pursue Catiline, 77, 79
    Battle of Pistoria, 108, 111
    Trial, 112
Arrius (Q.), 67
Atticus, (T.), 20, 37, 41, 45, 97
Aulus (Aulus Fulvius), 78
Autronius (P. Autronius Paetus),
    66 Consular Election, 24, 31
    First Catilinarian Conspiracy, 33, 34
    63 Consular Election, 57
    Involvement in the Conspiracy, 61, 78

Bellienus (L. Annius Bellienus), 3, 46
Bestia (L. Calpurnius Bestia), 61, 82, 105

Caecilius (Q.), 15
Caelius (M. Caelius Rufus), 57
Caeparius (M.), 86–8, 90, 103
Caesar (C. Iulus Caesar),
    Connection with Crassus, 42
    Proscription Prosecutions, 47
    Pontifex Maximus election, 61, 98
    Cooperation with Cicero, 65
    Given Custody of Statilius, 90
    Rabirus Prosecution, 93
    Piso's and Catulus' Attempt to Link Caesar to the Conspiracy, 96
    Character, 98–9
    Debate on 5 December, 98–9, 102–103
    Threatened with Death on 5 December, 102
    Relationships,
        Catulus, 96
        Piso, 96
Caesar (L. Iulus Caesar), 36, 89
Cassius (L. Cassius Longinus), 51, 82, 84, 90, 98
Catiline (L. Sergus Catilina),
    Character, xii, xiv, xvi, 1, 25–6
    63 Consular Election and Tabulae Novae, xiii, 50
    Ancestry, 2–3
    Youth, 4
    Service in the Social War with Strabo, 4–5
    First Wife, 9
    With Sulla in the East, 8, 13
    Gratidianus and the Proscriptions, 10–12
    Lepidus Rebellion, 13
    Army Service after Lepidus Rebellion, 14–15
    Alliance with Crassus, 26
    The Vestal Virgin Affair, 27–8
    Praetor and Pro-Praetorship, 28–30
    Second Wife, Aurelia Orestilla, 30
    66 Consular Election, 31–3
    The First Catilinarian Conspiracy, 33–4, 41
    Trial for Extortion, 37–8
    64 Consular Election, 41–2
    Trial for Involvement in Sullan Proscriptions, 46–7
    Manlius and the Sullan Veterans, 47
    Cicero's chicanery, 55–7
    Defeat, 59

The First Meeting of the Conspirators,
    59–62
The Start of the Catilinarian Insurgency,
    62, 64–5
Aims of the Conspiracy, 63
Betrayal, 65–8
Senatus Consultum Ultimum, 68
November 7 Meeting at Laeca's house, 71
November 8 Meeting, 71
First Catilinarian, 72–4
Departure from Rome, 74–5
Last Letter to Catulus, 75
Activities in Etruria, 77
Military Manoeuvring, 107
Impact of Discovery of the Conspiracy,
    107
Battle of Pistoria, 108–11
Flowers on his Grave, 112
Reasons for Failure of the Conspiracy, 114
Relationships,
    Pompey, 4–6
    Catulus, 10–12, 14, 27–8, 39, 75
    Crassus, 14
    Metellus Pius, 15, 32–3, 37–8
Cato Minor,
    64 Consular Campaign, 52–5
    Prosecution of Murena, 79
    Grain subsidy, 80
    Debate on 5 December, 101–102
    Seeks Tribuneship, 104–106
    Vetoes Nepos' Bill to Recall Pompey, 106
    Gives Cicero the Title of *Parens Patria*,
        106
Catulus (Q. Lutatius Catulus),
    Exile under the Marians, 10, 13
    Lepidus Rebellion, 13
    Vestal Virgins, 28
    Last Letter from Catiline, 75
    Attempt to Link Caesar to the
        Conspiracy, 96
    Debate on 5 December, 101
    Relationships,
        Catiline, 10–12, 28, 75
        Caesar, 96, 102
Cethegus (C.),
    Character, 60

Leading the Conspiracy, 81–2
Meetings with the Gauls, 84
3 December, 86–8, 90
Attempts at Rescue, 97
Brother Votes for Death Penalty, 102
Death, 103
Chilo (Q. Annius Chilo), 61, 90, 98, 103
Cicero (M. Tullius Cicero),
    Non-noble Ancestry, 1
    Consideration of *coito* with Catiline, 11,
        41
    Praetor and Manlius Trial, 35
    Character, 39–40, 93
    In Toga Candida, 42
    64 Consular Campaign, 44–6
    Pro Murena, 52–3
    Cicero's Chicanery in the 63 Consular
        Campaign, 54–7
    Electoral Reform Legislation, 53
    Crassus' Letters, 65–7
    Warnings of the Insurgency, 67–9
    The Murder Plot, 71
    The *First Catilinarian*, 72–3
    The *Second Catilinarian*, 76
    The Gauls, 84–7
    3 December, 87–91
    The *Third Catilinarian*, 91–2
    Cicero's Dilemma 92–4
    The Senate Debate, 97
    The *Fourth Catilinarian*, 99, 101
    Cicero's Motion, 102
    The Execution of the Conspirators,
        102–103
    Struggle with Nepos and Bestia,
        105–106
    The Aftermath, 111–12
    Pro Sulla, 112–13
    Relationships,
        Catiline, 5–6, 57–8
        Pompey, 5, 10, 45
        Gratidiani, 11
        Crassus, 26, 95–96
        Clodius, 37, 40, 58
        Anthony, 58
        Caesar, 96
        Torquatus Minor, 112

Index   207

Cicero (Q. Tullius Cicero), 21, 94, 101, 113
Cicero (Terentia), 23, 43, 67, 94
Clodius (P. Appius Claudius Pulcher), 58
   Catiline's Extortion Trial, 36
   63 Consular Election, 52
   Catilinarian Conspiracy, 78
Considius (Q.), 71
Cotta (L. Aurelius Cotta), 24, 81
Crassus (M. Licinius Crassus),
   Proscriptions, 13, 36
   Sullani, 13
   Character, 26, 95
   Military Ability, 26
   Political Activities in 63, 49
   Letters Warning About the Conspiracy, 65–7
   Given Custody of Gabinus, 90
   Tarquinus incident, 95
   Absence from Senate Debate on 5 December, 98
   Relationships,
      Catiline, 14
      Pompey, 26
      Cicero, 26, 95–6
      Caesar, 42
      Murena, 51, 69
Curio (C. Scribonius Curio), 102
Curius (Q.),
   Character, 60
   Love Affair with Fulvia, 67
   Betrayal of the Conspiracy, 68, 71, 76
   Loses his Reward, 112

Fabia, 27–8
Flaccus (L. Valerius Flaccus), 85, 90
Fulvia, 67–8, 71, 76
Furius (P.), 90, 98

Gabinus, 82–4, 86–7, 90, 103
Gracchus (Ti.), xiv, xvi, 56
Gratidianus (M. Marius Gratidianus), 9, 10, 43

Hortensius, 13, 31, 44, 79

Lentulus (C. Cornelius Lentulus Sura),
   Character, 60, 81

Leading the Conspiracy, 81–2
Decision to Enlist the Gauls, 83
Meeting with the Gauls, 84
3 December, 86, 88–90
Attempts at Rescue, 97
Death, 103
Lepidus, Major (M. Aemilius Paulus Lepidus), 13, 70
Lepidus, Minor (M. Aemilius Paulus Lepidus), 70
Lepidus (Man. Aemilius Lepidus), 70
Licinia, 27
Lucceius (L.), 46, 94
Lucullus, 49, 52, 57

Manilius, 35
Manlius, (G.), 47–8, 50, 54, 59, 62, 65, 67–9, 110
Marcellus (M.), 70
Marcius Rex (Q.), 50, 69–70, 114
Marius (C.), 7–9
Metellus Celer (Q. Caecilius Metellus Celer), 69, 70, 105–106, 108
Metellus Creticus (Q. Caecilius Metellus Creticus), 69
Metellus Nepos (Q. Caecilius Metellus Nepos),
   Pompey sends to become Tribune, 104–105
   Attacks Cicero, 105–106, 111
   Proposes Recall of Pompey to Deal with Catiline, 106
Metellus Pius (Q. Caecilius Metellus Pius Scipio), 81
   Character, 15
   Command in Spain, 15
   Catiline's Extortion Trial, 32–7
   Crassus; Letters incident, 66
Murena (L. Licinius Murena), 49, 52, 84
   Trial, 79

Nero (Ti. Claudius Nero), 100, 101
Niger (L. Novius Niger), 111–12
Nigidus (P. Nigidus Figulus), 87, 92

Orestilla (Aurelia Orestilla), 30, 78
Orestinus (Q. Mucius Oretinus), 42

Petreius (M.), 108–10
Piso (G. Calpurnius Piso), 45–6, 88
   Relationship with Caesar, 96, 102
Piso (Cn. Calpurnius Piso), 14
   First Catilinarian Conspiracy, 33–4
   Manilius Trail, 35–6
Pompeius (Q. Pompeius Rufus), 69
Pompey (Gn. Pompeius Strabo Magnus),
   Siege of Asculum, 4-6
   Spain, 14
   Wars with the Pirates and Mithridates, 31, 49
Pomptinus (C.), 85, 90, 107
Prosopography, 27

Roman Republic,
   Problems, xiv, 47–8
   Fall of, xiv–xvi
   Political Framework, 16–25, 53–4, 56
   Differences between Roman Law and Anglo-Saxon Law, 9, 28, 37–8

Sanga (Q. Fabius Sanga), 84
Sempronia, 51–2
Servilia, 101
Sestius (P.), ix, 78, 91, 105, 108
Silanus (D. Junius Silanus), 52, 88, 97, 100, 101
Sittius (P.), 32
Statilius (L.), 61, 82, 103
Strabo (Gn. Pompeius Strabo),
   Siege of Asculum, 5

consilium, 5, 111
   Death, 6
Sulla (L. Cornelius Sulla),
   Character, 7
   Early Military Career, 7–8
   Command Against Mithridates, 8, 10
   Sullan Civil War, 10
   Proscriptions, 10
   Death, 13
Sulla (P. Cornelius Sulla),
   66 Consular Election, 24, 31–2
   First Catilinarian Conspiracy, 33
Sullani, 13
Sulpicius (Ser. Sulpicius Rufus), 52–4

Tarquinus (L.), 95
Torquatus Major (L. Manlius Torquatus),
   66 Consular Election 24, 31–2
   Catiline's Trials, 34, 37
   Cicero's *Consilium*, 94
Torquatus Minor (L. Manlius Torquatus),
   P. Sulla's Trial, 112–13

Umbrenus (P.), 82–3, 90, 98

Vargunteius (L.), 60, 71
Vettius (L.), 60, 71
Vestal Virgins, 27–8, 43, 94
Volcatius (L. Volcatius Tullus), 32
Volturcius (T.), 85–7, 90, 96, 97

Index of Geographic Locations and Wars

Aesernia, 14
Africa, 18, 29, 30, 31, 33, 131
Allobroges,
   Involvement in the Conspiracy, 82–5
   Appearance in the Senate, 85–8
   Revolt of, 107
Amiternum, 123
Apennines, 107, 108
Apulia, 63, 69, 78, 86, 104
Arpinum, 7, 39

Arretium, x, 54, 77
Asculum, viii, 5, 6, 111, 116

Brundisium, 104
Bruttium, 78, 113

Campus Martius, 16
Capua, 69, 78, 105
Cilicia, 8, 14
Cisalpine Gaul, 45, 63, 69, 78, 79

Etruria, xvii, 47, 48, 56–7, 62, 65, 67, 69, 70, 71, 77, 107

Faesulae, 47, 54, 56, 62, 76, 78, 107

Lucania, 104

Massalia (Marseilles), 75
Mt. Falernus, Battle of, 5
Mulvian Bridge, 85

Nuceria, 62

Paelignum, 63, 111, 113
Palatine Hill, 2, 103, 113
Picenum, 24, 63, 69–70, 78–9, 108
Pisaurum, 78
Pistoria, x, 107, 114, 116, 123
Placentia, 2, 108
Pontus, 8
Praeneste, ix, 14, 68

Remus Road, 108

Sicily, 10, 39, 45
Spain, 14, 15, 81

Thurii, 113
Transalpine Gaul, 78, 82, 96, 107–108
Transpadana, 63
Tullianum, 92, 102–103

Umbria, 63

Via Aemelia, 108
Via Aurelia, 75
Via Cassia, 107–108

Wars,
   Punic, xv, 2
   Macedonian, 3, 8, 9
   Mithradatic, 3, 9, 104
   Social, 5, 8, 16, 117
   Cimbri and Teutones, 7–9
   Sullan Civil, 10, 14

Index of Authors, Books and Speeches

Adnotationes super Lucan, 11, 118
Asconius, 11, 31–2, 34–7, 41–2, 44, 78, 95, 117, 128

Badian, 8, 14
Batstone, 125

Cadoux, 27
Camelot, 136
Cichorius, 14
M. Cicero (as an author and not a historical figure), xvi, 2, 37, 41
   In Toga Candida, 11–12, 31, 33, 42–3, 46, 118, 128
   Pro Murena, 33, 52–3, 56–7, 79, 118, 120
   Pro Sulla, 33, 118
   Pro Cornelio, 35
   Expositio Consiliorum Suorum, 95, 117–18

Catilinarians, 100
   First Catilinarian, xiii, 1, 18, 33, 36, 73, 118
   Second Catilinarian, 18, 37, 76, 118, 120
   Third Catilinarian, 90, 92, 120
   Fourth Catilinarian, 99, 100
   Reliability as a Source, 118–21
   De Consulatu Suo, 118
   De Temporibus Suis, 118
   Pro Caelio, 119, 131, 136–7
Q. Cicero (as an author and not a historical figure), 17, 19–21, 44, 117, 121–2
Commenta Bernensia, 118

Dahl, Robert, xvi
de Ligt, Luuk, 48
Dio Cassius, 34–5, 47, 50, 61–2, 64, 95, 117, 127 131–2, 139

Diodorus Siculus, 74, 117, 126
Drummond, 91

Gelzer, 20
Gruen, Erich, xiv, xv, 36, 45–6, 67

Harris, Robert, 136
Hin, Saskia, 48
Hortensius (as a historian and not a historical figure), 117
Hutchinson, Lester, 136

Ibsen, Henrik, 135

Jonson, Ben, 135
Juvenal, 134

Keaveney, Arthur, 8, 12, 15

Levick, Barbara, 5, 44, 65, 132, 138–9
Lewis, R.G., 27, 123
Livy, 11, 34, 117, 127–8, 132
Lushkov, A.H., 127–8

Marshall, 47, 128
Maurenbacher, 14
Meier, Christian, xiv, xv
Mommsen, Theodor, 137

Namier, Lewis B., 23

Orosius, 27

Palazzo Madama, xiii, 134
Phillips, E.J., 36
Pollio, Asinius, 126

Plutarch, 7, 12, 42, 56, 64, 74, 94, 103, 117, 119, 128–31

Quintilian, 117

Rich, J.W., 48
Sallust, xiii, xiv, xvi, 4, 7, 9, 11, 24–5, 27–8, 30, 32–3, 44, 47, 50–1, 59–65, 69–70, 73–5, 84, 91, 95–6, 99–100, 109, 113, 115, 117–18, 124–6, 129, 132, 136, 138–9
   Bellum Catilinae, 1, 70, 74, 96, 100, 117, 122–6, 135
   Historiae, 14–15
   Reliability as a historian, 122–6
Saylor, Stephen, 136
Seager, Robin, 24, 138–9
Spartacus, 136
Stockton, D.L., 99
Stone, A.M., 64
Suetonius, 34, 47, 112, 117, 130–1
Syme, R., 9, 24, 34, 96, 126

Thucydides, 62

Valerius Maximus, 11
Virgil, 134
Voltaire, 135

Waters, K.H., 138–9
Woodman, A.J., 32, 64–5, 124

Yavetz, Z., 51

Index of Latin Terms or Anglicized Latin Terms

Aerarium, 120
Ambitus, 53
Amicitia, 6, 10, 49, 51

Bona Dea, 28, 92, 94
Boni, 22, 138

Catilinarians,
   Description of Groups Composing, 76
Centuria, 16–17, 21, 44, 47, 53–4, 93
Clarissimi, 32
Clientela, 20
Clientes, 15, 20, 23, 54, 71, 81, 84

Index   211

Coitio, ix, 11, 12, 20, 41–3, 46, 57, 123
   Cicero and Catiline possible *coitio*, 41
   Antonius and Catiline *coitio*, 42, 43
Collegia, 44, 97
Comitia Centuria, 16, 93
Comitia Tributa, 16, 23, 93, 105, 106
Comitium, 33, 34, 36
Commentarii, 121
Concordia ordinum, 45
   Cicero's concept of, 39
Concursus honorum, 42, 60
Consilium, viii, 13, 28, 32, 94
   Of Gn. Pompeius Strabo, 5, 111, 117
Consulares, 32, 37, 46, 70, 72, 88, 90, 98, 102
   Rank in Senate, 98
Contio, 35, 76, 82
Curia, 84
Curule Aedile, 18, 47, 98
   Importance to Consular Candidates, 18

Decemviri, 2
Deductio, 18
Dignitas, 8, 18, 19
Divisores, 21

Eques, xiv, xv, 3, 5, 12, 17, 20, 21, 22, 37, 39, 44, 54, 56, 60
   Support of Cicero, 44
Exordium, 99

Factio, 24, 39

Gens, 1–3, 18, 30
Gratia, 20

Hostes, x, 72, 77, 100, 106
   Legal Significance, 97

Imperator,
   Requirements for Title, 110–11
Ingenua, 123
Inimicitia, 96
   Catiline and Metellus Pius, 15
   Crassus and Pompey, 26
   Catiline and Clodius, 37
   Catiline and Cicero, 54, 57
   Caesar and Catulus, 96
   Caesar and Piso, 96
Inquilinus, 1, 43

Latifundia, xiv, 48
Legatus, 3, 8, 14, 15, 18, 108
Leges, 93
Lex Cornelia, 46
Lex Manilia, 35
Lex Plautia, 70, 111
Lex Porcia, 93, 99
Lex Sempronia, 93, 99, 100
Lex Tullia, 53
Lex Valeria, 93

Maiestas, 35

Nomenclator, 18

Opinio, 34
Optimates,
   Principles of, 22–3

Parens Patriae, 103, 106
Patrician, 2–4, 7, 24, 31–2, 36, 41, 52, 121
Patronus, 84
Perduellio, 9
Plebeian, viii, 3, 4, 31, 41, 52, 69
Pontifex, 27
Pontifex Maximus, 44
   Catulus Loses Election for *Pontifex Maximus* to Caesar, 96, 98–9
Popularis,
   Principles of, 22–3
Praetor, viii, 1–3, 8, 35–6, 40, 42, 46, 60, 67, 69, 86–8, 101, 105, 108, 112
   Duties of, 28–9
Praevaricatio, 37
Prensatio, 18
Princeps Civitatis, 32
Princeps Senatus, xvii
Pro Praetor, ix, 32, 107, 122
   Catiline in Africa 15, 29–31
   Duties of, 2–3, 29

Proscriptions, ix, 9–10, 13, 26–7, 43, 46, 48, 63, 66, 76, 111, 116, 122, 134
    Description of, 12
Provocatio, 93
Publicani, xiv, 29, 30, 44

Salutatio, 18
Saturnalia, 74, 81, 88, 107
Senatus Consulta, 120
Senatus Consultum Ultimum, ix, xvi, 22, 68, 79, 93, 106
Sequestres, 21, 42
Sibylline Oracle, 84
Socii, 4

Sodalitates, 19
Spolia, 127
Suasoria, 122
Sullani, xvii, 12–13, 15, 63
    Description of groups making up the *Sullani*, 3

Tabulae Novae, 50
Tabulae Publicae, 121
Toga Virilis, 4, 5
Tribuni Aerarii, 37
Tribus, 5, 16, 19, 20
Tumultus, ix, 67